"This book is an innovative and forward-thinking project that pushes us to reimagine what a committed feminist book on the American West might look like in our current moment. It includes lively and informative interviews that emerged from insightful questions."

—Susan Kollin, author of *Captivating Westerns:*
The Middle East in the American West

"*Living West as Feminists* is a book filled with illumination, inspiration, and intimacy. Each of Krista Comer's in situ conversations casts a thoughtful and nuanced light on complex subject matter, cumulatively granting access to an enlarged (and still-growing) portrait of seriously engaged academic and personal investigations into the relationships between place, history, identity, and some movements (again both personal and collective) toward forms of restorative justice. A highly recommended text for academics and non-academics alike."

—Elizabeth Rosner, author of *Third Ear: Reflections*
on the Art and Science of Listening

"How many ways can we answer the question, 'What is the where of here?' For Comer and her contributors the question takes us to many worlds, many intricate and dense connections, to relations that trouble settler assumptions and open paths toward reparations, toward an ethic that attends to the care of where. This beautiful, intimate set of reflective conversations offers stories of feminist struggle, of gardens, and of hikes and friendships between surfers. It's a joy to read and a promise that another world is possible."

—Mary Pat Brady, author of *Scales of Captivity:*
Racial Capitalism and the Latinx Child

"In *Living West as Feminists* Krista Comer leads readers on a road trip through the politics of place, engaging in a series of conversations with scholars, educators, activists, and feminists about the U.S. West, a region that is not only geographically vast but also a contested space and a contested term. As a passenger on this journey, I found myself thinking through Comer's questions about how we live in specific places—and especially how we pay attention to the ways we live on specific lands. They feel like a challenge as well as an invitation: How can coalitional feminism inform our relations to place? How does rootedness in place call us to be in coalition with others and with land and home? These questions, and the ensuing conversations, will stay with me for a long, long time."

—Lacy M. Johnson, author of *The Reckonings: Essays on Justice for the Twenty-First Century*

LIVING WEST AS FEMINISTS

Conversations about the Where of Us

KRISTA COMER

University of Nebraska Press

LINCOLN

Publication of this volume was assisted by the School of Humanities and the Office of Research at Rice University.

The University of Nebraska Press is part of a land-grant institution with campuses and programs on the past, present, and future homelands of the Pawnee, Ponca, Otoe-Missouria, Omaha, Dakota, Lakota, Kaw, Cheyenne, and Arapaho Peoples, as well as those of the relocated Ho-Chunk, Sac and Fox, and Iowa Peoples.

Library of Congress Cataloging-in-Publication Data
Names: Comer, Krista, author.
Title: Living West as feminists: conversations about the where of us/ Krista Comer.
Description: Lincoln: University of Nebraska Press, [2024] | Includes bibliographical references and index.
Identifiers: LCCN 2024021599
ISBN 9781496229533 (paperback)
ISBN 9781496241139 (epub)
ISBN 9781496241146 (pdf)
Subjects: LCSH: Feminism—West (U.S.) | Women's studies—West (U.S.) | Feminist theory—West (U.S.) | BISAC: SOCIAL SCIENCE / Women's Studies | SOCIAL SCIENCE / Feminism & Feminist Theory
Classification: LCC HQ1191.U6 C66 2024 | DDC 305.42092/5279—dc23/eng/20240628
LC record available at https://lccn.loc.gov/2024021599

Designed and set in Lyon Text by K. Andresen.

For my mother, Jean Houston Comer
a woman who never met a road trip she didn't like

CONTENTS

ILLUSTRATIONS

THE INVITATION

Note: In November 2020, immediately following the U.S. presidential election, I invited a group of colleagues into a "conversation project." The conversations commenced through in-person individual interviews in the summer of 2021 and were completed in summer 2022. What follows is the invitation.

You are invited to participate in a "conversation project" that asks scholars to reflect on how we live in place and live our feminisms in place. How do you inhabit your feminism and how does it inhabit you?

I will come to you at a place of your choice accompanied by Chicano/a studies scholar José Aranda who will videotape our discussions. Beforehand I will pose loose questions to guide us, but the important thing is to follow topics and leads important to you and to the moment. An open-ended back-and-forth rather than a prepared or rehearsed format promises generative work that others can learn from. I imagine interviews to be personal and reflective as well as intellectually engaging. Taking a cue from the feminist ethical commitments of two oral history projects—*Chicana por Mi Raza*, directed by Maria Cotera with codirector Linda Garcia Merchant, and *Women Who Rock: Making Scenes/Building Communities*, a collaborative initiative headed by Michelle Habell-Pallán—you are invited to review and edit materials.

Our collected conversations will be showcased in a book that updates the cross-cutting histories of feminist work about the U.S. West and how our perspectives change understandings of "feminism" and "the West." Feminism in popular debates and scholarship invokes contested meanings, conflicts between women, and disparate histories and political priorities. "The West" is contentious for its naming of a dominant geopolitical settler space that erases the people and histories of Indian Country and their sacred relations to land. As a collective speak-out about these difficulties and our lived efforts at work-arounds, the project wants to let breathe relations between our lives, places, and work. Inviting more embodied discussions of ourselves might help better situate the types of feminist analyses we invest in.

In the now-time of this invitation, in the aftermath of the 2020 election, *Living West as Feminists* hopes to share with a broad readership the standpoints of specific people in specific places. The extreme divisiveness of the current national scene and devaluation of the humanities in higher education, all made worse by the COVID pandemic, require innovative forms of research accessible to broad audiences. Sharing our personal and scholarly stories, conceptualizing for nonspecialists how we live in place and do justice work, offers new paths for scholarship, feminist placemaking, and political alliance.

The general public needs whole-person pictures of feminist Wests that come together even as we distinguish between feminists who write about womanism, Black feminism, Indigenous feminism, queer Chicanx feminism, materialist feminism, and critical regionalism. Our conversations encourage white feminists to speak about themselves and their white and feminist histories as strategies of undoing white supremacy.

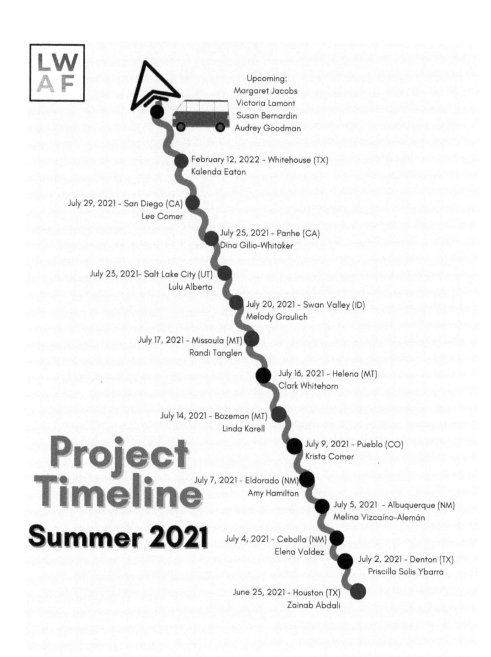

LW A F

Upcoming:
Margaret Jacobs
Victoria Lamont
Susan Bernardin
Audrey Goodman

February 12, 2022 – Whitehouse (TX)
Kalenda Eaton

July 29, 2021 – San Diego (CA)
Lee Comer

July 25, 2021 – Panhe (CA)
Dina Gilio-Whitaker

July 23, 2021– Salt Lake City (UT)
Lulu Alberto

July 20, 2021 – Swan Valley (ID)
Melody Graulich

July 17, 2021 – Missoula (MT)
Randi Tanglen

July 16, 2021 – Helena (MT)
Clark Whitehorn

July 14, 2021 – Bozeman (MT)
Linda Karell

Project Timeline

July 9, 2021 – Pueblo (CO)
Krista Comer

July 7, 2021 – Eldorado (NM)
Amy Hamilton

July 5, 2021 – Albuquerque (NM)
Melina Vizcaíno-Alemán

Summer 2021

July 4, 2021 – Cebolla (NM)
Elena Valdez

July 2, 2021 – Denton (TX)
Priscilla Solis Ybarra

June 25, 2021 – Houston (TX)
Zainab Abdali

Fig. 1. Project Timeline Summer 2021. Created by Zainab Abdali.

Project Timeline
Summer 2022

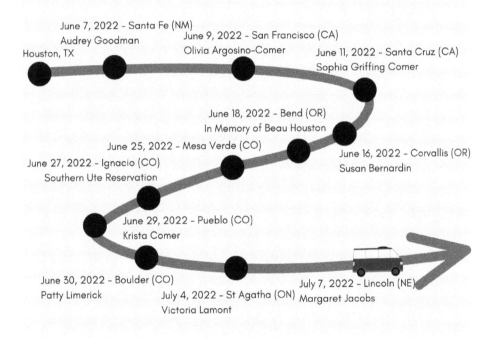

June 7, 2022 – Santa Fe (NM)
Audrey Goodman

June 9, 2022 – San Francisco (CA)
Olivia Argosino-Comer

Houston, TX

June 11, 2022 – Santa Cruz (CA)
Sophia Griffing Comer

June 18, 2022 – Bend (OR)
In Memory of Beau Houston

June 25, 2022 – Mesa Verde (CO)

June 27, 2022 – Ignacio (CO)
Southern Ute Reservation

June 16, 2022 – Corvallis (OR)
Susan Bernardin

June 29, 2022 – Pueblo (CO)
Krista Comer

June 30, 2022 – Boulder (CO)
Patty Limerick

July 4, 2022 – St Agatha (ON)
Victoria Lamont

July 7, 2022 – Lincoln (NE)
Margaret Jacobs

Fig. 2. Project Timeline Summer 2022. Created by Zainab Abdali.

FEMINIST ROAD-TRIPPING AND OTHER INTRODUCTIONS

The best-known feminist road trip in American popular culture, *Thelma and Louise*, famously ends with its two BFF (queer?) protagonists promising each other to "keep on going" as they plunge into the Grand Canyon, law at their heels, in a 1966 baby blue Thunderbird. Like so many Westerns whose outlaws live on the wrong side of the law but on the right side of justice, or enough on the right side to create sympathy, Thelma and Louise are escaping to "Mexico." Mexico in American cinema is where the good, the bad, and the ugly go when storylines need a change of subject, when tellings of U.S. history need new bearings.

In my own memory of cinematic Mexico, I see men wearing chaps and dark hats. They need a shave. The shots are shadowy interiors, bars, guns, scuffles. Am I thinking of *The Wild Bunch*? In memory I see surf footage too. Director Bruce Brown takes California blondeboy surfers for a ride into "Old Mexico," surf surfari! There are the literary road trips too across the Mexican border. Legendarily, Kerouac's *On the Road*. Cormac McCarthy.

Predating all, the territories and worlds of Indigenous people.

Let me clear the table by way of introduction to say that the travels chronicled here, the feminist road-tripping conceptualized in the *Living West* project, is aware of these tales. Too aware. I raise them not to recenter them as origins for us but because I anticipate the associations readers likely have with "road trips" in their families and in American cultural life. Any of us exposed to America's tales of itself will have been trained to love them.

The West of classic lore conjures a legacy of open roads, beautiful country, a search for self, adventure, and fortune. It easily crowds out thinking that the contributors here are trying to eke out. You might say that's the West we "deal with" as feminists, as white women worth any salt as allies, as women of color, as Indigenous women. Because ask yourself: who actually crosses the border in the opening examples? And isn't the Trail of Tears, the many trails of tears of U.S. history, also a road trip?[1] We hope to take you elsewhere.

Feminist road-tripping as it emerges from the evidence of our collaborations amounts to somewhere else than the places created through those stories and amounts to someone else. The somewheres and someones, the lived histories and political understandings of lives lived, our lives, come from other sources. While there is mutuality and not naivete on the score of contradictory influences, familiar road trip tales do not help much to tell the where of us now.

LIVING WEST AS FEMINISTS IS A LIVE AND ONGOING PROJECT beyond the first and last pages of this book. It is as much about people and our relationships with one other, including our own histories, as it is about grappling with "the U.S. West" or the histories and practices of feminism. To the extent this book advances an argument proper, it argues for feminism as a relation, a system of relationships, more than a set of ideas committed to this or that vision of a future. It takes as its point of feminist reckoning the question of how we live and notice our living in specific places, on specific lands. Such reckonings with the politics of place have been the ongoing work of feminist critical regional analysis and theoretical frameworks.[2] *Living West* contributes a relational methodology to that evolving body of cultural theory.

During a couple of summers, in fifteen places over thirteen thousand miles across today's U.S. West and into Ontario, Canada, José Aranda and I met with people in places chosen by them. Who is José Aranda? My partner in life and husband, occasional work-partner, a Chicano/a studies scholar, and a mentor to graduate students. A feminist. José and I met with participants in backyards, in state parks, on intergenerational family lands, on county roads marking childhood memory. We met at Panhe, the place by the water, in the Acjachemen language. We visited a sheep farm, camped in the shade of the Tetons, were welcomed into Missoula's magnificent new public library and into the gorgeous gardens at the Georgia O'Keeffe Research Center in Santa Fe. We set up in front of a ceramic mural at the Sangre de Cristo Arts Center in Pueblo, my birthplace.

José Aranda loves to drive. More miles, for him, is a good day. He steered us through whiteout rain, hairpin turns in the Cascades, switchbacks over Berthoud Pass across the Continental Divide. He kept a

characteristic cool through miles bumper to bumper in the boggling traffic of the Mojave Desert coming west toward Los Angeles. Fires, wind,
smoke, haze, flying rocks, birds, deer, and sunny brilliant open skies. Of
course, the prize: big skies, sunset skies, barely lit skies of early starts.
But also white nationalists in Montana running a cheap motel we slept in.
A white Wyoming state trooper wearing the token mirrored sunglasses
who stopped us for not slowing down fast enough as we came into a small
town. After seeming over-interested in the Brown Hispanic man driving
a cargo van with Texas plates, and triple-checking our documents, the
trooper waved us on, friendly-ish. Another victory for our strategy of
Krista performing nice-white-lady-with-blonde-gray-hair? In an era of
total-wired living, a cell phone the basic equipment of First World life,
it's surprising how much of the United States is intermittently off the
grid. In the expanses of Wyoming or valleys of the Rocky Mountains, one
expects no signal, but not along the stretches running east of the Silicon
Valley. José drove on.

"The Invitation" that begins this book exhibits a one-page statement I sent to people who I hoped would participate. I invited scholars I
knew; some were younger scholars who had been graduate students of
José Aranda, others I know from surf research. Many I've known a long
time as members of the Western Literature Association. Who else but
people already connected to one another would be up for this experiment in knowledge-making that was also an experiment in new forms
of friendship?

Like me, the scholars I invited have overlapping interests in research
about place, gender, culture, and/or Native America, Black Wests,
Chicana/x and queer studies, and environmental or Indigenized environmental justice. For people with these interests, doing a self-study-in-place
made a kind of sense. Nonetheless, even for those with much in common,
questions about the places that we love or belong, or don't belong, and
who we are in them, are far from straightforward. Answers require "I"
responses, a blending of the personal, intellectual, and political. Most
people I invited to participate said yes. Others I wanted to invite but did
not, worrying I didn't know them well enough to ask. Questions about
the where of us are not casual, it turns out. They involve who one's people
are, to whom we feel accountable, and how any of us are making peace

with the itinerant, often displaced lives of most university faculty. Industries of higher education oblige university workers to go where jobs exist, another layer of complication in our relations to place.

Immediately before the pandemic and the summer of George Floyd, a version of *Living West* was beginning through conversations with colleagues Priscilla Solis Ybarra, Dina Gilio-Whitaker, and Martha Pitts. At the 2019 Western Literature Association conference in Estes Park, Colorado, we did a panel together, "Climates of Violence: Feminism and Environmental Justice." What was significant, more than a timely topic, was the chance to work across queer Chicana, Indigenous, African American, and what many women of color and Indigenous women call white feminism. As the white feminist of the group who at the time was writing toward "white troubles" in recent feminist films, I was all in, notwithstanding anxieties about mistakes.[3] After the Estes Park conference, encouraged by the goodwill and honesty of our exchanges, we kept meeting. We seized on the chance because, well, such an opportunity so rarely happens. When the political climate worsened, learning from each other seemed an obvious path toward a better, more collective feminism. The term "coalition" arose more frequently for us, and beyond us. If the term seems old-school, dated, or "1980s," the act of working across difference toward a common vision persists as the hardest and most important political work to sustain. Activists and scholars were resurrecting the term for today, and we joined that effort.

It is something of a truism to say that building feminist coalitions raises tensions about who feminism speaks for, the communities to whom it is accountable, identity politics, and the very notion of community itself. The term "feminism" is often pluralized, as in "feminisms," a move I do not make in this writing out of a sense of claiming feminism as a collective enterprise, coalitional at its sources. "Coalitional feminism" arises from links between justice movements and political thought, and for me it is preferable, as a theoretical premise, to the widely used term "intersectionality."[4] Returning to the question of feminist accountability under current political conditions brings unsettled debates about histories, needs, and alliances to new times of crisis. Coalition-driven actions like Black Lives Matter (#BLM) and No to the Dakota Access Pipeline (#NoDAPL), led by Black and Indigenous feminist visions, show the efficacy of alliances that can hold up against the most entrenched histories of violence. But conflict and lack of mutual understanding is also entrenched. Antagonisms, for instance, between Indigenous and African American activisms and justice priorities. Or the persistent "trouble with white women" and white racism in the women's movement revamped with new spokespeople like Ivanka Trump, who promotes her father as a feminist and models wealth-seeking as a feminist ideal.[5]

As an act of accountability, our group cowrote a symposium proposal focused on building better feminist coalitions within and across our communities. The idea was to bring lessons from earlier thinkers into coalitional work today. A reading list to guide us included Linda Tuhiwai Smith's *Decolonizing Methodologies* (1991), establishing that accountability to Indigenous communities is a core ethic for all research involving Indigenous people. The Combahee River Collective Statement (1977) and landmark *This Bridge Called My Back* (1981) by Cherríe Moraga and Gloria Anzaldúa clarified that differences of race, class, geography, and sexuality between women bear critically on white women's accountabilities. Bernice Johnson Reagon's "Coalition Politics" (1983), as true a statement now as it was forty years ago, teaches that coalition isn't warm and fuzzy. It's not "home." Coalition is what's necessary to stay alive. Not in that moment but later I would think of Minnie Bruce Pratt's acute confrontation with her own white racism in "Identity: Skin Blood Heart" (1984).

The above writings speak to the asymmetry of coalitional work and to histories of white feminists subsuming others' justice priorities. As a corrective, Priscilla Solis Ybarra urged our group to invite as speaker the philosopher Kristie Dotson, who along with Elena Ruíz, offers a more tempered sense of being "on the way" to coalition.[6] Another invitation went to Tiffany Lethabo King, whose concept of offshore "shoals" intertwines histories of genocide and slavery and helps map organizing challenges of the present.[7] Elsewhere King draws from a dialogue in Zainab Amadahy and Bonita Lawrence's "Indigenous Peoples and Black People in Canada: Settler or Allies?" (2015), which conceives coalitional practice as "how the substance of political work is not always about 'getting it right, but about committing to the process.'"[8]

Looking back, I see that others believed, as we did, that the moment demanded we step into fraught conversations. Woman Stands Shining

(Pat McCabe) and Carolyn Finney took up the challenge of bridging red/black divides in "Conversation at the Crossroads: The Intimacy of Rights Relations" (2020). A couple of us attended that conversation and witnessed how earnestly McCabe and Finney reached for one another, refusing to separate (as they put it) stories of stolen land and stolen people. Another grappling that has since been much celebrated is the very personal as well as political and intellectual exchange in letters between Robyn Maynard and Leanne Simpson in *Rehearsals for Living* (2022). Through their self-conscious relationality and commitments to a broad vision of justice that explicitly fights anti-Blackness alongside Indigenous land dispossession, they suggest a path forward in which abolition politics serve as enabling frameworks for sovereignty.

Ultimately, though, even as our symposium was funded by the Rice Humanities Center, all the pieces did not come together. The COVID lockdown was in full force and the very communities we hoped to gather were hardest hit. The symposium did not materialize.

I wonder whether we were or I was ready to lead the process.

Instead, when COVID restrictions eventually lifted and vaccines made travel less risky, I came up with a plan for a feminist road trip. Happy for time behind the wheel, up for (as he says) being a roadie, José Aranda volunteered as both driver and videographer. The plan drew on coalitional impulses by jump-starting reconnections with scholars through in-person and in-place interviews. Wherever someone wanted to meet, we would go. I had questions in mind—they had been brewing. But my desire to head out didn't happen overnight.

I have written a fair amount over the last ten years about the challenges of working from feminist perspectives on the U.S. West as a settler region and the changing status of "regionalism" under globalization.[9] Specifying the feminist stakes of gender/sexuality arguments in the field of U.S. West studies, and indeed in any field, is an important expression of accountabilities—to people and places, and to the politics always present in scholars' ideas.[10] In the last five or so years, in the Western Literature Association, scholarly conversations about feminism and place had seemed to stall. Scholarship generally was making a needed paradigm shift to understanding the West as a settler colonial space that attempts, historically and in the present, to eliminate Indigenous places, people, and knowledge. Histories of women and attention to gender analysis were central to the paradigm shift, though how or whether feminist stakes were part of research accountabilities was usually unstated. Meanwhile, as an organization, we held a series of painful and important sessions over a couple of years centering on histories of sexual harassment within the association itself. I was part of that team. We established a "Code of Conduct" to express no tolerance for sexual violence, trans* and homophobia, xenophobia, and racism.[11] A larger political climate clearly ignited some feminist concerns but not others. Why?

In contexts of meltdowns in national and global politics, the rise of patriarchal authoritarianisms, the Global Women's Marches, #MeToo, ubiquitous eco-grief, and on and on, a lot of organizing was on the ground. New feminist priorities had emerged from organized and grassroots sources with younger women of color, nonbinary people, and Indigenous people in the lead. Significantly, the Women's Marches leadership published a seventy-one-page "first intersectional policy platform" in 2019.[12] Specific policy initiatives, with next-step plans, include an end to interpersonal and state violence; advocacy for reproductive, racial, economic, and environmental justice; support for LGBTQIA, disability, civil, and immigrant rights. Three goals topped the list: Universal Health Care, passage of the ERA, Ending War. Given the policy directions of this movement, Mikki Kendall's bestselling *Hood Feminism* (2020) seemed to hit a popular chord when she defined feminism for *these* times as a feminism that cares about fundamental needs, food security, housing, incarceration, education access, medical including reproductive care, and livable wages.[13]

Then came the January 6 Insurrection at the U.S. Capitol. While the insurrection was shocking and dangerous, the action also bore familiar outlines of extremist activities that U.S. West researchers have been tracking in Oregon, Idaho, Nevada, Utah, and Washington state. NPR's Kirk Siegler connected the regional dots. In "Roots of U.S. Capitol Insurrectionists Run through American West," Siegler characterized a masculinist "Western ethos" behind previous stormings of federal buildings and threats against elected officials, with trivial legal consequence.[14] Insurrectionist actions in the Capitol had had practice in the administrative offices of western states. They had dress-rehearsed the insurrection consulting a western settler playbook. The difference now was that ethnonationalist militiamen had a powerful patriarch in the White House egging them on. Again, I wondered and worried. Where were we as feminists and scholars and university people working on the U.S. West in relation to these events?

I had my hunches. But I didn't want to "have a hunch," make an argument, or organize conversations through strands of feminist theory. It felt urgent to hear from people themselves about their own particularized, messier feminism. I wanted to get to know us better in our ideas about, and especially our troubles with, feminism. Troubles are legion in feminist thought, and I speculated about the why of cautions in U.S. West studies. But what was on people's minds as they themselves reported it? I was not sure how to initiate that conversation, or that once initiated, I knew how to let it take its course. A radical change was called for. It needed to get personal, and public in its personalness.

Leaving aside for a moment the question of who talks about place issues in scholarship, let me ask first: who talks about themselves at all? Challenges to scholarship as either objective or neutral are far more common than before global social movements of 1968 changed how universities do knowledge. But a look at graduate programs including in my own department or at major humanities journals shows that things have not changed very much. Scholars create reputations, satisfy standards of promotion, when they generalize knowledge and abstract authority into sequences of claims which speak toward an everywhere, not from an "I" somewhere. In a million small and large ways, we learn to scrub the "I" from our work. An "I" is implied in our pages, on every page. In book introductions, scholars are allowed, expected, to explicate an "I" that clarifies argumentative stakes. But then we are supposed to get on to the real business at hand: our claims and contributions to fields that are other abstracted bodies of knowledge, not people in particular. Though we might actually know these people, at times well.

In college, in graduate school, as years go by, the writers we are get estranged from the "I" doing the work, and the "I" living our lives. I am talking about myself here, for sure, and I have been reasonably successful at maintaining an "I" in my writing. Lately I've had help in seeing how much the process of assimilation into higher educational institutions de-skills individual scholars when it comes to the "I." In my home

English Department, a cluster of recent hires of very collegial and talented creative writing faculty have brought into my daily life lots of conversations about modes of writing, the process of teaching, and humanities missions. Together a few of us saw through a several-year process of curriculum redesign (blending creative and critical practices) and team-teaching our yearlong senior research seminar and writing workshop. Lacy Johnson and Ian Schimmel particularly have taught me how to lean into ways of writing less driven by argument as it is classically conceived. Embracing and challenging the "I" who writes is an important avenue into knowledge-making and is conducive to the issues so important to this book, accountability and relationality.

Of course, not all schools of scholarship are antithetical to the "I." Feminist and Indigenous scholarship offer many exceptions to a rule of authority without an "I." From the 1980s on, the move to acknowledge an "I" pulling strings in research and writing has been a premise of feminist social scientists and humanists. Situating oneself, establishing "positionality" as creators of knowledge, results not in less rigor but in a tougher standard for objectivity in knowledge, "strong objectivity" as Sandra Harding calls it.[15] It also pulls back a curtain concealing the authority of those who need not say who or where they are. Because who is the social actor who needs no introduction? Only the Euro-centered white masculine speaker. He is the royal "we."

The "I" of Indigenous studies, like the "I" of feminist studies, understands research to be linked and in relation to the presence of the researcher. In terms of purpose, while a broader critique of colonial or settler colonial masculine authority may be an outcome of Indigenous research, its aims are directed usually to Indigenous community flourishing. The "4Rs" of Indigenous research ethics—to respect Indigenous knowledge, create responsible relationships, engage in relational reciprocity, and conduct research relevant to Indigenous people—insist an "I" relates to a "we."[16]

In feminist scholarship, interestingly, those who most often talk about "the where of me" or place issues are women of color, postcolonial scholars, Indigenous scholars. That move seems both enabling but also at times a requirement for the writer to speak. How is it that some women are in place, while others apparently are not? To invent herself as a writer and thinker, for instance, Gloria Anzaldúa invents the place she comes from as a U.S.-Mexico border-dweller. Her book title *Borderlands/La Frontera* teaches readers the where of herself as a framework for theories of border consciousness, hybrid national histories, spirituality, and Chicana queer feminism. Like so many women of color feminists, Anzaldúa's move to locate an "I" from some unrecognizable outside or border place to a "we" is a move that connects personal to historical legacies. When the "I" becomes a "we," the halls of knowledge-power can be entered and altered.

But what about white progressive feminists? Placing oneself in history, tracking legacies that apply to specific places may be an unflattering process. Our life stories, those of our white kinfolk, often do not live on the right sides of history as much as we would wish. Bringing this background to the fore of our public selves, listening carefully for our own "white stories as such" might seem to nullify anti-racist and/or decolonial commitments of today, to add injury to injured parties.[17] It might seem better not to claim feminism if it requires locating and naming ourselves as white women and sorting the complications. Without consciously agreeing to the thought, we might feel disqualified or muddled about justice convictions. So much suspicion exists among white settlers, Indigenous people, people of color, women and trans* people, feminists, and feminism. Won't putting white histories into this mix, won't spotlighting white stories as such, agitate mistrust rather than help us know one another better as a way to become better neighbors?

What I find hopeful about the *Living West* project is its attempts to put these questions, among others, inside a relational network. It is very difficult to talk about whiteness without it taking over all the molecules in the room, as Susan Bernardin puts it in her interview. Still, the simple demographics of U.S. politics and histories of organizing suggest that white women and white feminists constitute a critical mass in any justice struggle. The more any of us figures out how to speak about our white histories, not be tempted into silence or passivity in the face of them, the more coalitional aspirations might be advanced.

To me, one of the great surprises is the well-being our work has generated among participants. By virtue of the kind of live project it is, we consented, before the fact, to reach beyond the differences of feminism and nurture what we share and learn from unlike histories. You might say we agreed more to be in relation to one another than to "do interviews." The concept of "feminist rest areas" that has come to animate these conversations is a way of imagining paths on the road trip that offer alternatives to conflict, offramps to being stuck or without a place (so to speak) to be together. "Feminist rest areas" as a term was devised with José Aranda and Zainab Abdali, who is the research assistant for the project. The three of us kicked around many ideas, this one among the first big ideas. Rest areas put group attention on relationalities that sustain us and provide security. They might offer actual rest or time to reflect, but they are more than a right to rest, as serious and important as that right is for women. Rest areas are about taking a break or having breathing space with company, not doing it alone, and focusing on what is good, what is working, between us. They are places where sometimes, possibly, as individuals or as a part of a collective, we might find perspective on the conflicts that consume optimism about solidarities.

Our visits and interviews allowed us to take time out from what younger people call "grind culture"—the crisis of exhaustions endemic to twenty-first-century hyper-capitalism and its violence.[18] Pretty immediately, the idea of "feminist rest areas" got bandied about as a way to pause and notice the strength and sureness that came from a beautifully and spontaneously prepared breakfast, for example. Or a story unexpectedly gifted by someone's elder mother about grave difficulties in a life history. Each feminist rest area moment grew from the quality of attention to the topics at hand, the connection created via conversations, thinking, and listening. Traveling to people's homes, meeting children, partners, parents, animals, finding street addresses and texting about logistics, sharing meals, going to beloved restaurants, driving in someone's car or them driving with us in the van, sometimes staying overnight in a spare bedroom or in a bedroom vacated especially for us—these moments infuse the where of us. Through them flowed rest area securities because connections and generosities are not transactional exchanges; they are small justice moments creating affective bonds.

In retrospect, serendipitous timing factored into the sense of group well-being. The COVID period frayed, delayed, and changed social life in ways we are yet coming to know. Increased awareness of mental health needs as well as opportunities for some to work differently, including working remotely, created openings amid great hardship. In universities, people were less in their offices and in department meetings. By meeting in state parks and backyards and family lands, conducting research in deinstitutionalized contexts, we lucked into shortcutting the "ugly feelings" as Lisa Duggan calls them, the hyper-competition and passive aggression driving so much university social life and productivity today.[19]

The perspective of relationality, the commitment to feminism less as a specific argument or set of claims than as a relation, seems to be a bedrock of group well-being. Public reporting about U.S. feminism cannot say enough of how feminists don't get along and implode their own initiatives, and I have hoped instead to hold true to the idea that our relations are as important a resource as anything else. Without solid relational foundations, the ability to listen and keep talking, one cannot sustain pushes for a different world. In my own white, raised-Protestant history, the idea of relationships as inherently precious and not measured by functionality and efficiency goes against the grain of norms and behaviors supporting achievement and upward mobility. It takes time to be good neighbors, both quality and quantities of it.

I am reminded of a story that is important to my own sense of justice, told by the feminist Silvia Federici. She is working in Nigeria, where her colleagues at university shake their heads to hear her define her major life security as the wage. The wage! How insufficient! Who will support you during hard times?[20] This story hits home for me and for my sense of the priority concern wages were for me as a young feminist. I was not focused on "equal pay" as much as economic autonomy, my ability to control my life because I could fund it. So I do not discount the wage as autonomy at all. But that was as far as an upper-middle-class imagination trained toward independence went. Federici's colleagues identify other sources of both security and vulnerability. What happens when self-reliance fails, they ask, as it must, eventually? A deep security, for them, is the presence of trustworthy others, community members and friends. Surely as an insight, the idea of banding together for mutual need is supremely obvious. It is the building block of social movements. But for me, and I daresay many white middle-class people schooled very primally in independence, it involves a fundamental retooling of the self. Because the people who support us when things get difficult, or who we support, are the people with whom we have accountability relations.

On this topic of security and vulnerability, I want to close by pausing on a few moments when the women around me taught me what I needed to learn in order to grow. A lot of my learning has happened through university life; going to talks that open new thinking; figuring out curricular change; teaching students, which always is mutually enriching; and experiencing the reading and discussion of feminist theory groups. But my education has also taken off in new directions through integrating university feminism with work I've been able to do through the Institute for Women Surfers (IWS). The IWS is an international public humanities project I direct; it was cofounded in 2014 with the world champion surfer and activist Cori Schumacher. Since 2015, it has been advised by a Steering Committee. The purpose of the Institute is feminist political education, and a curriculum can be found online for IWS trainings in California, Europe, and Oceania.[21]

In one of the earliest versions of these moments when the women around me were my teachers, before the Institute was formalized, I spent time with Farhana Huq and Mira Manickam. Farhana was in the process of founding the social change organization that became Brown Girl Surf.[22] In 2011 I learned with much surprise that surfers had read and were sharing my book *Surfer Girls in the New World Order*. They were reaching out to me with requests to collaborate in surf activism. Farhana was the earliest to reach out. We talked by email, then Skype, and eventually I would travel to Oakland to meet with her and scheme and laugh a lot and plan events designed to change surfing. This process is how we began to collaborate. I remember walking around Oakland close to Farhana's home with a group of her friends who were advising about Brown Girl Surf. All of them were younger, and none had children. Farhana was asking about "our passions." It was a group think, a go-round, one of Farhana's signature forms of leadership.

What bothered me was, when it came to me, I answered the question so feebly. I thought the question was naïve. In my university sophistications, I felt like, "There go the surfers, talking about living the dream." I did not consider my own happiness enough at that time—that's what

I took to be under discussion via "passions." There are times in a long university life when one bends to the job, and I had been bending for a while. In my alienated relation to my own for-real happiness in universities, in the distance that I could tell was accumulating over time to places I loved and knew myself best, I felt distance from Farhana's group. Theirs was a discussion about what it cost to live that dream, to surf a lot, to organize one's day and life around tides and wind, the foregone securities related to employment, health insurance, financial regularity. I had a steady income, children, a partner, but there were other costs to me of a financially secure life. How unrecognizable my spirit had become to myself, given the tenor of an earlier life with so much living outdoors. It was all taking a toll.

The experience with surf activists in Oakland lingers because I knew then, and continue to know, that I was distant not only from the group but from the previous me. I very much wanted to live the dream—not of surfing as a way to organize life, but of living close to the water as a way to organize purpose and a life lived in the body and the spirit of certain singular places. I left one place, Silver Strand Beach, to pursue education, because there was no feminist life I could figure out there. I chose to move toward a feminist life as it seemed to be unfolding. It was not much of a choice—I had to do it. But the choice broke something in me. Probably the broken spot was already there. It had to do with relations of self to the female body and to the spirit of place, and my inability to hold them together.

Which brings me to Sara Ahmed and the feminist killjoy—a term for those who get blamed as joy-killers when they bear news of sexism. Where does feminist theory end up? Ahmed asks. Where do *we* end up with it? In "Once We Find Each Other, So Much Else Becomes Possible," Ahmed offers her reflections. The "we" she addresses are women of color who might find possibilities for persisting when they find one another. She is talking about relationality as a buffer against the whiteness encountered in universities that are structured so they do not understand themselves as white. I have loved working with this bit of Ahmed's thinking in contexts of the Institute for Women Surfers because she upholds the significance of everyday archives, the lived archives "built from our experiences of walls, what we come up against."[23] Ahmed urges the "we" who are outsiders to build from the "creativity and inventiveness that is behind us" and that cannot be separated from "a survival story."[24] In the Institute's events, both in Wales and Australia, I have written this quote on the paper "board" we post to the wall to talk about seas of whiteness and maleness in global surf culture. The idea is to appreciate archives built from the everyday "us," meaning outsiders to institutions not designed for our flourishing. Ahmed's regard for an outsider archive that values the knowledges of other worlds discourages assimilation as the entry fee for intellectual growth or belonging. I love this quote because it cherishes the material from before, whatever someone's "before" is. Ahmed does not ask, nor want us, to leave former selves behind on the way to now.

All the stories and conversations moving through the *Living West* project show what they are built from, the histories and places where our archives root and take hold or have trouble rooting. Our earlier stories, those from before the we of us today, deserve respect and affection and whatever honest feminist telling we can bring to them. They deserve our thanks. They got us here.

THE BLOG LAUNCHES US

Even before José pulled the van out of the driveway in Houston, the project was live. The blog had launched our relationships in public.[1] Along the way, we became aware of one another. People who didn't know I stopped drinking young, now they could know it. Not everyone read everything. But most of us read something.

Excerpts from two initial blog entries will follow shortly as a way to give a picture of posts, what putting ourselves out there meant as examples for others who would be interviewed later. Because of COVID and remote instruction, graduate students at Rice had not really met Zainab Abdali, on the project as a graduate student research assistant, until they read the blog about her journeys from Islamabad to Syracuse to Houston. And until now and the blog, I had never found a right moment to return to memories of mine about the West Coast Women's Music Festivals.

When I conceived the *Living West* project, I had developed a website and worked on Facebook on behalf of the Institute for Women Surfers. Not as much as I should have, but for me it was a lot. I practiced writing outwardly, let's call it, toward the audiences who were Institute participants. Our trainings are open to the public, so some of the people attending I did not know until they applied. Naturally I learned to write toward this public the hard way, because of upsets of those who needed to see themselves being represented and I hadn't done it well enough. Or learned fast enough. Feminist representation should err on the side of very conscientious recognitions.

For scholars, I sensed a blog would force a different issue—to put ourselves on the page as us. Most of us have been hesitant, uncomfortable. Unlike surf activists, we're not sure we want an audience. Still, crises in the humanities, and all of that, we need to leave our shells behind. Blogs lend themselves to the present tense, evoking immediacy, transparency. They seem interactive and friendly. They invite informality. You can ask people for pictures from family albums. You can ask questions of people as researchers, tease out claims and evidence, but encourage sharing it in personalized, nonspecialist language. Especially if you do the same yourself.

The decision to craft this project as both a blog and a book has helped dramatize various conditions imposed by academic forms of writing. The mandates for "field interventions" and "arguments" as rationales for writing scholarship and creating new knowledge takes researchers down certain paths at the expense of others. It's the other paths we've had a chance to explore instead. Hence the project's intervention is in service of feminist relationalities and solidarities in process. I have faith that knowing each other more than we did can help us understand others' priorities differently and better.

Blogs and books are not substitutes. Books have their own lives, networks, and presence in institutions and libraries. Books are important as archival sources and travel through different circuits of readers and reviewing protocols. They create credibility. It's beneficial to have both a blog and book. It's possible they generate nonoverlapping discussions, knowledge, and audiences.

A few last notes are in order about the book's structure before we turn to my excerpt, and then Zainab Abdali's. Interviews have been edited from original videotaped materials as well as from their blog versions. Readers are invited to see them as linked but discrete conversations. The blog entries can be found on the *Living West* blogsite, and they have lots of photos and chattiness, standing as moments along a road trip. The book versions of each interview are condensed for publication and more curated.

For the book, in addition to introductory and concluding chapters, I have created intermittent short entries named "Road Finds." These entries point to the discoveries or "finds" of travel; some of them uncover problems, preview ideas to come, or contextualize long-standing convictions now seen differently from the perspectives of many miles, specific places, and once-in-a-lifetime company. These "Road Finds" call to mind detours and side trips that end up being the point of things, memorable as reckonings.

Visual entries on the blog are a delightful record of dogs, prom dresses, teenager-hood, birds, land, kin, and colorful picnics. For the book, a single visual that conceptualizes "feminist Wests" has been submitted by each contributor. These visuals collectively offer glimpses into the range of definitions of feminism, of Wests, and of ourselves embodied within places. Finally, each interview begins through an introduction by me that previews scholars' work and the background of our relationship. The conversations then proceed via the principle organizing the project, what I call "the where of here."

To the question of audience. A lot of people one may not expect have read the blog. Zainab Abdali's childhood friends are reading the blog, from Islamabad. A family member unknown previously to Kalenda Eaton contacted me to reach Kalenda, after reading about family lands in Whitehouse, Texas. My dear friend Bonnie Leonard, dean when I was an undergraduate at Wellesley College and someone who came to my wedding and with whom I still keep touch, is reading and telling me what she learns. For the record, my mother is reading.

Excerpt of "Heading Out," *Living West* blog
KRISTA COMER

When I was twenty, twenty-one, twenty-two . . . I don't know exactly. I think the year was 1980 or 1981. There's a lot of stories I could tell, no single moment of political consciousness. But all of them are stories about places.

My early place orientations owe everything to the southern Colorado prairies running up to Pike's Peak, the fact that my aunt was afraid to ride her own horse, and the fact that from about ten years old on, I became a rebel girl with no sense of why.

Later for our road trip, when we get to my birthplace Pueblo, I will be interviewed there by José. I am from a family that, on both sides, was a business family in an era of postwar prosperity. In the businesses, the family women had roles to play. I am the eldest of five sisters, but in Pueblo we were only three sisters. In photos I am a six-year-old with a pixie haircut, smiling prettily in a blue velvet dress, white stockings, black patent leather shoes.

But as a launch point for our project, what came to mind is a story about a different road trip taken out of battles with myself and trying to figure out how to think about the world.

My introduction to the West Coast Women's Music Festival was not seeing women walk the slack line naked. I have no memory of a slack line. I would not have recognized what it was or the talents it requires. What

Song and Celebration at the West Coast Women's Music Festival

Jamming and Jiving Under Yosemite's Golden Boughs

by M.A. Karr

GETTING THERE

THE ROAD IS deserted and dark, closed after the summer rush to Yosemite. The sky, well-brushed and wistful, is full with a harvest moon. Thousands of women are southbound on Interstate 5, with nowhere to turn for 30 miles, following a ill-begotten and half-hearted map. "If this turns into a dirt road, we're going back, I don't care what you say," a companion complains.

In the middle of the road, there are women in day-glo construction vests sporting flashlights, giddy-business, brandy-mit-coffee and new toy walkie-talkies. "Robin, honey, bring us more coffee out. Where is it, sweetie? Out." Finally, directions to a place where the cabin might be. We stumble through the dark, trees silhouetted above. A canceled press party becomes a jam session. There's wine in styrofoam cups and Gwen Avery on the piano. Tired and bleary from the dust, sweatered women stroll in the late night cool, city-conditioned ears buzzing in the silence. Then sound checks in the morning—"testing, testing." Dusty mattresses and night birds . . . dew-soaked pantlegs . . . and satisfied fireflies.

FRIDAY

Although the festival is supposed to be three days long, nothing much happens on Friday. Breakfast is fruit and yogurt on the cabin porch steps and a hot shower. Most of the women will arrive today—their Hondas, VWs, trucks and campers kicking up the powdery dust, choking carburetors and noses, jockeying for a spot in the remote horse-pasture parking lot. Dykes-on-Bikes line their mounts up across from the information area and stumble, growling, to their campsites or cabins. Women in wheelchairs, with guide-dogs, with children, arrive and hustle; the soft sounds of German, Danish, French and Spanish voices float

The ADVOCATE (Ticket Section), January 8, 1981

Over 2,000 women gathered for the first West Coast Women's Music Festival this past September.

from the footpaths and latrines. Sleepy noises in the early morning cool.

As the day grows warmer, shirts come off and women wander to the lake—icy cold mountain water full of fist-sized tadpoles curious enough about warm flesh to take toothless nibbles. The women swim naked and lie on the clover. Impromptu jam sessions start in cabins, campgrounds and under trees. The Orchestra Sabrosita, a San Francisco salsa band, join forces with members of Alive!, a San Francisco jazz group, and hot Latin rhythms blast-out under the noon sun.

By late afternoon, craftswomen have set up their wares. The campgrounds and cabins are full, almost everyone has found friends, and the migration over to the main lodge for dinner begins.

The many Friday night workshops range from a Matriarchal Shabbat Ritual, a Festival choir, and Incest Survivors workshop, to Z Budapest's White Blessing Circle. Alix Dobkin, a lesbian singer, activist and performer at the festival, airs her opposition to boy children on the festival grounds during her workshop. While members of the press are briefed at Robin Tyler's cabin, an idyllic weekend suddenly becomes very hectic.

Essential information: **Robin Tyler** and **Tori Osborne** are co-producers of the festival; the seed money came from an accident settlement; it took three to four months to organize the event; and *everyone* worked while there. The organizers had even built ramps for wheel-chair accessibility for the approximately 50 disabled women in attendance.

Tyler and the lead singer for the Orchestra Sabrosita dash from the press conference to open the weekend with a salsa dance in the cool Yosemite mountains. Sabrosita is a big group (violin, trumpet, sax, piano, bass, percussion) and they're decked-out in San Francisco Mission District finery laced with punk. It's a professional sound, a great presence and everyone sambas in their down

75

Fig. 3. Article on the West Coast Women's Music Festival in *The Advocate*, January 8, 1981. *The Advocate*, 1981. Used with permission.

I remember is a white woman, maybe in her late thirties, beckoning me into the festival's grassy parking expanse. A few women staffed the edges of the festival grounds. This woman wore an orange construction safety vest, open, no shirt, no bra. She had on baggy shorts, and boots, and her walkie-talkie chattered as she made her way to my car window, leaned way in, and with a smile said, "Hey honey, over there," nodding toward the spot where I was to park.

I was twenty-one, twenty-two? I already had the feminist bug, the fever.

My boyfriend at the time—we built houses out at the beach, him the builder and me selling them—was crushed by the trips I took. Maybe I had learned about this music festival on an earlier road trip, also taken solo, to Oakland, or Berkeley? I was hearing strange news. I remember hearing the term "the matriarchy." I did not assess it as outlandish. I was only surprised anyone talked about the whole of history. I had never thought to make any claim about history, including my own.

I remember how I was driven to pursue "it," this thing I was doing, this act of feminist travel. What havoc and confusions it caused between my boyfriend and me. I remember calling him on the road, calling home to Oxnard, where we had a stucco house with carnations in the flower box across the street from the sand at Silver Strand Beach. Our world of ocean, dogs, a vision of how to live alongside the water, dreams. Maybe I was at a phone inside a cabin in the Sequoias?

I must've pitched a tent on the festival grounds because I remember trying to find it later in the dark, walking past other women's campsites after a show under a starry sky. Drunk. *This again*, I remember feeling. Drunk, lost in the dark.

The West Coast Music Festivals were where I first saw women put up their hands in staggering numbers when a speaker asked, from the stage, how many had experienced sexual violence. I remember meeting Z. Budapest and Starhawk. They had tables set up and I spent a long while listening at the edges of their conversations. Did I understand what I was hearing when Bernice Johnson Reagon schooled the crowd with the "Coalition Politics" speech? I saw lots of women's bodies, their shapes, across ages, across race. Nobody was shaving. Swimming, holding hands, laughing loud, running the stage lights, the communal kitchen, the parking, the show.

The feeling of the place was easy, unselfconscious. *Herland* before I knew names like Charlotte Perkins Gilman, a world away from the Southern California bikini culture of home. I was wary of the bikini; it was hard enough to evade guys' attention with my clothes on.

The outdoor grounds of the festival were a feminist reprieve and I hadn't known I needed one. I remember the signs directing us to "Women Only" spaces, "Women with Boy Children" and, vaguely I remember, "Women of Color" spaces. I was amazed anyone had thought of such categories. Reading newspaper reporting on the festivals since, including Michigan's, I recall some of the conflicts during my own earlier times there, over the boy children. I did not understand or approve of a need for separate spaces for boy children.

When I got home to Oxnard, to my boyfriend and our dogs, I doubt I had language for what I had learned at the festival, what I had seen, how scared I had been and doubtful I could even find that off-road remote place. Did I have a map? I must have. I had no coherent thinking to share with him, and I would not have said how much confidence those women in orange safety vests gave me.

I imagine there was beach walking when I got home. Troubled sandy walks where we did our apologizing and trying to make sense of things and especially our making up. Those beach places cemented our him and me, the textures of our bonded life. I was sorry, so sorry, to be such a problem. I could not explain the feminist fever, why it made me turn our life upside down and quarrel with all his friends.

He did not deserve the drama of my feminist coming out. Many things I did not deserve. He cut me off once we parted ways, and our beach house and other work together was sold.

When my younger sister Lee moved in with me during her high school years, I was still living in that beach house and watering the carnations, it was before everything changed and I left town to return to school at Wellesley College. I took Lee out of class and we drove up together to a later music festival, maybe 1983. A sisterly gift I was trying to give. I need to ask her about it. My memory is it was messy.

The break with my boyfriend was a break with place, with that beach, our foggy morning walks, the world of musty ocean and treks in the little truck with surf racks to away-spots like Jalama Beach for surf. It was a break necessitated by the young feminist I was becoming because being feminist was not optional. The festival was an official place of consciousness. Women like Starhawk and Z. Budapest, Sweet Honey and the Rock, initiated me into ways of living and thinking I desperately needed.

All that urgency and heartache and dawning "movement consciousness" is mixed into those festivals, the outdoors of Northern California cold water mountain lakes under big piney trees. Drunk or not, I was proud of myself for getting there.

Excerpt of "Islamabad→Syracuse→Houston," *Living West* blog
ZAINAB ABDALI

This "feminist West" conversation has been making me think about the feminist communities that I wouldn't think that I would be a part of, in the West.

I grew up in Islamabad in Pakistan. My parents are from Karachi, Pakistan, and my grandparents are from India. They were migrants in 1947 when Partition happened. But my "there" really is Islamabad. Because I grew up there. I felt very connected to Islamabad, I was there 'til I was seventeen. But I knew that my forefathers weren't from there. But the "there" they were from is not a place I can go to again, or ever. I can't go and my parents haven't been either, to India. So Islamabad really was home to me. When I left Islamabad, I was seventeen. I went to Saudi Arabia for a year. I finished high school there. And then I moved to Syracuse, New York. Syracuse was my first home in the United States, and by the end of my four years, it did feel like home as well.

I have very conflicted feelings about Syracuse. They are good at student outreach, incoming student outreach. But Syracuse itself. There were a lot of unwelcoming aspects about Syracuse. There were very few people of color at Syracuse University. The dorm I was in was majority white. There were definitely incidents and things that happened that made me feel unwelcome. But over the years, through the effort of other Muslim students and my efforts, we were able to build a Muslim community. So by the end of my time there, I felt like I belonged. You create a place; you carve a place for yourself.

Honestly, it was Muslim women, who were older than me, who took me under their wing. And there were very few. There wasn't much happening at the university, but people took initiative. Graduate students mentored me even though they didn't need to—I wasn't in their department or anything. And then, after me, I mentored the younger people. I had very nice kind friends. My roommate and the people on my floor really did try to help me. I was very new to the United States. But I had to take some part in creating community myself.

Getting off campus, I felt more at home. I started volunteering at the Northside Learning Centre. It's a refugee education center. I fell in love with that place the first day I walked in. They provide English-language learning for adults and children. It was initially supposed to be an adult learning center, but the founder told me that if you want to do an adult English learning center, the women won't come because they have children. So they opened it to everyone. The founder said we're open for ages four to seventy-four! For the children it was more tutoring than learning because a lot of them had been in the United States for a while.

When I started working there, I found a sense of community. And it was my first year and I was like, "Wow, okay, I can feel like I'm at home," even though there weren't any Pakistanis. My students were all Somali and other East African students, a few Ethiopians, a few Burmese students. By the end, it was a lot of Syrian students. I mean, I can talk about Northside forever, because I loved that place. You're surrounded by these young Muslim girls, and the whole center was a lot of different languages and different people. A really happy place.

I never thought that that's the community I needed. When I came to Syracuse even in the beginning, I was like, "I'm fine. It's okay. I have very nice friends." Two weeks into my freshman year, a student who lived in my dorm sent around a Snapchat photo of me to other folks who lived on the floor and captioned it "bomb threat." I remember that really shook me—I didn't know how to respond to it. I didn't have a community to turn to. I was so new to the university and to the country itself. There wasn't really anybody, any figure of authority or university resource, who I felt like would have supported me.

But honestly all those years in Syracuse, it was the classroom environment that felt most hostile. I sat in so many classes where the instructor would have us debate the pros and cons of drone strikes in northwest Pakistan, or whether Muslim immigrants should be allowed to enter the

Fig. 4. Image of Mosque Isa Ibn Maryam (The Mosque of Jesus, Son of Mary), formerly the Catholic Trinity Church, in Syracuse, New York. Part of the complex of the Northside Learning Center. Courtesy Dina Eldawy.

United States, or whether "some countries" have cultural differences like honor killings that make it impossible for migrants to assimilate to American culture. Stuff like that. And students would say this while I'm sitting right in front of them, in my hijab, visibly Muslim, and the professors would not intervene. They encouraged these debates.

I remember one sociology class where there was a debate at the end of the semester about Susan Okin's article "Is Multiculturalism Bad for Women?" I remember half of the class coming up with carefully prepared points for why Muslims can't assimilate, and how Muslims are uniquely oppressive toward women, and then I had to rebut their points. In those moments I was so, so angry at the students who said this stuff, but now in hindsight I can't believe how irresponsible the instructors were.

I did not identify with "feminism" until I got to college. In high school, in Pakistan, I really did think of feminism as something not for me, but something for, like, white Western women. I associated feminism with a white savior idea, about "saving Muslim women." But my parents are very open-minded, considering how religious they are. My dad raised me very strongly to believe in economic independence for women. We are four sisters and my parents gave us freedoms that I didn't see other girls of my age getting. But I didn't associate that with the word "feminism," maybe "women's rights" or "women's equality," but not "feminism."

When I came to college, I took a class on Native American women and feminists. Dr. Sally Wagner was teaching us about how Indigenous women influenced the activisms of Susan B. Anthony and Elizabeth Cady Stanton. She made us think about feminism for each of us individually. At the end of that semester, I did a project on a tribe in northern Pakistan, an Indigenous tribe of that area, the Kalash, on Kalash women. That class made me think about being Native in non-American contexts. At the end of the class, I shared that I felt comfortable calling myself a feminist because I had been exposed to women of color feminisms that allowed me to look beyond the prior associations I had had about feminism. I found my way to feminism, to a Pakistani Muslim feminism, through Indigenous women's feminisms.

Today my feminism is abolitionist and anti-carceral. I've been thinking about abolition as a great framework for the way I approach feminism. It is connected to prison and police abolition, and then also to ending the "War on Terror." There is a Muslim advocacy group that put out a call recently, maybe last year (2020), to "Abolish the War on Terror." That's a really broad vision and so ambitious. They frame anti–War on Terror organizing along the lines of prison abolition. Their materials quote Ruth Wilson Gilmore. I find that to be a promising and clarifying way to go about it. Angela Davis's *Freedom Is a Constant Struggle* and *Abolition Democracy* are works that place the War on Terror and the torture in Abu Ghraib or Guantanamo Bay along the same continuum of domestic prisons and policing in the United States. Connecting the figure of the criminal and the figure of the terrorist, connecting policing and warmongering—this work speaks to the *absolute necessity* of abolitionist feminism.

LIVING WEST AS FEMINISTS

PART 1

SUMMER 2021

The Relations Holding Us, with Priscilla Solis Ybarra

Fig. 5. A bumblebee with pollen-covered legs climbs out from a yellow bloom—it dots the bank near a lake in the lands of the Wichita and Caddo Affiliated Tribes in a place for-now called North Texas. "Spanish Gold." Courtesy Priscilla Solis Ybarra.

In the last couple of years, Priscilla has been taking a lot of photos. She posts them on social media sites as #ChicanaBirder. The photo of the flower "Spanish Gold" contributed to the playwright and director Virginia Grise's project on Instagram to welcome the spring equinox in 2021. Grise's activist art lately inspires Priscilla's writing. She's just published a piece about watching Chicanx theater with her mother and what they teach one other.[1] The play tells of an urban farm in South Central Los Angeles founded after the 1992 Rodney King riots.

Priscilla is one of a handful of Chicanx scholars who have been making the case for relationships between Chicanx communities and environmental studies, and the necessity for decolonial relations to the land and land use. Raised in a family that worked the fields as migrant laborers, she and they know about growing food.

When José and I arrive at Priscilla's house in Denton, it is Friday, July 2, about 2:00 p.m., and she is waiting for us in the street. She greets us while taking a photo of one of three juvenile Mississippi kites perching on a tree limb.

Priscilla is a "soft landing" as a first official interview. It has been a huge push to get ready to travel, arrange for our younger son to look after our house, just get out the door. We have not done this kind of long venture, ever. Too many responsibilities—but even our young adult kids agree it's time for us to go! We have traveled north from the coastal plains of Galveston Bay in the Gulf of Mexico through Houston and further north. At about Conroe, we see the beginning of southern pines associated with the Big Thicket.

We arrive in pretty decent shape, psychologically and physically, and part of our wellbeing is Priscilla and what she means to us. José was her PhD director at Rice, and I have worked with her and learned from her. For over a decade, José and Priscilla have conducted semi-annual "Tallers" or writing workshops to develop Chicanx scholarship. El Taller has nurtured younger scholars' work and invited the debriefings needed to get through the rocky road of university life for Chicanx faculty and graduate students. Running Tallers has given José and Priscilla practice at crossing the personal and scholarly with the political. The interviews we do together for Living West as Feminists *has a core Chicanx foundation. All that saturated relationality and trust holds us.*

"Relationality" means María, Priscilla's mother, is a force in our project. She and Priscilla live together these days, and María is full of joy to see us. She takes instant comfort that this white woman carrying in her bags to spend the night, who comes with the much-beloved José, speaks passable Spanish and cares about talking to her. I have met María, but this visit is not in a lecture hall or restaurant but in her place, her home, with the colors and photos of their lives. What food they have made! Peach and tomato gazpacho. María chops vegetables all morning. A Southwest succotash appetizer of lima beans, corn, squash, red peppers, cilantro, cumin. This feminist care ethic, informed

by everything that Priscilla believes and that her mother teaches her, connects our talk of tomatoes and today's rainstorms to the land and to the ways we are with one another.

The Where of Here: Clear Creek Natural Heritage Area

Krista: Let's back up and tell folks about conversations we've been having since we arrived at Clear Creek. And we will record for posterity that Priscilla has let us know that when there's some bird photo that she *must* take, she will. [laughter]

Priscilla: This is one of my favorite places—it's called Clear Creek Natural Heritage Area. I've been coming here at least fifteen years, walking dogs. It's developed over time into a trail system. It runs along the Clear Creek of the Trinity River. I've always liked to hike here. But one of the things that I've been doing in the past two years is a lot of birding. So when we were pausing at the beginning of our filming, we heard a cardinal and a pretty loud summer tanager. And an indigo bunting that hopefully will fly close for us to see.

The past pandemic year and a half, this place has become even more important to me, which I thought wasn't possible. I could come here and be safe because I was outside and people were masking while hiking, being really respectful. And I was learning so much about the birds and the plants and trees and the grasses. I've done a great deal of travelling during my entire academic career, even as a graduate student. But the pandemic really made us slow down. I'm from north Texas, I was born in Dallas, I went to college here in Denton. And now I've been teaching here at the University of North Texas for ten years. But I've gotten to know this place, this spot on Earth, this land, so much better in the past year and a half. I feel much more of a relationship with this place, and this Heritage Area has played a big role in that.

Krista: We are talking in the "Pocket Prairie," and looking at flowers here and one of them—

Priscilla: The lemon bee balm. Yeah, all kinds of wild flowers here during the seasons. This is a prairie we're sitting in. Then there's the post oak forest. There's a wetland, and a creek. Lots of different bioregions in this one place. There's a big garden. Schoolchildren come here for environmental education.

Krista: An interesting question for people's relationship to place is where they feel safe, where they feel they belong, what things or to what places or lands they feel they belong. Sometimes the way people think about that question is they know where they're not supposed to be, where they feel unsafe or unwelcome or out of place.

Priscilla: This is a municipal "Heritage Area," but these are the lands of the Wichita and the Caddo affiliated tribes. Comanche also would come through. The city of Denton is named after John B. Denton, a big perpetrator of genocide against the Wichita and Caddo people. I do bring attention to that history through speaking engagements, with my students, especially these days over Zoom. That attention has been growing in the past two years.

I've had the rare privilege as an academic to live in a particular place for most of my life. I was born in Dallas, in the Trinity River watershed. I was raised close to the Brazos. I've had the privilege of being close to my family. Still, it's hard to talk about "a sense of place."

It's like a deeply rooted familiarity with the feeling of the air, what it's like when it rains, what the air feels like when there's tornadoes, how hot it gets, and it's getting hotter and hotter. In winter, there's always going to be at least one ice storm. I know those kinds of things in my bones in a way that when I've lived other places I didn't. I feel a comfort level with the oak trees. An oak tree is a tree to me, you know—like, that's what a tree is. I know there's tons of different trees. But an oak tree is the tree, my uber tree. Oh, that's a yellow-billed cuckoo. You hear *cuckuckuck*.

I'm trying to answer your question. But I'm not really answering your question. It's a growing question for me too. Your question was broader— like, what does it mean to feel like you belong? My sense of belonging is of the air and the sounds and the rain and the weather. The weather patterns and the smell of the soil and the shape of the water, its creeks and rivers and reservoirs. All of that is what makes me feel at home. And I haven't even had to think about it that much. Because I've basically always lived at home. You know, even Houston, it's not this—it's a very different bioregion.

Krista: And you're not the only "belonging being" who matters. Creatures matter. That's something that we're listening for as we talk.

Priscilla: Yeah, this is the dynamic that I've been thinking about. It's always been important to me, but until recently I have not given myself permission to think of myself as someone who "does that." Who factors in the "other beings." I have a developed idea of belonging, and not belonging, as a queer Chicana, as an academic, in the social sense. But I'm thinking these days about place and the degree to which I've not given myself permission to be a naturalist, a natural historian. I've always been cultivating that, but I hadn't crossed over into it the way that I've let myself over the past two years.

Krista: And does being a natural historian belong to someone else? That set of knowledges?

Priscilla: It has belonged to someone else! But I decided that it belongs to everyone, that we all access that knowledge to one degree or another. I really hate the idea that "natural history" has been categorized so narrowly.

Krista: Do you want to put a couple of guardrails on what you're talking about? Names or traditions or organizations?

Priscilla: I don't even really identify as a birder. I put it on my Instagram, #Chicanabirder.

Krista: The natural historian and the Chicana haven't automatically lined up?

Priscilla: No, and, interestingly, I found two other Chicana birders and—I know, this sounds so millennial!—we're the only ones in the Instagram universe who have used that hashtag for our posts. One of them is in Seattle, and the other one is in Southern California. We found each other and had whole conversations through Instagram messaging. That is so rare.

I don't identify as a birder or a natural historian or scientist or even an "environmentalist." Because those categories are too constrained. They suggest a kind of authoritativeness and mastery, and though I have the ability to do all kinds of things, "master them," I do not identify with that hierarchical sense of what it means to be a scientist or natural historian.

Krista: I wanted to hear your thoughts about whether your sense of place is related to some large entity we might call the "U.S. West."

Priscilla: "Region" has been dodgy for me, historically, because Texas is hard to pin down in terms of regions. Where I grew up here in the northern part of Texas, it borders on the Great Plains, and feels very southern, feels very western. It feels very Texas, growing up in the public school system cultivates a distinct sense of identity as a Texan.

My sense of place has been more in relationship to Texas, as a historical entity, the way that it has changed politically and socially over time, and completely in relationship to Mexico. Because of history, but also because of my mother's immigration from Mexico. I have always existed on a map that's more in relationship to that north/south vector than the east/west vector.

Krista: So we're not in the West, we're in "Greater Mexico"?[2]

Priscilla: Absolutely.

Krista: What do you think about linking those two? Is it useful for you analytically?

Priscilla: Yeah, especially in terms of Manifest Destiny and the relationship with the history of Greater Mexico. Environmentally, I think about the evolution of the politics of humans' relationship to where we dwell in this country. It's been about the history of U.S. imperialism and takeover of half of Mexican lands and the way those lands become the imaginary of American environmentalism.

The West as "an environmental place" has always been, still is, Greater Mexico, of course. But the environmental conversation does not see it as Greater Mexico. That's part of why I wrote *Writing the Good Life*, to map the Mexican onto the environmental in terms of regional imaginaries. So, as an analytic, the U.S. West helps us become aware of larger dynamics. The West becomes an imaginary for environmental thought and policy and all the national parks, and activism, monkey wrenching, tearing down the dam.

Krista: Let's talk about feminism, and how you understand your own feminism.

Priscilla: I've always practiced the "redefinitions" that feminism brings us. My mother is a very strong character. To me, she's always been a feminist. I think my father, at least with me, was practicing feminism in terms of the way that he wanted me to become exactly who I wanted to become. I grew up in a very fundamentalist Christian church, but my home was not very patriarchal. Once I was about fifteen, my mom told me, "You can go to church or not."

There's a woodpecker in that mesquite tree over there. Just flew over there. I think it's the downy woodpecker. On the right, the mostly dry mesquite tree, right in the middle, upper branches. It's on the side—it's hard to see. I saw it fly into the tree. I wasn't sure what it was. But now that it's on the side of the tree, it's pecking. I can see the motion. I might be able to get a picture. The lighting is really weird. Oh, no, it's a red-bellied woodpecker. That's a pretty big woodpecker.

I didn't identify with feminism until I came to college, at the University of North Texas (UNT). I was in the first women's studies course ever offered at this university, 1994, maybe, my second or third year of college. It met on Wednesday evenings, for three hours, and instead of having a particular professor, we would go to professors' classes, or they would come to our class. We learned from political scientists, from English professors, philosophy professors, psychology professors, the whole range. I learned fundamentally that women's studies is interdisciplinary. We did have one textbook. Even with the core group, it was not just one approach. I started to recognize things in my life that I could identify as feminist.

But I still wasn't able to connect how my mom was able to do what she did, apart from the histories that were being told to me. It didn't map on. My best friend in college, Sarah Oglesby, her mom was in the feminist movement, in NOW [National Organization for Women] so it mapped right on, right? And she was my English professor, and became my colleague and good friend, Barbara Rodman.

One way "feminist identification" often happens is that one learns about feminism and says, "Oh, these were all the ways in which I was constrained, growing up. And now I'm going to do things differently." But my parents cultivated my independence. The genealogy was fundamentally different.

Krista: Can we talk about ways in which a sense of place has feminist dimensions for you? You're talking about a feminism that has at its core a sense of autonomy for women or a sense of possibility, independence. What would you characterize as a feminist vision for you about environment or about place and *this* place?

Priscilla: One of those things that goes deep in my life experience, but I wasn't always able to connect the dots, is autonomy, nonpossessiveness. A deconstruction of hierarchy, or a distributed power, not hierarchical power. My mother always cultivated in me a sense of autonomy. She would say she never wanted me to be dependent on a man. That I should always be able to leave, whenever I wanted. That's about nonpossessiveness in a relationship, no control.

The priority then was to cultivate financial independence through education. But part of that was learning about autonomy more generally. In relationship to place and relationship to land, it is recognizing the way that we dwell in community with one another. And that's really the better way to approach our relationship to place and other beings, a nonhierarchical, nonpossessive relation. It's postcapitalist, as a way of thinking about land and place. That then is fundamentally "environmental." But I wasn't able to make that connection for a very long time.

Krista: Are you thinking of postcapitalist in the way of feminist theories of postcapitalism? As in Gibson-Graham, *A Postcapitalist Politics*?

Priscilla: Not really that so much as "post" all those systems. The way that I was able to find a place for myself and my family story, and my relationship to place, was through Chicana feminists of northern New Mexico, from the 1960s and '70s. What they were writing about was a rejection of possession and control over land and women's bodies, fundamentally. Enriqueta Vasquez and Betita Martinez, who died just days ago. Maria Cotera is going through all of Enriqueta Vasquez's papers right now. What an amazing archive.

I was very drawn to those writers and wanted to read the newspaper they founded and published for the land grant movement in the '60s and '70s.[3] The most visible leader of that movement was Reies López Tijerina. In writing my history of Mexican American environmental action and thought, he looms very large. But I found the writings of these women who identify as feminists, Chicana feminists, to be much more rewarding of my time and investigation. I eventually figured out I was interested in them because they said the land grant movement was not just about people who owned the land and now other people own the land. It's about that nobody should own the land. That's really radical.

Recently I came across some of Enriqueta's writing, where she documented the fact that at the famous Chicano Youth Conference in Denver, they came up with this idea of land banks, to create communal property within the movement. Not the land back movement that we're seeing today with Native nations. Instead of saying, Oh, well, after the U.S.-Mexico War, so many Mexican American families lost their land, and we're going to sue the United States to get possession of the land for these particular families, this was a different thing altogether. She's invoking alliance with Native nations too. This practice invokes Mexican American Indigeneity but also cooperation with Native people.

Krista: I wonder if you would tell a story about yourself, a feminist story of place.

Priscilla: Maybe this is a little abstract, but my commitment to this place, to living here, and I feel like it's a very feminist practice, has everything to do with my family. For most of my life, I've prioritized my career, education, and job, my endeavors as a scholar. But once I came back home, it was very clear to me that the priority is to be home. That is about care and not about ambition or status or success or even financial reward.

Krista: So then, a story about your family?

Priscilla: That's a big question.

Krista: Anything that comes to mind, a little thing. We could begin by talking about this afternoon with your mom if you want. Or maybe we could talk about the work you're doing with Cara Mia, the theatrical group?

Priscilla: One story that I can tell about my family is . . . I'm always abstracting. Ugh, this is hard.

Krista: It is. I was saying before, it's slippery, and that's why I came up with telling a story about "feminist relations to place" because we're all trained to abstract.

Priscilla: For most of my life, I was the satellite among all the children of my mother. I was doing my own thing, and my brothers were the ones that were close to home and taking care of things. That role has shifted now that I've committed to being in this place. It's been a process of learning how to inhabit that role in my family. I've had independence in the family, but not authority. Now I'm in a place in those relationships where I carry more authority because of the responsibility that I'm taking as the primary caretaker for my mother.

My feminism plays a role there because if I didn't have the structure, or the analytic of "care" as a priority, that one can commit to care, and it's a position of strength, it would be harder for me to own the decisions that I'm making about how I'm structuring my life.

Krista: It would seem like classic women's exploited labor?

Priscilla: Right. And that I should prioritize my career or my scholarship or both. If I had kids or a husband, not a queer life . . . the kids would be in school and everybody would just assume, "Oh, yeah, of course, you're gonna live there. Because your kids are in school, or your partner's career" or whatever. But I am here because I have done this on purpose. "Care" is a real position of strength—it's not just human to human but also to this place.

I think so much about shifting from privatization and possession, towards a sense of community and dwelling together. That looking through that lens at just about anything is fundamentally transformational. I think about all the time that I've spent learning about history and politics and literature and theory, and it really comes down to that. That analytic can help negotiate any number of challenges, and really reinvent any number of relationships. And I think that's something that my mother has known for a really long time.

Fig. 6. Elena V. Valdez watches as her daughter holds a camaleón in Cebolla, New Mexico. Courtesy Elena V. Valdez.

It's the day before the Fourth of July and we are driving north from Denton toward the Llano Estacado. José is behind the wheel, and I'm not sure who of us first says that Priscilla's house was for us a "feminist rest stop." We are beginning to put this language of the blog into use, feeling out what it means. We are talking about the well-being of Priscilla's and María's care ethic, the ways that care infuses connections to land, food, and to mutual ways of being with one another, listening to one another across generations. We feel secure knowing we have Priscilla's lunch tucked away for later on ice in our cooler.

Immediately outside of Denton the trees change, become scrubbier, bushier, and a sense of distance on all sides tells us we've entered the southern plains. We're in cattle country, passing through Park Springs, Chico, and signs for The Jackson Spread, The Shaw Ranch. A water reservoir paralleling the Texas 101 is filling up with today's rain. We do not take the roads toward Waurika, Oklahoma, Chickasaw country. Close to Harrold, Texas, the wind farms begin.

We are headed for Santa Fe and spending time with Elena Valdez. And with Zenaida, nickname Zeni! Zeni is the ten-month-old daughter of Elena and Matt Pacheco. We are going officially to interview Elena, and see Matt too, but we can barely contain ourselves looking forward to Zeni. We will stay at their place. Elena and Matt have been cooking, asking us what we like to drink, are we hungry after six hundred miles on the road? The answer is yes. When we get close, they wait for us in the driveway.

Visiting Elena means visiting, broadly speaking, Elena's world as someone deeply embedded across generations in the history and place of Santa Fe. Today she works as a Hispanic Education Specialist, part of the Language & Culture Division of the New Mexico Public Education Department. Since she left Rice with her PhD in 2019, Elena made the life decision to decline a Vanderbilt postdoc and return home. She intends to connect what she learned in the academy to other publics like her family, neighbors, and former classmates, as well as thinkers who are doing the work for communities of public policy. On behalf of the Center for Education and Study of Diverse Populations at New Mexico Highlands University, in 2021 she wrote "Reclaiming Our Past, Sustaining Our Future: Envisioning a New Mexico Land Grant and Acequia Curriculum," to reflect on conversations about acequias and land grants unfolding in New Mexico. "Acequias" are communal irrigation systems. Elena directs policymakers to great examples of how to take more of a lead from existing curricula coming often from Indigenous sources like the Pueblo Indigenous Wisdom Curriculum Project and Tewa Women United.[1]

Our interview takes place in Cebolla, a drive up from Santa Fe into the mountains over rough, gravelly road. En route Matt and Elena's windshield gets pockmarked from loose stone on the highway, as does ours.

We pass Bode's, a spot known to folks in these parts. We stop. The place has everything from nightcrawlers and fishing rods to woven blankets, enamel cookout pots, and wide-brimmed hats. It's the Fourth of July, and a lot of 12-packs of beer are under the arms of guys passing through the doors. Matt gets bottles of water.

"By the way," Elena tells me, "This place is not O'Keeffe country." We have just passed Abiquiu and a sign on the road proclaiming "O'Keeffe Country." Recently the state of New Mexico produced promotional ads for tourism that angered a lot of people. In U.S. popular imagination, people associate Abiquiu with O'Keeffe and surrounding landscapes. The ads quoted O'Keeffe saying, "I saw this land, and it was mine, I knew it was mine." Three Sisters Collective, a Pueblo Indigenous women–centered grassroots collective, pushed back, describing the ads as "romantic settler voyeurism" that erase Indigenous presence.[2] *This controversy about artistic traditions that locate some in place while signaling unaware takeovers of place for others goes to the heart of feminist Wests.*

After the interview, inside the coolness of the Cebolla house, we have a picnic and bring out the last of Priscilla's food. Sharing it, we connect Denton to Cebolla, Priscilla and María to Elena and us. We wait for Zeni to come back with her father from visiting his family nearby. Later we have dinner and time with Elena's parents. We saw them at Elena's PhD graduation on Zoom, but we haven't seen them in person since Elena's and Matt's wedding!

The Where of Here: Cebolla, New Mexico

Krista: We've been talking about the *chamiso*.

Elena: We're surrounded by chamiso. This is where my dad grew up, this area, not this house, but in Cebolla. My father's side of the family is from here. I don't know at what point they all arrived. They're some of the first settler colonial, Spanish colonial, and Mexican people to come here. I recently learned that some of my family members may have been among those people from Abiquiu who were enlisted to defend territory, even though they were detribalized. A group of people living in Abiquiu came here to be a buffer between the Spanish Mexican empire and Native people, because this was Native land.

Krista: We begin with a place where you feel welcome. Recognizing the complications, the mixings of Spanish settler and Indigenous backgrounds and claims on land.

Elena: There's lots of complications in northern New Mexico. But this always felt like home to me. The smells, the sights. It's been open to me, to listen and learn and observe, and look for *camaleones* [horny toads]. I spent so much time being by myself and playing out here, climbing the trees, listening to family members because we're in an area where many of my family members who live in other surrounding villages . . . if they pass by, and were to see that my mom and dad were here, they would stop and come and talk and eat.

Krista: And today we brought Zeni with us. She went right into the chamiso, touching the flowers, squatting to pick up rocks.

Elena: Yes, this is her first visit here to Cebolla and to our house, my grandparents' house. I hope she forms the relationships that I formed, to place, to the mountain. One day I hope to tell her more.

Krista: Let's talk about the mountain, and the place of here.

Elena: I smell the dryness. The dirt has a particular scent. The chamiso, the juniper, you smell that. There's a kind of animal smell—elk, cows, horses, sheep. People keep sheep.

Krista: Yeah, we hear mooing.

Elena: There are always living things crossing through here. We are close to the Carson National Forest and the Trout Lakes. I've spent lots of time fishing there with my family and hearing stories about people who were once alive and where they lived and what they did. This place contains lots of memories embedded in things.

Krista: Does one come to mind for you?

Elena: My own memory or somebody else's?

Krista: Yours—though memories, "our own" memories, travel through other people's memories.

Elena: Lots of my memories seem melded together of the time I've spent out here. I haven't spent the kind of time I used to, now that I'm an adult and working and having a child. But I remember going to the pond in the neighboring property that belongs to my uncle and looking for camaleones, the frogs, and just admiring the little, tiny, tiny frogs and being amazed by how they can live in this environment that is so dry. Nothing is certain—we don't know if there will be enough water to fill up the pond, but they come back. It's like a miracle.

Krista: One of the questions for all of us is the relationship of these places and spaces to the U.S. West. I wonder if you would reflect on that.

Elena: In this part of northern New Mexico, I felt so embedded here, rooted, for the longest time. My parents did a good job of teaching me that I do belong here, so that my understanding of the U.S. West and the United States in general and New Mexico's place in it was very different from that of people who grow up in other places in the United States, or even children who grow up in the cities in New Mexico. Because I had an awareness that this used to be part of Mexico. That's why my family speaks Spanish, right? This was a Spanish Mexican territory, and before that it was and has been a Native place, and continues to be. We have different customs that are our practices, our words, always connected to that history.

Krista: Does a word come to mind for you?

Elena: Off the top of my head, *camaleone*. I don't know if in Spanish that actually refers to a horned lizard the way it does here. It's very specific. When I've looked it up on the web it literally translates to "chameleon" or "lizard." But here it's the horny toad. Probably, it has to do with the fact that when Spanish-speaking people came to New Mexico and saw it, they may never have seen one before. The word stuck.

Krista: Are you saying that this was a place apart from the U.S. West?

Elena: From the U.S. West, writ large, the popular U.S. West? Definitely. Though always my experience of this place has existed in tension with what I've read and learned from people who aren't from here. And from popular histories, narrative, even the concept of "O'Keeffe country."

Krista: Is there utility in talking about the relationship of this place to the U.S. West? I hear you saying this is part of Greater Mexico. We were having that conversation with Priscilla.

Elena: As a Nuevo Mexicana from northern New Mexico, I feel like this was never "West" to me. This was my center. My mom has said jokingly that for my dad, Cebolla is the *ombligo* [belly button] of the universe. It really is because we're so connected. The utility for someone like me, in talking about this space as part of the U.S. West, is being able to have conversations with others who don't understand who is who. This is not their center, right? This is their West perhaps. The "U.S. West," the concept of it, tells us how we got to this place, and how it continues to shape lives.

Krista: As you say, "this is their West," all the land masses, and the idea of O'Keeffe, the group of photographers and painters that popularized this place, and has become "my West" for so many people.

Elena: Right. So many vacation homes—it's a struggle for people who have been from this place to live here, especially now, and it's hard to find work. A lot of people commute to Los Alamos, to the labs, if you don't work for local government. That's how it's been for a long time— artists move to Santa Fe. The contemporary O'Keeffes, the German artist Gustave Baumann, a puppeteer from the thirties. I get frustrated when people talk about "the housing crisis" in Santa Fe. It's too expensive for people who've lived there for generations! For immigrant families it's too expensive to afford a house. In my case, the only way we could afford a house was Matt's VA loan. We didn't have to make a down payment.

Krista: Can we talk about your relationship to the term "feminist Wests" and if there's a certain image or visual or some history that comes to mind for you?

Elena: I've been helping my family clean out a house of my other grandparents, my mother's parents, in Albuquerque. They moved there in the 1950s from Las Vegas [New Mexico] and Wagon Mound, and lived there until they died, just recently. It's sad. It's been hard to see their land, their yard that was so beautiful, just die. They had apple trees and peach trees, apricot trees. Roses. Every kind of plant, native plants, non-native plants they picked up from everywhere they came from. My grandpa built almost every part of that house, because they had seven children. So they had to have room for those children. He did his own plumbing, electricity. He knew how to use things, and make a home, and make a life, and my grandma too. They did it together.

I connect that to feminism because my grandma took such care with soil that has no nutrients. She and my grandpa grew the most beautiful things, and feminism is cultivating something and enjoying your family, within nature. Those are important things, relationships to people, to spaces, to practices like gardening. That's how I've come to know feminism. And from here in Cebolla, from the trips that I would take with my parents to the mountain. I loved hikes, and hearing about plants, what is good for what ailments. People here look to those resources as very important. And that knowledge, I never thought about it as necessarily feminist, but in the way I carry it, and transfer it, that's the feminist practice. I want to protect it, that's crucial to me, to protect it and to show it to Zeni. These things are part of her, and part of our way of being here.

Krista: You've written about land use knowledges that are coming back from the colossally problematic displacements of them by classic forms of settling the West. We might think of this as a feminist care practice, really. Or the action of taking your PhD from Rice to engage in public education about acequias.

Elena: Recently I wrote what was supposed to be a recommendation for an Acequia and Land Grant Curriculum in the K–12 public school system. It was done on behalf of the Center for the Study and Education of Diverse Populations at Highlands University. But I wasn't formally involved in the stakeholder listening group, so the paper became my personal recommendations. I could see blind spots with the ways in which conversations around acequias and land grants unfold. It was a process of thinking about what can or what should we not forget? Who should we follow? Who's doing this work already and has great examples of how to incorporate a curriculum into the public schools? It's a lot of the Indigenous people here in New Mexico who are actively involved in their communities on their nations, in their sovereign nations, but also in broader New Mexico education system with the Pueblo Indigenous Wisdom Project.

Acequia is a term from— it's "Moorish," people might say. When the Moors settled Spain or colonized Spain, a lot of their culture transferred, and at the time New Mexico was being colonized so much of that culture, Islamic cultural knowledge of living in other places, transferred here. That's very much part of our heritage in New Mexico and in the very word *acequia*. Acequias are ancient irrigation systems where one digs ditches from a main primary water source to water crops. It's done communally. Everybody is responsible for taking care of each other and ensuring there's equal share of the water. Some of the way it's been written about here in New Mexico often notes, "Oh, well, it just came from Spain." But Pueblo people were irrigating too. The settlers here, Spanish Mexican, survived only because they learned from the Native people. This traditional form of cultivating crops has evolved here in unique ways.

Krista: *Querencia*, let's talk about the term. Because we aren't talking about just a practical water project, right?

Elena: Querencia can mean lots of things to different people. My understanding of it is a deep sense of being rooted in place, and being part of place, of loving place. In that love, respecting place. You know how to live in balance with nature and the other living things, right? Acequia culture, experiencing it, living it, is about querencia. Because you know how sacred water is, you're not certain how much you'll get, especially with climate change. It's like a holy attachment to place.

I have always felt, even entering into the PhD program at Rice, and going on that journey, that I wanted my work to be connected to the broader public and to people like my family, my neighbors, my classmates. I try to find the connection between what I was doing in the academy and those publics. I think it's useful to pay attention to what other people are already doing, who may not be scholars. Because there are a lot of great thinkers who don't have PhDs who aren't working in institutions of higher ed doing great work!

Paying attention to what's happening there, and trying to form partnerships and make connections, it's important to be prepared to explain how one's scholarship or knowledge could be of use. Having an imagination and being prepared to act, being prepared to have a vision and say: I can help the public education department perhaps, to think about things differently. I want to be prepared to listen because in the academy, some of us can think we know everything. But we don't always know.

I pay attention to Tewa Women United. Corinne Sanchez is there. She has a PhD. There is a lot of wonderful work in Española and the surrounding community. Lots of Indigenous women have done that kind of work. I follow Indigenous scholars, Indigenous women here in New Mexico who're doing similar things. I may not know them personally, but they've been kind enough to accept my social media requests. Daphne Littlebear posted something recently about how difficult of a choice it seemed at one point to get an education, but then go to her home pueblo. The world makes it seem like, "Well, you should get out," right? To "be successful." She posted: "This was an active choice that I made, to come back and raise my children here so they can know their community and where they're from." I feel similarly.

When we think about feminist Wests, I ask: Are we paying attention to all the different types of feminist West that exist? Are we citing people who are thinking about these things and are working in those areas? Are we translating that to activism in ways that can benefit the communities we write about and think about all the time? That's important to me, as a feminist, always.

Remaking the Heart of Aztlán, with Melina Vizcaíno-Alemán

In a pretty amazing accident of good timing, Melina's very recent essay "Growing Up Chicana in the Heart of Anaya's Aztlán" gives our conversations an edge and a focus. The piece is a tribute to the great educator and writer Rudolfo Anaya, a man particularly treasured in his hometown of Albuquerque, and a longtime mentor to Melina. As someone who was bookish, a reader, Melina's tribute to Anaya is an occasion to consider the impact of coming-of-age narratives on young readers like her. As a middle-school girl she read his second novel, Heart of Aztlán, *and the vivid hope of the story, about Aztlán "being in the heart," was just romantic enough for a youthful mind. Even though, she cuts in, her own youth "was no romance."[1]*

Allowing this critical piece to turn personal, she tells us: "Soon I would become a teen mother, like my sister and mother before me, and my grandmother and great-grandmother before us. We lived the realities of growing up Hispanic and female in Albuquerque, not so much in the Aztlán of Anaya's fiction."[2] She moves out of the voice of the scholar, authority, and resituates this homage to Anaya on Chicana feminist and more personal grounds. The task of the essay then is to balance her appreciation for the road map to political consciousness provided in Anaya's work and in coming-of-age tales centered around Chicano young men with other female-gendered challenges and expectations she and the women of her family knew from their own lives. The challenges are still there and it's her work as a Chicana feminist to make them her business.

Don't be misled by my introduction that we launch instantly into these weighty matters. No! Along with Jesse Alemán, the man Melina married who is a Chicano literary scholar and associate dean of graduate students at University of New Mexico, José and I are ushered to a spot set up on their airy back porch. Melina brings a tray of chips and two dips: one a chunky fresh avocado mix and the other a blend of mango, jalapeño, onions, and tomatoes. There are drinks too. Jesse has dinner marinating for a BBQ. Lightness, and humor, and especially Melina's laughter! These sounds and feeling mark the moment as one of friends returning to one another, reminding me of other dinners with Melina and Jesse, our long evening after Elena Valdez's wedding in Las Vegas, laughing at who can remember what while sharing the trials of parenthood.

Melina's sense of place is indelibly mixed with domestic life and legacies of teen motherhood, along with herself as a young thinker. She searched in the world of ideas and texts for ways to be and know, willing herself to become an exception to rules of the teen mom legacy. Melina continued education as a first-generation college student, then completed postgraduate study. Questions about "the where" therefore have to do with regions of the mind and intellectual aspirations superimposed over places of homelife and motherhood. They do not map easily onto one another. No surprise perhaps that Melina's homage to Anaya puts on the table the larger problem of teen pregnancy in New Mexico.

Melina's places involve transformations both of intellect and of her relations to family in a place she has lived all her life, where her young adult children and grandchildren live today. We do not begin, as in recent interviews, with "place" as a hallowed natural world, a source of well-being through smells, air, histories of family stories interwoven into a tradition of belonging that should be handed on. Melina will not tell you that story.

The Where of Here: Albuquerque

Krista: I thought we'd begin with the "where of the here," but since you've shown us such beautiful refreshment and welcome . . . I thought we might bring that pitcher over here, put it on camera. [laughter]

Melina: Yeah, I'm going to drink out of it! This is my specialty drink. It is a watermelon *agua fresca* with lime juice, a squeeze of agave and some tequila. It's a very nice and fruity and festive drink. Look how pretty it is!

Krista: It's beautiful.

Melina: This comes from my kitchen.

Krista: It's perfect for the where of the here. It's hot in Albuquerque! What a refreshing drink for the backyard in the summer. And Jesse Alemán is over there, drinking with José!

Melina: We've been hosting here for eighteen years. We got married in 2003, the same year we moved into the house. The house has changed, the kids are grown up. And now my son has kids. So we have grandkids coming to the house. It's just amazing how fast time moves. Eighteen years ago, I was a different person. Obviously, I was younger, we were just starting, the kids were little. In and of itself, that was going to be an adventure, being a new family, a "blended family."

We needed to purchase the house before we got married because I had already been married before to the kids' dad. You know, terrible credit. All kinds of domestic things, baggage, carried over from the previous marriage. We were under the gun and really trying to get into something before we actually got married so that Jesse would be the sole owner and they wouldn't take into account my own credit background. We got into the house the day before we got married. It was very intense. So much has happened here. We raised our kids and now we have our grandkids coming over and we looked everywhere in the city.

I grew up in the South Valley, so I had an attachment to the valley and never really lived in the city proper, though I came to school in the city. It's very close. We were just looking everywhere and we discovered that this neighborhood is where my dad grew up. At the time he grew up it was on the outskirts—it was the edge of the city. Technically we're in Northeast Heights, in terms of Albuquerque geography. A lot of people refer to it as the "Northeast Whites"—that's the kind of reputation this part of the city has. But there are a lot of Chicanada, a lot of people of color, a lot of blue-collar, middle-working-class people. We didn't expect that or anticipate it, but that's the way this city works. Albuquerque is metropolitan—it's a city-city. But it's also a small town. You can have a small-town feeling to it, and you end up knowing someone, or you end up knowing an area better than you thought because it's a very small town, spread out.

Krista: Listening to you about the where of here, it's a domestic place, it's a place for family. We're at your home, we're in your backyard.

Melina: Absolutely.

Krista: And it's a place of feminism, of feminist advocacy and thinking. We've been having conversations about places people feel they belong, or don't belong, about claiming places. You talk in the piece "Growing Up" about living in Albuquerque all your life. Still, it's not straightforward what "place" means.

Melina: I've never lived anywhere else. And I've lived here, and only here, for very domestic reasons. I was in a first marriage—it didn't last, it wasn't healthy. It wasn't a good relationship. I had two kids out of it. So it's kind of like a life sentence. That sounds awful to say, but I made decisions in my life when I was young when my brain wasn't fully formed, having kids at eighteen and nineteen. Being an adult without being ready to be an adult. That is also a part of the place where I grew up, because being a teen mom was the family tradition, passed down for generations. What would be an interesting project to figure out is to trace it, even in my own family. I know it goes back at least three or four generations.

Krista: In your essay "Growing Up," you say life can seem at times unpredictable, but retrospectively you look back and see patterns that are actually predictive of certain outcomes.

Melina: "Belonging" was really conflicted. It was getting pregnant young and getting married because that's the solution, right? If you get pregnant, you got to get married, because the thinking is very Catholic. You can't have a baby out of wedlock—that's unthinkable. So there are certain traditions that we adhere to in a very complicated way. That's how we belong in a certain community. There was a moment for me, long after I decided to leave my first husband and get a divorce, where I realized that I never felt like I had a different choice. That collective identity felt familiar, because from my mom and my sister to my cousins, to my niece to myself, you know, we're all going through the same experience.

Krista: It was a normative life cycle?

Melina: Absolutely. There's those narratives about having your consciousness raised. Going to school, being the first in my family to go to college and actually take that seriously. And to become aware. That is what happened with my own journey becoming Chicana. I wasn't a Chicana before college. I didn't have that awareness, consciousness, or critical thinking that one has to undergo in order to feel comfortable claiming that identity. There's a certain point where you can take control over your identity, rather than your identity controlling the terms of your life. And that, to me, is what it means to be Chicana. But what's that leap? It does raise the question of what happens with the droves of girls who don't become Chicana, don't find a place for themselves in the way that I found one. They don't come to that awareness. We have a huge high school dropout rate, and education isn't really valued on a collective scale in this state. Of course, then we say they were undereducated, and I would say in my own family that's true. So, it's not like the first generation makes it to college, and then everything lifts up. It's a much harder struggle, and I'm dealing with it with my own kids.

There's that first gen that makes it, but there isn't always a path, following it. So it feels lonesome and lonely. Because having awareness actually can make you disidentify from your community of origin. In some ways, you have to. I had to, in order to grow as a person, and to get out of those patterns of unhealthy behavior. I use my first marriage as an example. The person was abusive, and we were not good to each other. But even after we were divorced, I had internalized that negative attitude and did something to myself psychologically that it takes a long time to get out of.

Krista: I deeply appreciate this conversation. The impulse can be to claim places that affirm us, or they affirm family and family traditions, especially traditions that are pushed to the margins or undervalued by white settler culture. It can be harder to put on the table the way in which we disaffect from places because to have survived them required steps that actually took you away.

Melina: There's a lot to be said about understanding the importance of disassociating ourselves from places so that we don't come to think that we own a place. That's our responsibility as intellectuals and academics and educators: to not claim a place in order to own it, but to understand that we're dwelling here. There are traditions that tie us to Albuquerque, but they are tied to histories of violence, conquest, conflicts that divide people. My family, they carry on a very colonialist narrative about belonging here, and being here for seven generations past. As someone who identifies as Chicana, the colonialist narrative is not one that I accept as true. But I understand it is a prevailing narrative that defines this place and that people associate with it. That's how they feel like they belong. But in identifying as Chicana, I separate myself from it and my own family. "Chicana" is not a word that my mother or father or sisters are familiar with, or identify with—which, again, can be alienating. But it's important to contest those Spanish settler colonial narratives.

You had a question about how you belong in a place? Is it a feeling? Is it a memory? Because, it's funny, I often forget that I've been in a place until I actually go to the place. One story memory that I have is when I first went to Madrid, New Mexico, with Jesse. He asked me if I'd ever been to

Madrid before, and I said, "No. I don't think I've ever been there." So we go, we get there. And we sit down in a bar, and all these memories start to come back. I think I've been here before, I have been to this place, with my ex-husband. Because it's a biker bar. We used to go because he was part of a biker club with his dad. We would go on Sunday drives, which I never liked.

I'm cerebral. I've always been an intellectual even before I was an intellectual. So the last thing I want to do is spend a Sunday afternoon on a motorcycle. But there was a kind of motor memory, I had this extreme—like a vision—remembering that I've been here. It was so intense that it made me sick. So the way I've learned how to cope with certain traumas has been to forget. You forget, but then you don't forget. Because once you get there, then it's like seeing a picture, and it revives all these memories. I'm very sensitive—I feel through my gut. Literally, so everything just . . . all my lunch came up.

There are places or sites of trauma, original sites of trauma. They are tied to my family and to these very intimate childhood places and homes where I grew up. I continue to return to them in my dreams and so I'm very much attached to place. But it's not always celebratory.

Afterword: Chosen Kin and New Stories for Girls

The camera is off, interview done. Right before it's time for the BBQ, the rain that's teasing actually lets down and waters everything, Melina and I are musing about reshaping relationships along lines more chosen than inherited. Meaningful relationships for her with women today often take place in other women's homes, kitchens, at the kitchen table. Sharing stories, photos, recipes, work, and art. The term "feminism" has not been an automatic or obvious one for Melina to claim, and developing relations with women of like minds is part of her current feminist journey. These women are friends who are chosen family—*comadres*, sisters, grandmothers. She has sought them through her work, and her interests as a Chicana academic. Most of them are older, such as Teresa Márquez, a librarian with immense institutional memory and knowledge who also worked with Rudy Anaya. She passed on in February 2022, and Melina is grateful to have had a chance to interview her.[3] Rigina Wright and

Fig. 7. Artist Carlota EspinoZa in front of her mural *Mexican Heroes* (1966), housed in a storage room at the time of this photo and currently on display at the Rodolfo "Corky" Gonzales Library in Denver. Donated to the Denver Public Library by its original owners, Carlos and Anita Santístevan. Courtesy Melina Vizcaíno-Alemán.

Carlota EspinoZa, too, are like sisters, though they are old enough to be her grandmothers.[4]

Melina tells me that for her, Chicana has "feminist" built into the term. In contexts of the Southwest, "Chicana" issues a critique of settler Spanish colonialism. Unlike Rudy Anaya's gender order, Chicana perspectives doubt whether marriage structures and traditional family structures are going to hold everything together. The reality of the institution of marriage and motherhood, its structure of gender inequalities in domestic realms, means that for many Mexican American mothers, the ideal of family without gender hierarchy is not a possibility. Chicana feminist analyses of family identify the perils of institutions of motherhood for both girls and for boys who grow up without a sense of alternative possibilities.

Where do girl readers encounter stories of alternative lives? Melina talks about not finding a book that really spoke to her particular experience as a girl. Probably they existed but she didn't have access to them. The book that she did have was *Heart of Aztlán*. Later *House on Mango Street*. If *Mango Street* was authored by someone who was "nobody's wife and nobody's mother," as the book jacket famously proclaimed, what wisdom did it offer the girl who *is* somebody's wife and somebody's mother?[5]

Melina tells a different story through sharing her own life. She offers different counsel and wisdom than *Mango Street*. Through scholarship, teaching, and leadership as a faculty at the University of New Mexico, she provides pathways for young women and men whose stories, too, may be different.

Feminist Homing and Unhoming, with Amy Hamilton

Amy Hamilton cares about Indigenous grasses and the problem of invasive species—which turns out to be a perfect metaphor for our deep talks about growing up white in the West. How whiteness relates to feminism and issues of communal accountability is on Amy's mind; it's been on her mind for years because she is a white woman who teaches and writes in the field of Native American studies. Our conversations pivot around early teenage feminist consciousness, the inevitable whiteness of our histories, and especially how to contend with that whiteness, not to disavow it. These are trepidatious conversations. We worry over talking about whiteness, knowing we will get things wrong.

How precious to have this chance to interview the incoming editor of Western American Literature.

It's early in the day, cool, and José and I make our way to Eldorado, a community a few miles outside of Santa Fe. We are meeting at Amy's parents' home. They have lived there seven years, after forty years living in town where Amy grew up. She is there for several weeks with her sons and her husband, Chris. It's a great spot to meet—quiet for an interview, and meaningful to Amy.

Our van turns into a long private driveway, and we crunch over gravel and park at its end. The house seems cut into the hillside, built to nestle. Were she living, my aunt Adrian from Pueblo, whose life companion hung paintings by Taos artists in the home they shared, would talk approvingly about the architecture, the wide-angle view of the mountains, and the scene's calm. We step down from a gravel driveway into a shaded series of connected courtyards, scrubby trees exuding a dry fragrance.

Amy opens the front door, and there are her boys! Bright-eyed, welcoming, sitting on big sofas in a shaded living room. They are hanging out a minute while their dad and granddad get ready to take them swimming in the community pool. Chris comes out for introductions. I see skateboards and ask the boys whether the local skate park is welcoming? I'm trying to get them to laugh at the expense of their dad, who also skates. They say there's a guy "even older than him" who's teaching kids to handplant. The guy has skills, but their dad gets along all right.

Very nice vibe going this morning in Amy's family.

The Where of Here: Eldorado

Amy: One of the things I've been mulling around over the last few days, about "the where" of this conversation is that my experience of Santa Fe, at this point in my life, is like a palimpsest. It's layers. Layers of memory—connected to experiences and stories, connected to the place itself, the feeling of being here, the feeling of the air, the kind of light that's here, unlike light where I live in northern Michigan. There are the layers of what it means to be back here now. I feel that this is my place, but I also am here temporarily, I'm here as a summer visitor. The place is continuing on without me. My old dentist office, pediatric dentist . . . is now a gallery. Right? Of course.

Krista: Only in Santa Fe!

Amy: In Santa Fe, everything becomes a gallery. There's a house downtown that a friend of mine grew up in. I used to go to birthday parties at this house. It's a bank now. It's odd, but it's so familiar. Layers of knowledge.

I was on sabbatical in the 2015 to 2016 academic year. We lived here in my parents' house for the year. This is where I wrote *Peregrinations: Walking in American Literature*. That year was so wonderful, full of writing and reconnecting with friends and family that I've known my whole life and my children going to school here. Not at the school I went to, but going to school and making friends they see in the summers, and experiencing a very different culture from the upper Midwest. That's a whole other layer of memories and experiences. It's a funny thing to think about Santa Fe for me. It's at once something that I could talk about forever, but also something that's really difficult to articulate because it's so deep, it's so felt.

My parents have been in Santa Fe a long time. But they are never going to be native to this place. Or they're never going to feel like this is *their* place in the same way that it's my place. Because they grew up elsewhere. My mother's from the East Coast, from Maine. My father grew up in Southern California, in Riverside. Their sense of home place is connected to those landscapes. Mine is connected here. And even though my sons spend a lot of time in New Mexico—because we're here every year for some time in the summer, and then every other year we're here at Christmas. And then that sabbatical year.

But my sons' place, their home place, is the Upper Peninsula of Michigan and Lake Superior. And it's a very interesting experience to have that separation. Especially growing up in Santa Fe, where there are so many families here, both Indigenous families and Chicanx families who trace their families way, way, way back. It was not an unusual experience in high school to go to a party with one of my friends and she would talk to somebody and say, "Oh, wait, I think . . . are you my cousin?" That was a very common experience. And for me, I think of this as connected to whiteness.

Krista: Yes, this is the discussion we were having before we turned on the camera, and that we want to tease out as much as we can.

Amy: Yeah. My parents had the ability to move here from California when I was a baby. I was born in LA, and 1970s LA was . . . the smog was horrific. My parents didn't want to raise their family there. There was also the problem of commuting and the long commutes on the freeways in California, which is much worse now in Southern California. So they moved to this place. My dad is a lawyer, and he worked for the highway department. He now works for a private firm. My mother was able to continue her career in education. They had that mobility.

I grew up with many other children from families like mine. Parents who were hippies or hippie adjacent. My parents were more hippie adjacent. [both laugh] I grew up with lots of friends whose families moved here to live on some of the communes that were popping up in New Mexico in the sixties and seventies. I have friends who were born on the Hog Farm in Taos and in other places. That was my primary community as a small child. I was in playgroups with those people, with these primarily white families who moved here to raise their children and had this idea about what it meant to raise their children in New Mexico. In some cases, they had a romanticized vision of what it meant to be growing up here. There's a lot of New Age stuff in the community that I lived in. Not my parents so much, but definitely there's a lot of that viewpoint, crystals and . . .

Krista: Crystals were a part of people's sense of relation to land, or to the universe?

Amy: To the spirit of place, the sense of place. We were connected in this New Age way. That was very much my experience in childhood. Not in my own family, but in the community that I was part of.

Krista: What about the American West, and romanticized ideas about Santa Fe for white hippies or white hippie-adjacent families?

Amy: There was a dialogue with the U.S. West, absolutely. That prominent idea about space and land and *available* land, *available* space that was here, or was imagined to be here. And ways of becoming part of the communities that were already established here often in problematic ways. Adopting acequia culture, for example. Or adopting the stories of this place as your own in a way that was often very problematic. It was unconscious, very naive, hippie communes not recognizing the communities that they were impinging upon, who often pushed back and thought that the hippies were kind of funny, kind of teasing them. A lot of eye rolling.

Krista: Do your friends talk about being "native" in a way that is more complex for white people to say these days? People who are aware of other claims on land and place?

Amy: There's a definite understanding of those complexities. This history has always been there. You think about Black Lives Matter and the attention to monuments that has happened this year, and in Santa Fe the obelisk downtown recently came down. It was a four-sided obelisk that was in the middle of the plaza. Three of the four sides commemorate New Mexico's role in the Civil War, for example the Battle of Glorieta Pass, which was just this way [pointing] from where we're sitting. It was the furthest western battle of the Civil War.

And the fourth side of the obelisk had the language of "savage Indians" on it. Years and years ago, I believe in the early 1970s, somebody took a chisel and chiseled out the word "savage." So there was a blank rectangle. I don't remember it ever being anything but the blank rectangle, but everyone knew what had been there. It's about the success of the U.S. Army in turning back the Indigenous people. And so when there was this resurgence of attention to monuments, and more focused attention to monuments, and after a lot of foot-dragging about removing it, a group of activists came together, tied ropes to the top of the obelisk, and pulled it down, and it broke. They destroyed it.

We talk about the history of this place, and what it means for me to claim this place and be a part of that history. I am able to claim this place because of that history. Growing up, we knew this history, but Santa Fe markets itself as a place where three cultures exist harmoniously. That's never been the reality. There's segregation here. Not completely, but there's a fair amount. And there are absolutely tensions.

In *Braiding Sweetgrass*, Robin Wall Kimmerer talks about becoming Indigenous to place. And I think about that a lot and about what she's getting at with that, because there is a way of taking that permission to claim "native-ness." I used that word earlier, and it's not the right word. Kimmerer is talking about responsibility. To become Indigenous to place is to recognize your responsibility. That's how I understand it. Responsibility to a place includes an acknowledgment of and a reckoning with separations, distinctions.

Krista: For me, the term "responsibility" raises accountability. Can you talk about your sense of feminism?

Amy: It's a really difficult question for me. I'm not sure why it's as difficult as it is because I've always identified as a feminist, although what that means has changed over time. I'm currently serving as a director of gender and sexuality studies at Northern. My undergraduate degree was English and women's studies. I'm surrounded by these conversations, and I'm immersed in them. I'm part of them. When I go back to the beginning of my feminism, it comes back to growing up in the community I grew up in. We would go to the crystal and New Age bookstore, and I think that's where I bought my first book that was a feminist book, which was *Women Who Run with the Wolves*.[1]

Krista: These early feminisms are so important to not reject, not renounce. We get trained away from them, trained to critique them. Sara Ahmed talks about coming into universities with the selves we already are.[2] We bring our histories, we don't arrive unformed. She is talking about women of color, but it's true for most of us. We get taught to distance ourselves, to "know better." We don't tell stories about the earlier us. They're not dear. We begin to disavow or go quiet out of shame. Perhaps it's a white woman's tendency even more so? Can you talk about your relation to the term "feminism" as difficult, elusive? Let's talk about you buying that book *Women Who Run with the Wolves* and what it meant, and the crystals.

Amy: I think that was where I felt a sense of empowerment. Like oh, this is something that I can belong to. This is something I can identify with. This is a place where I can find community and power, right? I was probably [my son] James's age, fourteen or fifteen.

Like, who am I? And how do I understand that identity in a community, the specific community that I live in where, you know, I have peers with connections to Indigenous cultures or . . . many friends of mine who could trace their identity back through the generations to the Conquistadores.

You want me to tell you a story of those days? There wasn't a lot to do in Santa Fe for teenagers. Except get in trouble, which we did plenty of. But my best friend and I used to go for drives into the mountains and get out of the car, not to go on big hikes, but just to walk away from the car, away from the parking lot, and into the woods, into the land, and spend an hour hanging out. We often went during the fall, when the aspen leaves were changing. We'd take the leaves and put them in our hair. There was absolutely a sense of the two of us being women together in the woods. That sense of friendship and connection was a part of my earliest feminist identity. Feeling connected. This was our place, where we could be whomever we wanted.

Krista: For you, it was about women, bonds with other women. It wasn't a way to stave off male attention? Men weren't all over you?

Amy: Bonds with other women, a kind of empowerment. At that point it was more personal, not about men. And a sense of land and place.

In college, I started reading Willa Cather, Mary Austin, and Georgia O'Keeffe—growing up in Santa Fe, Georgia O'Keeffe is always in the background. She's always here and her experience of the land, her experience of Abiquiu, that place, that kind of connection became very, even more crystallized for me.

Krista: Crystallized, as a verb.

Amy: Right, you hold the crystals and feel the spirit. When I was in college, studying women's studies, I was trying to figure out what that meant, I am thinking back on very cringey things . . .

Krista: But this is what we have to claim.

Amy: I know.

Fig. 8. Feminist homing in the Sangre De Cristo Mountains. Courtesy Amy T. Hamilton.

Krista: Let's cringe together because you are not alone.

Amy: What empowerment meant, how to become empowered, as a young college woman. I saw that through claiming my sexuality. I did a senior project—talk about cringe—a photography project for a women's studies class, juxtaposing elements that seemed to me to be unfeminine.

Krista: Unfeminine? Not unfeminist?

Amy: No, unfeminine, with a defiance. Here's the big cringe, right? This is the one I really remember because it was so cringey.

Krista: Oh, we should put this up as a picture in our blog.

Amy: I don't know where it is, Krista, I don't know if I can find it.

Krista: Oh, you're resourceful.

Amy: I don't know if it exists anymore.

Krista: Let's assume you are motivated.

Amy: It was a picture of me. I borrowed one of my girlfriends' tight red skirts, it was knee length. I put on high heels. The picture was me sitting on the toilet with this dress on, with these spike heels, reading Betty Friedan's *The Feminine Mystique*. [giggles]

Krista: That's pretty resourceful!

Amy: The project was about putting it all together, I am all of these things at once. I can be sexy, also studious, and also sitting on the toilet. [both laugh] That was how I was coming to some sense of . . . [both laugh] feminism.

Krista: What the hell, it's great! We should restage it now. Reclaim that eighteen-year-old out of respect for that history. In a twist on Sara Ahmed, tell a loving white story about her.

Amy: We see in those histories a kind of obliviousness to privilege, to our own histories, a flattening out of what, what it means to be a person, a woman. Really interesting to remember.

Krista: Lots of white women critique privileges without an ability to talk about the "me" of the white feminist. It would be good for the work on anti-racism if we could do that, not renounce it so much we can't remember it.

Amy: The fear for me is doing harm to someone else. Right? In that kind of feminism, in what it does not acknowledge, it actively does harm. And that's the last way I want to be in the world. And yet.

Krista: There's not an escaping of that legacy.

Amy: There's not an escape. The other major project I did my senior year was a thesis. In it I first started making connections between feminism and place. I wrote about Southwestern writers like Jimmy Santiago Baca, Rudolfo Anaya, Leslie Marmon Silko, Joy Harjo, and their representations of the land as feminine. That project introduced me to Annette Kolodny's work,[3] which led me to working with her at the University of Arizona and then to the Western Literature Association. So, in the midst of my fumbling, I was finding my way to the work that has defined my life and my career.

I was thinking about the section "Heading Out" on *Living West as Feminists* blog, where you talk about the "I" and using the "I." It gets buried, right? What does it mean to bring it in? How uncomfortable it can be to bring the "I" back in! If I bring the "I" in, am I being rigorous in my analysis? But maybe using the "I" deepens analysis, complicates things. And, of course, the "I" is always there, whether we acknowledge it or not.

Krista: In feminist traditions of positionality, the "I" can be a way to situate our knowledge or take up a feminist standpoint. Stronger forms of objectivity are objectivities that locate the "I." I just did a theory piece on standpoint for Susan Bernardin's *Gender and the American West*.[4]

By the way, I love your entry in that same volume, your reading of the Layli Long Soldier poem "Whereas."[5] In my own reading of your essay, I think: "Here is Amy Hamilton implicating herself as an 'I,' as a white feminist. She is walking through the witnessing that piece does as an 'I' who understands white settler histories because she is a white settler."

Amy: My next book is going to be about grass. I've been thinking of shifting my approach, pulling out more of an "I" voice, which I used in the piece that I did for *Teaching Western American Literature*, edited by Brady Harrison and Randi Tanglen.[6] I've been thinking about how and where to make that personal perspective a more active part of my work.

With grass, one of the things I write about is Indigenous grass. And then the invasive. Such a metaphor there!

When I first started as an assistant professor, I was hired to teach Native American literature. Another white woman was hired to teach African American literature. And when we met each other, we said, wow. Wow. It's not necessary to go into why we were hired. But there's a responsibility to the material and to the communities and to the people and to the students. This actually comes back to the "I."

Because when I started, I didn't talk about my own racial identity in the classroom. And that led to students asking, "Well, are you Anishinaabe? Are you Indigenous?" Anishinaabe being the culture of the upper Midwest, where I am. By not talking about myself, I was creating a misrepresentation without thinking it through. I created this. I allowed for a misrepresentation of myself and where I would have to say, "Oh, no, I'm not."

So I started to think about what it means for me as a white woman to be teaching this literature. And the limits to what I know. That's a big conversation that I have in the classroom. Because when you're teaching Indigenous literature from multiple cultures, which is the way that it is taught at my university, there's nobody in the classroom who is an insider to all of those, right? I may have an Anishinaabe student, but that student may not have access to Diné storytelling traditions. We talk about what we can know, and how important it is to know more than we do know, as students, as humans, but also where the limits of that knowledge lie. There are places that you shouldn't push past that are not appropriate for you to push past. I'm also coming from Santa Fe where the Indigenous literatures of this place here are southwestern, Navajo, Pueblo, and I'm teaching up in Anishinaabe territory. That's also an interesting conversation to have with myself, and with my students and colleagues.

Krista: This is a very beautiful white feminist conversation to be having about the places we don't belong, and that we aren't welcome. It's not a problem. It's a way to know who we are, and where we should or should not be. Where we bow to someone else's belonging or their hospitality. What do they tell us is appropriate? How can we be a good relative?

Amy: One of the things that I am struggling with, trying to move into the public humanities, is where is my expertise, where can I contribute? And what is it that I know? I can speak with, I want to say authority, but that's not quite right. But where am I an appropriate representative?

Krista: What if you were to tease out the white woman part of that quandary? Would it make more sense?

Amy: Yeah, yeah. It's something I think about a lot. And that's why thinking about it with this grasp, maybe here in this place I can bring the "I." One of the interesting things about identity and growing up here in Santa Fe is that I didn't want to be a white girl here, I wanted to be a Sanchez. I wanted that sense of belonging that I observed. My early experiences as an assistant professor, where I was not bringing in my subjectivity, I sometimes want to interrogate that as: was there something purposeful there?

Krista: Was I trying to play Indian?

Amy: Yeah. Was I nervous to bring in my own subjectivity because I wanted to claim, not necessarily the identity, but maybe the authority of being able to speak about Indigenous literature? Or to be able to speak about the issues in the classroom, that I felt that I didn't have? I mean, what assistant professor does have authority, but you know.

Krista: Yeah. We have some reckoning to do there, as white women.

Amy: That's really interesting. Important.

Krista: Yeah. We need to stop taking a pass there.

Amy: Yeah. That level of appropriation. It's a remarkable and very problematic part of white identity. Yeah, talk about reckoning.

Krista: We're on a path right this minute. This could be a kind of resting place, I think, for white feminists with one another, actually, a rest area where we don't pretend otherwise. We do need each other for this.

ROAD FINDS
On Keeping Company

Pointing toward Colorado and knowing Montana is after, the feeling is isolation to be leaving Santa Fe and heading into more starkly white country. For both me and José, it seems the right time to remember who you're traveling with, the company to keep.

"Soft landings" is what I write on the blog about our time with Priscilla and Elena and Melina and her husband, Jesse Alemán. I contribute to the soft landing, I can bordercross. But the root is José and the sense of familia between them. Theirs is a bond of raza, of a Chicano/a standpoint. I am invited into it, and I live in it in many ways over many years even while I mind my racial manners. I call it "saturated relationality" in the write-up of the time with Priscilla. I do not exaggerate. The rest areas we occupy in the present of the road trip are indebted to histories and ways of living created by people of Mexican descent on the U.S. side of the border.

All that density of secure relationality is in the rearview mirror for now. Next stop: Pueblo. July 7 is seven weeks and change removed from an unexpected major surgery I've had once spring semester was done. There is a form of cancer among my sisters; two have had stage IV versions of it in their early forties. By comparison mine is minor. Maybe I trivialize, but cancer forebodings are relative among the Comer sisters. Seven weeks later, with medical blessings, I am down the road, no further treatment anticipated. Not strong but solid enough to get out the door, with a lot of help from José.

On the morning we leave Houston, our younger son Jesse is still asleep at his own place a couple blocks away and he will come over later to take care of our house until he goes to San Francisco for a new job. He has just graduated from Rice and we've had family in town for one after another festivity, which are followed a couple days later by . . . my surgery. But we're on the other side of it and Jesse assures us, yes, of course, he will water the bamboo, the wisteria, feed the fish in the pond, and do all the things an old house requires. The watering list I leave for Jesse is long—I'm too serious, inquiring again about it. As is his impish way he asks, "Wait, Mom, do plants need water?"

The last day and last interview in Santa Fe with Amy Hamilton at her parents' place in Eldorado, we put on the record our histories as white middle-class women and teenage feminists. Our conversation sticks with me—girds me. Amy is good company on the path of remembering whiteness to become more accountable to it.

In the essay ("Staying with the White Trouble") she is about to publish as the new editor of *Western American Literature*, I ask what white progressives can offer to white supremacists other than critique, superiority, or condemnation. Can feminists who are white (by descriptive definition, white feminists) not flinch at the term "white feminist," perhaps use it to engage the trope of "white feminism" that women of color feminists invoke as meaningful to them? Of the feminist thinkers I work with in that essay to think beyond white fragility, I didn't remember until recently the activist writings of Minnie Bruce Pratt, who was so important to me early on. How could I forget?

When I showed up at Wellesley College as an undergraduate in 1984, I was a self-funding young woman of twenty-five with a grown-up history. I had left a world behind in California to come east and start over in New England. I knew no one. Immediately I signed up for a women's studies major. A feminist in action and behavior but unschooled beyond the intense everything it had taken to live to that point, I had no inkling there was something called "feminist thought."

When I read Adrienne Rich, the statement from the Combahee River Collective (1977), and especially Minnie Bruce Pratt's "Identity" (1984), I knew I would never turn back to the previous life. Rich's "Diving into the Wreck" (1973) required reading skills I would need to develop, but Pratt's mix of politics with memoir was readable now. Place was a central fact of Pratt's life as it was mine. Her homeplace, Alabama, chased her away, and I had been chased away. Her heart was broken to leave the world of that place, but gone she had. She was talking about it straight up, holding her feet to the fire as a white woman. I too was trying to show up all the way. Pratt spelled out so many racist mistakes she was making in her organizing work, putting mistakes out there so others could learn. Her public reckoning spoke to me of leadership; she did not waffle, and she was honest. I gleaned from her a sense of what I could do with myself, what values I could hold.

Looking back, I realize I am putting language on what at that time was pure impulse. I didn't know where I was or who I was in relation to East Coast living. I felt like I had landed in a foreign country. I would go into Cambridge and wander on the weekends—I was in the vicinity so I thought I should. The first summer I took a creative writing class at Harvard because what else should I be doing? I had blown up my life with my partner on the beach. I now had a summer job and a rented room. Every day was a day to take steps in the new direction. I found a women's AA meeting where the participants were a former nun who had come out as a lesbian and did AIDS hospice, a professor from Boston University, a very high-profile critic of sexism in media, and a lesbian priest from the Harvard Divinity School. Later I asked her to officiate my wedding with José, but by then she was not doing weddings. There was a therapist with a practice devoted to phobias and behavior modification. Another therapist was in therapy herself with someone doing the new feminist cultural-relational approach, founded by Jean Baker Miller, at Wellesley's Stone Center. To say these were different influences than anything I had known is ridiculously an understatement. The AA women saw me for what I was—new in sobriety therefore vulnerable, resourceful, scared. They were kinder to me than were the creative writers at Harvard who could not countenance feminism in a beach story, indeed seemed insulted by the thought, and around whom I felt so unserious it's a wonder I kept going to class.

I did quite a lot of therapy.

The early 1980s feminist circles that I was finding in Boston were dead serious about racism in the feminist movement. The need for white women to get exponentially more aware preoccupied seemingly every conversation. I was around a diverse group of women, not all white, and many lesbian feminists, and it was the white women who schooled each other about racism. It's hard to know how much the harshness of that education was northeastern condescension or the growing pains of a bona fide collective fight with white fragility.

Rereading Minnie Bruce Pratt recently, that feeling of 1980s feminism flooded back. It was an unforgiving time, no gentle arrivals. But not for me a time of regrets. Often one hears about second-wave feminism being clueless on topics of race difference, and though I saw limits everywhere including my own, and continue to see them, I can say some white women took to heart the lessons of a Minnie Bruce Pratt. As a student at a women's college reading what was current to the moment, it was understood that women of color feminists and conflicts within second-wave feminism were what made the movement grow, learn, change, and become a large justice vision. *That* was the object lesson.

After recently rereading Pratt with two white feminists whose company I keep in order to think about whiteness, we learned of Pratt's passing.[1] One of the bravest legacies she leaves for me is the degree to which all her thinking about white supremacy took place in relational contexts, under its pressures. Pratt walked the talk of relationality. She did not go away, "take space," or stop hanging in there. She readily admitted her fears while not giving in to them. When she realizes, as a married woman in her twenties, that coming out and divorcing will mean her young children will be taken away, she reflects, "I felt no one had sustained such a loss before. . . . I became obsessed with justice: the shell of my privilege was broken. . . . I was astonished at the pain."

It's the next line, about dealing with astonishing pain, that really speaks to me: "The extent of my surprise revealed the degree of my protection."[2] In a moment of the most intense difficulty, she learns the true lesson of how much the protection from difficulty had been a life assumption.

Outside the Picture Window in Pueblo, with Krista Comer

I am my only "interview" in the whole of Colorado. Without planning it, the days are a heart-filling personal journey. I pay respects to my aunt Adrian's windy gravestone in the lonesome prairie cemetery. José and I visit my childhood friend in Colorado Springs, Drew Wills, with his wife, Jeannie Wills. We have a six-hour catch-up, hearing about children and the exceptional heart of their athletic lives. None of us wants the night to end. The last time we were all together was 1993, at my father's funeral.

Up then to Winter Park the next morning, the van trudging the grade and switchbacks of Berthoud Pass, across the Continental Divide, to stay over with a friend and colleague from Rice. He's been coming to the mountains long enough, seriously enough, to have scoped out what probably is all of the backwoods. He puts us up with great food, an amazing lodge of a house, a late-day hike up to Bottle Pass where we appreciate the summit to Byer's Peak and a sunset hike down. I am very slow, but not bad, he allows, seven weeks out from surgery. A river walk in the morning keeps his barrel-chested canine and everyone else happy. With cookies in a tub, we head out for Steamboat over Rabbit Ears Pass. One of its ears has eroded. At the top it's hazy from wildfire smoke—no panoramas today descending into the Yampa Valley.

We stay at a local favorite, Rabbit Ears Motel. My parents and youngest three sisters left Southern California to live in Steamboat in the early 1980s. My dad built a mountain house modeled on the Swiss chalet and skied from its front porch down to the lift line. I lived there too in a condo with the old boyfriend and our dogs. Sandy Buchanan, from that California neighborhood, skateboarding surfer teenage girlfriend, tagged along to Steamboat, splitting her college years between quarters at UC Santa Barbara, Zuma Beach where she was a rare early-eighties female lifeguard, and Steamboat's ski season. Sandy lived with my boyfriend and me, then my parents. She met Tom Woods who builds log cabins, stayed on with him in Steamboat, skiing, competing, river running, mountain biking, hang gliding, becoming a nurse.

We meet up with Sandy and Tom, they make us dinner. We take walks, admire the craft of their log home, remember my father, hear about a rustic place out at Hahns Peak Lake. It serves as a base for easy outings on the stand-up paddleboard and for more serious treks in backcountry powder. We hear about Steamboat life—"in the bubble," as Sandy describes it.

Accomplished outdoorspeople, all of my friends, embodying lives lived in my homeplace of Colorado, filling me with admiration and a sense of the lives I wanted but did not choose and who I am instead at the crosshairs of those contradictions.

The Where of Here: Out on the Beulah Road in Pueblo

José: It's 10:30 a.m., Friday, July 9, and I'm here with Krista. I am going to ask her the questions that she's set up for everyone in the project. Let's talk about place or land we are on. Why don't you start with the where of the here? How do you feel linked to it? Any early memories with place or land in your family, as a child?

Krista: Thanks for doing the honors, José. In my family, we call where we are now "out on the Beulah Road." It's Highway 78, Northern Avenue. When I was little, my grandparents had that house over there [pointing]. It's off this road and tucked away, but you can see it—it blends into the prairie. Behind where I am set up in this lawn chair, you can see the Sangre de Cristo Mountains. The view behind me was the view that I grew up with. I would come out to this house. It was a special place. I would be with my aunt Adrian and my father's parents. I was five and smaller. My mom and dad lived on Elizabeth Street, in town, with my two younger sisters.

This view was my first orientation to what today I would call "the West." It was a view, out of a window, from a house built by, actually, my mother's father, Samuel Monroe Houston II, a Pueblo builder in the fifties and sixties. It is a one-story house; the color is what somebody might call "architectural," a studied dusty green-gray. The color of the prairie. The house has no 90-degree angles. It was understood at the time, and still is, to be "interesting," sophisticated.

Of course, you're talking about people who had money, who would build an "idea house." Or that's the impression they gave, about money. It was more of an issue than they let on. Money split the family up. But my grandparents lived well. I remember a sunken living room. From the floor to ceiling were huge picture windows. Out of the picture windows, we would see what's behind me. Cocktail hour, dressing for dinner, and the view. Cokes on a coaster on the glass top table for little girls. That was me, at five.

I came here to do the interview for this project because I have been searching for this landscape ever since our family left it. The writing I've done, the yearnings I have to be in specific places and not others, they harken here. Early in my life my family moved to California. They were so upwardly mobile. They wanted to get out of Pueblo. As a child, I didn't know that Pueblo was anything to get out of. I thought it was a place where people loved me and my grandparents and aunt lived and our neighbors thought I was, you know, charming. I could walk around our neighborhood, walk up the steps onto porches and knock on the door. The McCabes, I remember. The elder McCabe would open the door, in I would go for a visit. For me, it was home.

But my parents had a sense of how much money they couldn't make living in Pueblo and working in the family business. It wouldn't support everyone. My father had differences with his father about how he was running the business. His father was not an honest man.

We are here, abutting Imperial Cemetery. It's where my aunt is buried, and my grandparents are buried. My father wasn't buried there, he preferred his ashes be scattered. Some of his ashes were scattered in Steamboat. And my mom scattered them in other places. That's telling—the where of my father's places—they were many places, places he had adventures. He loved Austria and Germany. He skied the Alps as a young man during his time in Europe, in the Army, during the Korean War. He returned to the Alps into his sixties, still skiing, placing in friendly competitions. I have a great picture of him standing on the number-one block, a winner.

Imperial Cemetery used to be my grandfather's cemetery. It was called Valhalla. The family was in the funeral business. They had a funeral home in town also called Valhalla. When my grandfather died, my aunt inherited that business. She had been in it, running it for years already. At that point my father and mother had been gone to California maybe twenty years. My aunt changed the name to the Adrian Comer Funeral Home. Everyone discouraged her. They told her no woman should put her name on a funeral home. She didn't listen, and the business went on, great, until she retired.

José: What places do you feel comfortable in, or welcome? Or not? What places are your places, your people's places? Alternatively, on what land or lands do you feel you belong or not belong?

Krista: As a child, I understood that this is Indian country. I understood it because of the people I saw around me; some of them worked for my family. I understood it when we would be in town, or would go to certain restaurants or to the infamous "Stuckey's." I understood we were related to Indian country, but I personally was not Indian country. Though I had no concept of what any of it meant. And my parents certainly didn't have a concept of what that meant. What they taught us was that this was our place. It belonged to us. I felt that I belonged here, that feeling is still inside me. I feel what people have been talking about in these interviews. I feel the dry smell, if that makes sense, the dusty prairie color, the scrubby trees slightly piney. I recognize the Sangre de Cristos as close, "present."

José, you and I camped last night in a place that's a little north of here. Not at the base of Pikes Peak, but in the long lead up to Pikes Peak. It's undeveloped land. I asked one of the guys there about his off-road muddy truck and he told me, "That's not mine, that's what my girlfriend drives." That made me smile. His girlfriend's truck! It was important to me to come back to Pueblo in a different way than the way I left, which was on the inside of the picture windows, looking at "a view."

It was the wrong side of the window, to be inside, that's the feeling I've carried since. I so much wanted to be out of doors. It was great to be camping out last night, and I did feel I belonged to this land. And I say that, knowing that these are unceded Indian lands, and that I say that as a white person. And I say so not to dispute Indigenous ancestral claims or with any disrespect, but to try to come to terms with the ways in which I was raised to think this all belonged to me.

I have a piece coming out in *Western American Literature* in August about "Staying with the White Trouble of Recent Feminist Westerns," so I have been thinking about being white a lot. Coming from a certain amount of money, from aspirational backgrounds, the world really did seem to belong to me. Even as a girl. It was not as much as if I were a

Fig. 9. Campside at sunset. Fountain, Colorado. Courtesy José Aranda.

boy, but I was raised to believe the world belonged to me. Working-class people, the working poor, people of color, are not raised with that idea. José, you were not raised with this idea!

So a lot of places seem to be my place. I can be at ease in a lot of places. But when we moved, when I was six, to San Francisco, it was not my place. Cities in general have not been my places. We live today in Houston, Texas, and Houston is now my place, because our sons were raised there. Because you are from there, and your family is there. We've lived there a long time and I've made a decision to be in Houston—again, Indigenous lands, Karankawa driven away early—because it doesn't make sense not to be from where you've lived for a long period of time, and where your children have memories of growing up. That doesn't make sense to me.

But that has been a grown-up belonging, a decision. When I was living on the beach in California, and when we go to Galveston today, those places feel like my place. That is not a decision—it's unconscious. I'm sure they do because of the profound whiteness of beach culture in this country and globally, and in global cinema. And because of memory.

I am thinking about the Galveston T-shirt I wore today mainly for sun coverage because it's very hot. It's 95 degrees, maybe? It's really hot.

José: It's on the hotter side of 95.

Krista: [laughs] There's a breeze, fortunately. I have on a lot of sunscreen and a hat and sunglasses. I wore this shirt for sun coverage. Long sleeves. But you know, Galveston is a place I belong because of the children. We took them to the water, very early, swimming in the Gulf and feeling out the Gulf and the waters of the Gulf and what it's like when it rains and you're in the water and there's fish activity. Lots of people complain about the Gulf, especially Californians. My own California family has learned about Houston over the years and does not stereotype it so readily—which is important because when progressive people lecture about "Texas," they wipe out people who aren't white, or conservative, or speak other languages than English. Which is the majority.

I digress! About Galveston, it will be a place that I claim forever, because of the children, memory.

José: This sounds like a good moment to ask you about association of these places with the U.S. West. Associations might be feelings, memory, body of knowledges, historical cultural legacies, language or sound legacies, sense of kin, and ancestry, any of which might include violence.

Krista: When I was growing up, I didn't understand Pueblo as "the U.S. West." If you drive around, you see commemorative wagon wheels on advertising signs, you see guys in jeans and cowboy boots. My grandfather on my mother's side (the Sam Houston side) wore boots with dress slacks, but not a cowboy hat. But the more you get into the mountains, the Mountain West, it's marketed as "the West." When I was growing up, I didn't think anything about that.

When I left California to go to Wellesley College in 1984, I was an "older student" at twenty-four. I thought of myself as being from California. I really began to understand, by virtue of the culture shock, what it was to be on the East Coast with people who did not grasp me at all. They had so many stereotypes of me, from the beach, and about California beaches. I was exotic. Ideas about "feminism" couldn't embrace someone like me. I was very different from most of the women at Wellesley, or in Boston.

I began to understand myself then as from a different region. I thought of it as being from California and the beach, where I lived when I left, and where I'd been building beach houses and living a water life. Over time, and particularly when I went to grad school, I understood my history as being from the U.S. West. California, a lot of people would say, is west of the West. I was trying to come to terms with where I was from. My parents were so mobile. Mobility was so important to them. And living with a spirit of adventure.

When I moved to the East, people had a much better sense of where they came from. A lot of people I was meeting understood where they came from. They would talk about home through race or region or family histories or cultural practices. This is when Critical Race Theory as such came into my thinking. I remember in grad school there were parties where students would sing (one was an opera singer, another a jazz singer) or do performance poems important to their sense of history. One of the poems, I think it was Hughes's "The Negro Speaks of Rivers." I couldn't do that at all. What a lot of talented people my peers were! I fled those parties afraid someone would ask me to take a turn. It's as if my family was so mobile, I had no sense of how to tell my history. My first book, *Landscapes of the New West*, took off from that confusion.

I got interested in Wallace Stegner because he was one of the only writers whose sense of place matched something I understood. The whole orientation, that's what matched. He used the term "regional chauvinism" to describe his lack of credibility in East Coast contexts. I could see a version of that around me in my years at Wellesley and later at Brown. It wasn't only ideas that were at issue—it was my way of being. I took heart from his statement that to know where you're from is to know who you are. But how to theorize this for myself as a feminist? That was the rub.

It took me too long to understand that I could think of "place concepts" as significant theory work. That inability was part of the regional chauvinism of the Northeast, its authority, and northeastern feminism, which didn't have to place itself since it was the center of what mattered.

When I went east, I left behind my western body, and that was pretty terrible. That's pretty terrible. I didn't know that could happen. I didn't mean for it to happen. I'm asking other people these questions, so I know what the next question is: about feminism. I will say that when I left behind the West, I left behind how bad that place was for me, how crazy-making it was—no place was ever a feminist place. Well, maybe the Music Festivals. But not in the Southern California I knew. Every conversation that was even a little bit about—I don't know what I called it. I didn't call it women's rights. I don't remember the early ways I started talking about "feminism." But inklings of feminism were a problem. For other people. When I left those places to pursue something that was more intellectual, I got my feet on the ground. But I also left behind whatever was "the West," including my western body, my way in the outdoors, having dogs. The way I had dogs, which was a huge relationship, then didn't have dogs.

José: You've answered most of the questions that you've asked others, but I want to take you back to an in-between place, that moment where you're still living on the beach building houses, before you go to university out east and start to engage with what feminism looks like on the East Coast. What was the feminism that you encountered between the beach and between the east?

Krista: Yeah, thank you for the question. I think it was about being strong, self-consciously strong, in outdoor contexts. But strong women are not "feminists" necessarily—that's more about talking back to men who were, you know, always better at everything outdoors. Way better. Having ideas as a woman and talking about them, not being able to be other than a "killjoy," which was no term of pride. I was such a feminist killjoy, and it was a drag for the people around me. Not wanting guys to pay for things. Not wanting to do what was expected, go to college after high school. I seemed to be hardwired to think for myself and follow my own path. I didn't think with all the facts, mind you.

I remember all the times I drove back and forth from Oxnard to Steamboat, and then Steamboat to Oxnard or Oxnard up north, you know, Santa Cruz or points north. Always solo or with my dog. I used what was at hand, the road trip convention so familiar in my family, to figure out how to be a feminist. The reasons I went places, alone, were feminist reasons, needing to test myself against whatever was in front of me. Often it was impulse, I just did it.

My mom was trying to get some of that same power by that point in her life. She had been trying by taking my sisters and me camping on ambitious long trips before I left home. My mother loves to travel. But "seeing the world" as my mother loves to say isn't the same thing to me as getting outside the picture window. Leaving behind "the view." I did it as best I could. I did everything I could figure out to control my life and eventually what it meant I did was to leave that place because it couldn't hold me. It couldn't sustain me. You know, that was a terrible sacrifice.

Let's end on a different note than "terrible sacrifice." I did years of projects with the Institute for Women Surfers as a way to come back to the water, come back to that beach place I was ruptured from because I was chasing feminism.[1] And being in Pueblo, as part of this project, goes to an earlier life moment, before I felt any political overtone. I haven't talked about my parents doing a certain kind of business in San Francisco in the sixties, concerning the Vietnam War, and I've been writing about that for quite a while but have not been ready to publish material. But this place on the Beulah Road is before then. Coming back here, to a sense of what it feels like to be here, it's great. To return outside of the picture window, and to sleep out last night.

Deciding to Remember the Many Strands
of Home, with Linda Karell

I'm reading "Spokane Kitten" as we drive north toward Cody, into the Heat Dome.[1] *Hot, hot. Excerpted from a memoir in progress, "Spokane Kitten" tells the tale of Linda's Montana childhood spent working around a mother's addictions. José and I will be in Bozeman, then Helena, then Missoula. It's been smoky in the Colorado mountains but clearing up after last night's rain. Wyoming seems all country, long stretches where no cell towers reach. Lots of lone bicyclers, gear strapped to their bikes. All except one are young white guys with beards.*

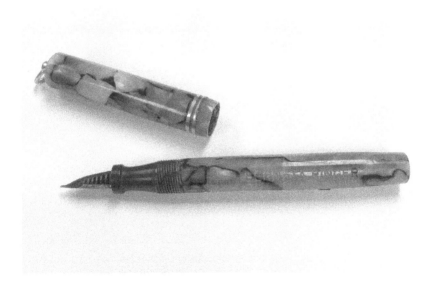

Fig. 10. A fountain pen gifted to Berneta Ringer Doig. In a rare acknowledgment by a male writer, in *Heart Mountain*, Ivan Doig attributes the origin of his writing to his mother. Ivan Doig Archive, Digital Collection, Montana State University (MSU) Library, Bozeman. Courtesy Linda Karell.

Watching all that road go by, I reflect on the visual Linda sends that says "feminist Wests" to her—a fountain pen, belonging to Berneta Ringer Doig, western writer Ivan Doig's mother.[2] She was a woman who was never not poor, in Linda's words, the pen a gift from husband-to-be, Charlie Doig. The pen speaks to women's stories, Linda observes, and also their silencing.

It's a first for me to visit Bozeman. I have been to three WLA meetings in Montana: two in Big Sky, one in Missoula. As WLA president in 2016, Linda hosted one of the Big Sky events. Memorably the conference was entitled "The Profane West."[3] Linda greets us with her therapy dog, Larry—so named because it's easy for hospital patients to remember. He's fun and frisky, an "exuberant little bastard."

We plan to set up our camera in her backyard but take our time getting there because the house stops you with its ingenious renovations. José comments that it has the feel of a feminist rest area. The bottom floor is an art gallery devoted to the work of Linda's spouse, Kenda Minter. Kenda's pieces are crafted from found items, one a delicate window covering made of wire and embedded colored glass lenses. We seat ourselves outside under a backyard tree. A bird feeder is affixed to an old upside-down fishing net, sans net. On the side of the garage is a decorative wreath made from, when you look closely, very compressed, layered aluminum cans. Linda recalls Kenda tucking cans under her car wheels and saying: "On your way out of the driveway, drive over these a few times, would you?"

The Where of Here: Bozeman

Krista: Here we are in your backyard, surrounded by all this art. All this found art and sculpture and compressed cans that Kenda has made come to life.

Linda: Yes, recycled this and that. It is an interesting yard. Kenda has done it all. I'm the one who drinks wine and appreciates. I sometimes fund plant buying, and I water, but I don't do the gardening labor. Kenda finds it meditative. It's a version of church for people who aren't churchgoers. I'm so lucky. I have a much better life because of that because I don't think I could do this for myself. I don't think I would do this for myself.

I'm much more of an indoor person. You were saying, Krista, that the place we do this interview depends on us. And I read these first blogs and people are taking you places, and I'm like: "Jesus Christ, I can't take you anywhere!" Like I don't go outside [chuckles].

Krista: Not everyone takes us places. What we are doing now is a way to engage place, we're talking about the where of here: your backyard. For you it's also indoors.

Linda: Yeah, and it's Bozeman. I'm not someone who gets "solace from open spaces" [riffing on Gretel Ehrlich's Wyoming memoir of that title]. It would never occur to me to go on a hike or go camping when I wanted to refresh myself.

No, I remember camping as a kid. I lived in a three-generation household. My great-grandmother owned the house; she lived upstairs. My grandfather and grandmother—and my grandmother had severe rheumatoid arthritis—lived on the main floor. When my mother was divorced, eventually we moved in. I had a room in the basement. I was tucked far away from people in my own little room that was completely private.

And my grandfather and my grandmother would go camping every summer, he worked for the railroad in Livingston. They had this little camper. To me, it just seemed like hauling all of your domestic work out into the woods where you didn't have the luxury of getting away from it. I watched my mom do most of that work because my grandmother couldn't. They would take us camping and for me as a kid, it was fine. It was getting the watermelon from the creek and running around with my cousins. But so much of my impression of places links to my mother's uncomfortable situation in place.

I don't like to be cold, I don't like to be bitten, I don't like to be burned, I don't like to be wind burned. A backyard is all the outside I need or want. Unlike what Ed Abbey actually did in *Desert Solitaire*—live in Arches National Park in a trailer as a Park Ranger—his philosophy of "Let it be there, you don't have to go see it," I'm all for that. I wish there were more restrictions on national parks. There need to be more safeguards for those places so that ecosystems and the communities of animals and insects in those places can continue to exist. I don't need to be in the middle of it. It doesn't call me or reassure me. I like to be cozied up under a blanket with a book.

Krista: That's a safe place, a good place?

Linda: Well, there is no safe place. But I think it's a good place. Even things like open-concept architecture, I do not get that. Give me a Victorian house with all sorts of little rooms so I can go be in these little rooms instead of a big space. I'm not sure what all . . . maybe it's my temperament. I'm not sure everything has to have an origin in childhood. But I'm not a camper. I'm not a hiker. I'm not a skier. I like to be indoors. And I like this backyard because it surrounds me. Impressionistically, it's one of the things I like about Bozeman. We are cradled in a mountain valley. In a geographic sense, there's a deep unconscious soothing, even though the presence of the mountains bespeaks geologic violence, eruption.

Krista: If I can pause you for a minute. When you said there's no safe space, there are a lot of ways to talk about that.

Linda: One piece of feminist scholarship that had a big impact on me was Biddy Martin and Chandra Talpade Mohanty's "Feminist Politics: What's Home Got to Do With It?"

Krista: The conversation about "home" in feminist politics and hopes for community.

Linda: Yeah. Taking home as a concept, whether it's identity, whether it's whiteness, whether it's feminism, whether it's the West, whether it's my backyard, whether it's my living room. "Home" maintains comfort for us; it welcomes by excluding others. So oppressive histories, that's always the work that is happening. The Martin/Mohanty conversation explained for me that the brilliance of feminism wasn't that any particular strand was correct. Many of the strands gave me language for why my life worked the way it did, and why my mother's life worked the way it did—language that filled in spaces that were terrified, or terrorizing.

I've taught the essay at different times. It's not conceptually hard to grasp. But I found students have a lot of trouble with it. They can certainly think about the community, any particular community, and the way that it excludes and includes based on certain identity properties, or beliefs, or locations. But they have a great deal of trouble then taking it and applying it to an idea of identity in which I'm not self-evident with myself. I'm not the same self that I was in the past. I won't be the same self that, even as I narrate to you a certain story, I'm leaving out things.

Krista: As in the disidentifications of someone like Minnie Bruce Pratt [whose essay Martin/Mohanty discuss]—from whiteness, or from her married self?

Linda: Right. The momentous pleasure of that could be *not* that we have lost something—the Freudian trope that we've lost something that we're never going to recover and so we're endlessly searching for the lost object and substituting things for it. But that the loss itself is interesting. That the losses, the gaps, are part of what constitutes us. They are necessary to political change and movements. That keeps me curious.

I think of Bozeman. I'm fortunate to be here. It's exactly where I want to be.

I left home when I went to graduate school at the University of Rochester. When I went there, I was never coming back. That was as far east of West as I could get. I was delighted to be there because I'm never coming home.

When I grew up, Bozeman, which is a completely different town now in many ways, was where we went for prom dresses. If you couldn't get to Billings, which is really the big city, this is where we came. This is also where we came to see Christmas decorations.

Rochester, I was never coming back. What was there to come back to in Bozeman? A very small railroad town in Livingston that the railroad had left. Bozeman wasn't the artistic center that it has become. And small towns, I find them frightening. I survived growing up in one. I went as an undergraduate to Montana State University, where I teach now, but got out. When the opportunity to come home happened, my mother and I had been estranged for a number of years because I was queer.

I felt if there was any hope for anything to happen with that estrangement, I had to come home.

Krista: Did you want something to happen? You've written about "deciding" to remember your mother. I'm moved by calling it deciding. It suggests a willingness to go somewhere that one has *decided* to go, otherwise one isn't going to do it.

Linda: Yeah, my mom had done things over the years that were indications of how much she loved me, even in the midst of her having a gut repulsion to queerness. For instance, I had a girlfriend in graduate school, and Mom sent us a double blanket. You wouldn't think much of that. But it meant something, like she blessed our relationship.

It's so tangled, because coming back to Bozeman, I had been a kid coming over to Bozeman for fun things like getting a prom dress.

Krista: Did you get a prom dress? Did you go with someone you liked?

Linda: Oh, yeah. Store's closed now. But I got a couple of dresses here. I dated a gay guy the last two years of high school, and that was wonderful. I have such a fondness for him. And a couple of proms I went to prom with a guy that I had a crush on. And those were not as much fun as going with my gay boyfriend who was my best boyfriend ever. I don't know how my mom came up with the money. At the time it was fifty dollars for a prom dress.

Bozeman is also the place where I went to live because Mom kicked me out of the house. Bozeman is where I got my undergraduate degree and first encountered feminism. Bozeman is where I came back as a professional. I've been so many selves here and it's been so many places to me. All of them allow me to think about the disunity of identity, the lack of safety in having any particular identity or any particular place, if what you need it to be is stable for you. Because it's going to be a different place and you're going to be a different person in it.

Literally, I'm talking under the crabapple tree that my mother-in-law bought for me that my mother's ashes are under.

Krista: Your mom's ashes are right here? Wow. [Proper pause.]

Can we talk about the American West and whatever ways you understood yourself to be a part of the American West?

Linda: My relationship with the West is fairly antagonistic. Deliberately. It goes back to that idea of however you define it, it's excluding. For my queer identity, when I moved here, there was "another lesbian" on the faculty. She talked about "the lesbian community." I was like, "What the fuck is that?" Because my experience of the lesbian community or the gay community was that I didn't fit. I was too femme, I wore lipstick, I wore makeup, I liked high-heeled shoes, I wasn't butch enough. Those were the operating identities when I was really coming out in the 1980s.

In any community I've ever been in, I feel this way about academia, about WLA, I've felt like I don't fit in. Yet as you get older, what you come to like is the not-fittingness of it, is the way that it allows a certain wonderfully dark humor, and a certain vantage point of seeing.

Krista: The Profane West—the title of the WLA Conference in which you were president.

Linda: Yeah, Katy Halverson came up with that name.

Krista: Oh, she did? I didn't know that!

Linda: She did! "You should name it this," she said. Katy doesn't swear. But she indulges me.

Not fitting in is a sort of Montana identity. It's very rural. There is a sense that I don't need to be in your business. And you can't come from a working-class background and feel like you fit in academia, you just can't. There's something essential about how it works—it's never disclosed to you.

Krista: Yes, it's an owning-class institution. It's never called that and you don't think it's that because it seems so progressive. It's confusing.

Linda: Right. That's one of the reasons I swear in class. It's a signifier of working class. It works well with students [laughs]. There's a pleasure in that stance that comes from my very ambivalent position as working class, not desperate working class, but someone who never anticipated going to college.

Krista: Really?

Linda: Oh, yeah. I got bored. I was a legal secretary. My boss was a lovely man. He owned property that constituted his income and he did very little legal work. I had nothing to do. He would say, here's the information, hand it to me on a yellow pad. I would write the will, I'd get two dollars and seventy-five cents an hour, and he'd get three hundred dollars. I was never going to be able to buy a car on that wage. So I went to college. But college wasn't on my radar.

I got to the point when I was living in Livingston, where I would make to-do lists and on my to-do list would be: read a magazine. I literally had nothing.

I'm constantly surprised by the fact I open my mouth, and I end up someplace else. That feels to me rooted in where I've grown up and in the "inside talk" of working-class people. We code switch. I love it when people underestimate me and think I swear because I'm crass or not educated. It's actually a strategy.

Krista: Your "feminist West" visual is of Ivan Doig's mother's pen. You read that visual as much about articulating a presence as about silence.

Linda: Any story we have is going to be partial. A half story. That doesn't mean it's not the story we need to survive at the time. If we are fortunate, if we're curious, our stories will change. We'll look back at our earlier stories and say: Oh, that allowed me to believe this or allowed me to do that.

Writing about collaboration, authorship, which I've done across a lifetime, was part of this idea. My first book, *Writing Together/Writing Apart*, was about the constructedness of "the author." I'm interested in dismantling this idea that we are unified and known to ourselves. Because if that were true, holy fuck, that would be boring. More than anything, feminism gave me the joy of being able to analyze something. I love to be able to think through, I find so much fun, in a deep satisfying way, to be able to think. Why is something like it is? Why am I feeling that thing? What sort of things go into the parts of my mother's story that I can't ever fully know? What difference does it make?

Lunch, with Clark Whitehorn

Our editor for this project, Clark Whitehorn, invites us to lunch. It's in keeping with our hopes to close distances between the personal and professional that we visit Clark, as we have visited others. We had interviews sort of nearby in Montana, so we drive over and spend an afternoon in Helena getting to know one another. Clark shows us around his place. We are talking bears, a favorite Montana subject, and he shows us a Joel Sartore photo of a grizzly bear running down a bison calf in Yellowstone.

I see a pull-up bar lodged at the top of a door jamb, reminding me of a less serious version we had for my youngest son. That I could use it even a single time! We find out later that Clark has gone running that morning. He is a book editor who is in shape. He is a book editor who was in the Coast Guard.

From the start Clark has been behind this project, excited about its on-the-road methodology and place-based interviews. Clark notices how few titles of books have the word "feminist" in them. He loves the van, the idea of the van, has offered good advice about insulating it, and also about visual stencils. I have yet to take that advice. Does the van have a name? he asks me, a couple of times.

Clark is telling us about the foods he has spread out on a cutting board. He carries them to a table set for we three, and then, stopping in his tracks, says, "My mother would be turning over in her grave!" Lunch plates, apparently. Already we were happy, everything is very nice, and now with lunch plates in hand, we can be happy again with no worries about his mother in the afterlife.

Local foods, Big Timber smoked sausage, and stuffed Greek olives from the International Market in Butte. Clark is talking about our lunch items but also about books, western studies and Native studies. One book he mentions, since I'm there and he's thinking about feminist-engaged research, is Neva Hassanein's *Changing the Way America Farms*. She is an environmental studies professor at University of Montana. Food

Fig. 11. José with Clark Whitehorn at his hospitable table. Author photo.

democracy, just agricultural practices. He likes that book, and checking it out later, so do I. We eat crackers, three different cheeses. José is fond of the sun-dried tomato spread. Clark points out the Flathead cherries grown in Missoula, and the Bing cherries. The ripe cantaloupe is not, he confesses, local. But it's good! He promises we can pick raspberries later from his bushes in the back and take them on the road.

Clark phones Charlene Porsild, his wife, who is president and CEO of the Montana History Foundation. It's late Friday afternoon, and does she want to come home early and chat? We are having fun, talking about women's history, and women hunters, and she can join in, have a beer. Like Clark, Charlene has a PhD in history with specialties in the West. Hers is the Canadian West, the Klondike, and her book *Gamblers and Dreamers* won, among other awards, the W. Turrentine Jackson Prize from the Western History Association.

We end up talking less about Western history or community building in the Klondike than "Montucky" or what we hear people call Montana's "white problem." Their own high school son, after the mass shooting at

Parkland High School in Florida, was a co-organizer of a school event designed to coincide with the March for Our Lives, a nationwide action for gun control legislation led by students. Clark tells the story of coming out of the backcountry, from a hunting trip, and turning on the radio. He hears his son Noah's voice on NPR![1] Noah and his classmates are part of Helena Youth Against Gun Violence. What both Clark and Charlene talk about is the high school culture of Helena, and its splits between hicks, jocks, goths, and "Capital H" boys who imagine growing up to be in a militia. At some point, they report, their son gets grief from other boys; he is assumed to be anti-gun—which is untrue, since Noah grew up hunting with his father. Apparently, he is the only guy among a group of female students who participate in the March for Our Lives in Helena.

I appreciate these tales of Montana today and the political insight of parents who are parenting in conservative states, as we do. I appreciate the language of "Montucky," which helps us articulate the important issue of whiteness for the Mountain West, including immediately in our next interview with Randi Tanglen, the director of Humanities Montana. We make good, at the end of our long lunch, picking raspberries from the backyard bushes, heavy with fruit. Charlene pulls out a jar of apple butter, made from their trees, which I will add to rice cakes later in the Missoula KOA where we camp out.

We stand on their porch, having had such a great lunch and connection. Clark offers a "next time, come and visit." We shake our heads over the smoky haze hanging over the mountains. From their deck we can't clearly see Mt. Helena, the Sleeping Giant, or Mt. Ascension. Maybe next time it will be a clear day. I still need to come up with a better name for the van! Clark tells me not to worry, the right name will emerge.

For Me, the West Is Rural, with Randi Tanglen

Missoula Public Library is Randi's chosen place for conversation. It is a state-of-the-art facility, created by local architects A&E Design in partnership with Minneapolis-based Traci Lesneski of MSR Design. The new library is billed as cultural house, makerspace, and center for lifelong learning. As Randi writes in "Guest Column: Sustaining the Humanities across Rural Montana," cultural institutions like museums and libraries have been essential workers, so to speak, in her own educational history. Raised in rural eastern Montana, educated at Rocky Mountain College in Billings before pursuing a PhD at University of Arizona, Randi knows firsthand the importance of cultural infrastructure in "keeping ideas, stories, and conversations alive and well."[1] As a homegrown culture advocate, she's a perfect fit for her appointment as executive director of Humanities Montana.[2]

Randi waits for José and me in the library foyer, bearing a box of cookies shaped as hearts from Bernice's Bakery in Missoula. "The heart," she smiles, "is Missoula." It's such a thoughtful Randi-like thing to do. I remember her bringing other treats to our "theory parties" in hotel rooms during a couple of academic conferences. "Party" isn't the right word for these gatherings of colleagues and friends who discuss feminist conceptualizations of place and region. Not enough wine. Randi has been a mainstay of the gatherings, always up for tricky conversations.

This extraordinary library space and level of investment in public learning centers is very hopeful at a moment when libraries are being closed or converted to other uses. Our own sons' high school library was converted to an eating space, its books mainly digital. Humanities Montana houses some of its programs in the library and when Randi shows us "The Democracy Project" banner, I get choked up. Youth initiatives that encourage young people to research issues they care about, how inspirational.

I understand, the better I know Randi, that facilitating complicated conversations is her calling card. When she was a professor at Austin College, in Sherman, Texas, Randi taught toward and has written about Sherman as a town where the first Confederate statue was erected in Texas.[3] *Her seminars showed how to teach classic nineteenth-century American literature (including Hawthorne, Poe, and Stowe) as types of Confederate monuments to ideologies of white supremacy. When I ask Randi for an early sample of her feminist work, she sends along the epilogue to her 2008 dissertation.*[4] *It reflects on the frustrated leadership attempts of her evangelical grandmother and herself, both of them faithful women whose talents warrant pastor or elder aspirations except that women are disallowed. This reflection piece is tempered foundationally by the particular white nativist vision of the afterlife. The white supremacy of evangelism is a cautionary tale Randi brings to her vision of feminism.*

The Where of Here: Missoula Public Library

Krista: You've been showing us around, Randi, telling us about the combination of state funds, private funds, that built this amazing place.

Randi: I wanted us to meet here because it's so connected to the type of work I'm doing with Humanities Montana—which is a State Council of the National Endowment for the Humanities. Our mission is to infuse the public humanities into the daily lives of Montanans. Libraries, public libraries, are central to that work. As you saw, one of our current initiatives, the Democracy Project, is housed here and in two other libraries in Montana. Young people are invited to research a local issue or something that they really care about. They use the information literacy skills that the library provides and create a solution for it that they can work on together to make them feel connected to their community and empowered to take action.

The Democracy Project is for high school students. For adults, we have programs about issues in civic engagement. We just wrapped up four virtual panels, from an initiative called "Why It Matters." This is programming on civic and electoral engagement about different kinds of political power that Montanans have. The virtual panels we did, during the pandemic, covered topics like, "The Purpose of Protests," "Rural/Urban Political Divides in Montana," "The Native Vote in Montana," and "The Political Power of Young People." Those are conversations we're having now.

The Rural/Urban Divide panel had almost three hundred people registered and attending. That was new, to be able to reach such a large audience. Especially in a geographically vast state like Montana with lots of remote rural communities, learning how to do the virtual programming on Zoom made our programming much more accessible. Before the pandemic, we were known for the one-on-one conversations that our humanities experts facilitated in libraries, museums, community centers, churches. Now we've been able to make our programming more accessible during the pandemic. Going forward, it'll be about finding a balance.

Krista: I hear and read about the public humanities as sometimes more alive than humanities in universities. It has the possibility of growing in ways that academic humanities are struggling to achieve. The defunding of the humanities in university budgets, the delegitimizing of humanities knowledge as STEM fields and professional training (law or business schools) take over the priorities of universities, bode very badly as higher education trends. Even when humanists figure out how to respond and transform what they do, it doesn't help as much as one might expect.

What are you seeing in Montana right now about the possibilities of public humanities versus the academic humanities?

Randi: I think about the question a lot. Our mission is to serve communities through stories and conversation. This could be taken, wrongly, to be a watered-down version of what we do in the academic humanities because it's not focused on discipline and rigor or writing or research. In university humanities disciplines (literature, history, philosophy, religious study), writing and research is organized around "the intervention," finding an argumentative niche and, frequently, throwing those who disagree or came before you under the bus.

When I talk to people and look at our programs and the impact that they're having, what people outside the academy are looking for is the multiple perspectives that the humanities provide. The different voices that the humanities are able to bring together and the nuance in differences those perspectives bring out. For the public humanities, the work is about the conversations of bringing the voices together.

A feminist method does more of that, of bringing voices together, experiences and stories together, like the work that you're doing in this project. I liked what you wrote in your About Us statement, of needing to find ways to listen to and learn from each other. I thought of that as an orientation towards public humanities that we're trying to do too at

Humanities Montana. At this divided political moment, and in a changing Montana that is becoming more red and more conservative and falling along the divides we see in national politics, it's so important.

Krista: Let's talk about "the white problem" in Montana. We heard from Clark Whitehorn, as you know, executive editor at University of Nebraska Press, and Charlene Porsild, CEO of Montana History Foundation, about "Montucky." They talked about cliques in high schools called "Hicks." The Hicks are white nationalists in training, a certain brand of gun rights defenders who can imagine themselves doing anti-government actions. At least in Helena, we heard, the cliques were the goths, the jocks, the Hicks, and the nerds. That category of "Hicks" must in its own way live in a lot of different places.

If we take up the idea of feminism as a theory that engages difference and conflicts between women, feminism as built out of that history, can you think about how feminist public humanities efforts can respond to Montana's white problem?

You know, I'll just throw that out there. [laughs]

Randi: Oh wow, thanks! My mind's going in a few different directions. I can speak to my own experience, of that "early feminism" you and I emailed about.

Krista: Yes, in the end of your dissertation, "Feminist and Religious Legacies," you talk about your grandmother, Rickey Tanglen, and her histories of evangelism in eastern rural Montana, with the Lutheran Church and the Lutheran home missions she founded.[5] She could not become an elder or preach; she was frustrated, angry. Your own feminism grew from what you learned about her and your own experiences.

Randi: I'll talk about that and it will bring us back to the issue of whiteness and feminism.

I grew up in rural northeastern Montana. Close to the North Dakota border. I was born in a town called Sidney. You've heard of the Bakken oil fields? It's out there. My family moved away when I was ten because of that classic boom-and-bust economy of the West. There was an oil bust, and my family ended up moving to different parts of Montana.

But Sidney is where my dad's family was from, and where my parents moved after they were married and started their family. My dad worked in the construction business, not the oil fields. Later on, he became a journalist at one of the local newspapers. My mom was a stay-at-home mom. With the economic realities of the oil bust, she eventually went to work full time, and had a long career in the federal government.

One thing important to me as a young person was being part of a church, the Lutheran Church I wrote about in the epilogue. It was a place where I experienced so much love and acceptance as a child. But then, as I got older, I started to see inconsistencies and especially the double standard around gender. I asked a lot of questions and eventually realized I couldn't ask questions without becoming a "black sheep." I felt rejected by the church, this place that had been so loving and accepting of me in this small community that I was raised in. I later found feminism, which also provided a place of belonging. It provided what religion had provided before, because feminism was something bigger than myself, something to believe in. It was right to my mind as a young person, a college student. I went to a really small college in Billings called Rocky Mountain College.

Krista: Can you remember a time you asked a wrong kind of question?

Randi: In my family, and my community, there was a lot of tolerance. When I asked, "Why can't women be leaders in the church?" the response was like, "Oh, that's Randi." Or "That's just Randi being a feminist." It was during the Rush Limbaugh era. It was like, "Oh, you're being a feminazi," teasing me, not taking me seriously.

Krista: Did you want to be a leader?

Randi: I did. When I was a young person, I would have seen myself as a pastor. I was really interested in theology.

Krista: Did you feel you had a calling? Thinking back to the young person?

Randi: I don't know. I think when I was young, I would have said that. But there wasn't a clear path for what that would look like. I think also that's why academia became an option and teaching spoke to that desire. In my teenage and early college years, I was going to church. After college.

Krista: This is a long-term faith path, and commitment.

Randi: Yes, and wanting to bring the worlds together, feminism and religion. In my dissertation, I was saying: "Hey feminists, you need to take religion seriously. It impacts what people do in the world." In academia, especially with feminism, there's a secularism; we don't know what to do with religion. Even now, we are blindsided because we haven't understood that religion shapes how people vote. It shapes how people live their lives and the actions they take in the world. That's something to take more seriously, so we can engage and be more effective as feminist teachers and as feminist intellectuals.

The other part that wasn't in my dissertation was that my mom was raised in a Mennonite farming community in northeastern Montana, even more remote than Sidney, in a small town called Lustre. This is where the whiteness piece explicitly comes in. The community is on the Fort Peck Indian Reservation. To this day, it's still not clear to me how Mennonite homesteaders in the early 1900s were able to get homesteads on the reservation.

There's that long history and dynamic too that as a young person, and now as a middle-aged person coming back to Montana, I really grapple with my Montana heritage. My mom and her cousins and her sister talk about it a lot—what it meant to be a white ethnic community on the reservation. And those legacies, what do we do with that now? And that gets to the cookbooks.

Krista: You are referring to the cookbook cover photos that you posted on your Instagram account. The "What's Cooking in Lustre" and the Blackfeet cookbooks. What should we know about them each, and also about them side by side?

Randi: When I was finishing my Master's degree here at the University of Montana, with Jill Bergman who passed away before I moved back to Montana, she was my mentor and a great feminist mentor,[6] I started thinking about the church cookbooks. My mom had some in her cupboard that were from Lustre, from the Mennonite Church. They recorded a lot of the food traditions from Mennonites who came to Montana from the Ukraine. I thought that was *fascinating*.

Jill had me thinking about historical recuperation work. I was thinking, where is the Montana women's literary tradition? At that time, I was thinking particularly of the immigrant women from communities like Lustre. Looking for women's voices and women's stories in unexpected places. I actually received a research grant from the Montana Committee for the Humanities, which is now Humanities Montana! I researched and did interviews with the women who made these cookbooks in eastern Montana. My question was: Did these cookbooks provide community for

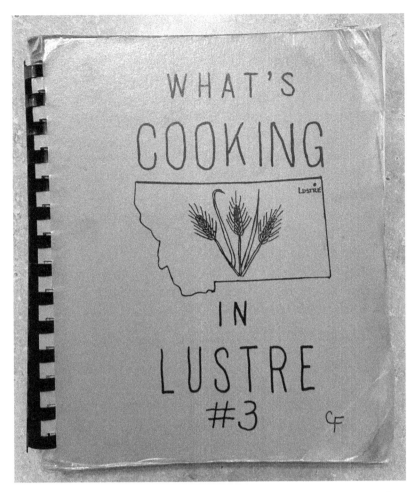

Fig. 12. Women's community through cookbooks. Courtesy Delores Tanglen.

women who were in remote Montana places associated with isolation and loneliness? What I found was that they provided unexpected leadership opportunities for women in very conservative communities that limited women's role in church and community organizations.

Those pictures on my Instagram were from community cookbooks at the Montana Historical Society Library in Helena. Looking at the earliest cookbooks, I think it was 1883, from the Butte area. Those strands of white women not receiving the recognition they deserved, and me wanting to help those voices come out. And then all the strands of feminist approaches, religion and family and places tied into one another by look-ing at how church cookbooks were an unexpected way for white women to assert leadership in spite of the traditional gender roles of their com-munities, and how these cookbooks served as literary, historical, and cultural documents. But the cookbooks I initially researched from white, homesteading communities in eastern Montana did not tell the full story of women's experiences in Montana.

A few weeks ago, I visited the Montana Historical Society. I had heard that their archivists were curating a significant collection of rural com-munity cookbooks, and due to my previous research and my new role, I was curious to see what they had acquired. I came across this "Blackfeet Cookbook," from 1969, which was a collaboration between out-of-state VISTA volunteers and Blackfeet tribal leadership, with an introduction provided by the tribal chairman. The aim of the collection was to combine "Blackfeet ways of cooking with the modern-day cooking." That cook-book from one of Montana's seven reservations raises a lot of personal and methodological questions for me as a white feminist scholar whose research—and identity—is so deeply invested in "place."

As a fourth-generation white Montanan, I struggle with the settler colonial legacies of my homesteading ancestors. The history of my family in Montana is a heartwarming story of church ladies and cookbooks, but also a brutal history based in colonization, removal, and genocide. Throughout my life I wondered how to make sense of the contradictions of my settler history. Can I have pride in and care about my ancestors? Can I have a deep connection to the eastern Montana landscape that shaped me as a young person, but still account for the injustices of the past and the present?

It makes me think of the essay "Looks Back," by Mandy Smoker (Assiniboine) who juxtaposes the version of Montana history depicted in classic C. M. Russell paintings with the life and experiences of her great-grandmother, Looks Back. She writes about the huge disconnection and asks where Montanans' stories converge and diverge. She wants us to contend with how that history has played out and been represented over time. Mandy's words mean a lot to me, because we attended grad school together at the University of Montana. She was born and grew up on the Fort Peck Reservation, where my ancestors originally homesteaded in

Lustre. She was the state poet laureate of Montana the same year I became executive director of Humanities Montana.

Similarly, Joanna Brooks, in *The Book of Mormon Girl*, a memoir, asks white scholars to grapple with the contradictions of history and lived experience and not to so easily valorize or condemn our ancestors. She talks about "actual human histories" including failings, tenderness, ignorance, arrogance. These are uncomfortable questions and over the years, like many white scholars, I've responded with anger, guilt, shame, denial. Fear. But when I step back from that fear, I wonder what types of conversations we, as a nation contending with racial injustice, could have. What types of relationships and alliances could we develop if we sat with and engaged that discomfort instead of trying to displace it? We ask that of our students and colleagues in the field—to engage and critically examine contradictions of identity and experience.

Krista: What a lot to ponder! Thank you, Randi. Did your mom cook Mennonite when you were growing up? What would be a Mennonite meal?

Randi: Yeah, that's why I was interested. Her aunts and grandmas would make these recipes for family events. You want an example of a Mennonite meal? Verenika—it's like a dumpling, like pierogi, but it has cottage cheese, and a heavy cream gravy. It's time and labor intensive. You have to fold over little pastries and pinch them together. My mom always observed: how did pioneer women find time to do that? The fact they did says that they were valuing something, or trying to maintain a sense of a culture or civilization in their homesteading life.

Krista: We began our conversation about the where of here through this library, the Missoula Public Library. But for you it's also eastern Montana, and histories of women evangelists in eastern Montana, and the issue of women's leadership.

Randi: In Montana they say there are six different Montanas. Living in Missoula in western Montana is so different than eastern Montana, which is plains and the prairies and the hills.

One part of the mission of Humanities Montana is that we push ourselves to reach the Sidneys and the tribal communities in eastern Montana too. Are our resources going to those places? That's hard to do based in Missoula. That's something we think about a lot.

Krista: A sense of place, for you, is Sidney? Plains and prairie?

Randi: Yeah, it is prairie and dry. And churchy and domestic space—female space was how I felt them.

I think a point of your research, Krista, is that the West is many Wests, the West is a contested space, and a contested critical term. For me, the West is rural, and coming from rural communities, that's where my sense of justice comes in. They are overlooked, underserved communities. One thing that I really like about my work now is that we're able to bring resources to those communities, especially through the American Rescue Plan and the CARES Act. To me, "West" is those eastern Montana spaces.

POSTSCRIPT: *IN SANTA FE, AT THE 2022 MEETING OF THE WESTERN Literature Association, Randi lets me know she is considering a move from Humanities Montana. It's a shame for them to lose her but unsurprising given Montana's political climate.[7] By the end of the year, Randi announces she is tapped to be the new Vice Provost for Faculty Affairs at the University of North Dakota in Grand Forks. That role charges her with being the chief faculty advocate at UND.*

In a lively interview about her new job a few months into it, Randi expresses gratitude for how welcoming she finds her colleagues.[8] She newly appreciates the toughness of North Dakotans. She had thought as a Montanan she knew about winter! She also talks about her love of the series Yellowstone; in fact, she is writing an article about the series' relationship to Montana's Confederate and Lost Cause legacies. The humanities and liberal arts, she tells the interviewer, are places to cherish for "civil conversations and deeper civic engagement, something that American public life is severely lacking right now."

ROAD FINDS
What Lingers in the Air

José sets up a lawn chair for me to sit in as he puts up the tent, puts in our bags, and gets our dinner. Thank God. I am exhausted. Grand plans with Randi Tanglen for dancing around the campfire at this Missoula KOA do not come to pass with fire bans everywhere in the Rocky Mountains. Wildfires burn ahead and behind us, and their names—the Cameron Peak, Sylvan Lake, the Muddy Flier—come in and out of conversations at gas stations and cafés in Colorado. They turn into the Anderson Hill and Harris Mountain fires at the check in desk of the Holiday KOA in Missoula.

This campground is one my mother knows well, where she brought five daughters and always a few friends. The KOAs of this country were havens for her in the 1970s. A decent feminist rest area for a woman driving cross-country in the summertime with a need to occupy lots of daughters. Like the character Alice (Ellen Burstyn) in the 1974 feminist road-trip film *Alice Doesn't Live Here Anymore*, my mother heard her own raw voice in the surround-sound of her children.

My father did not camp. But he loved the mountains. He loved alpine air, skiing. Aspen, Breckenridge, Vail, eventually Steamboat—dreamscapes of the good life. Given how thoroughly I was his daughter until I became my mother's daughter, they were also dreamscapes for me. The culture of lodges and après-ski. The ride up the gondola, finding friends at the top, disappearing down whatever run looked good. I was raised to be this kind of westerner. To recognize "views" and know self in outdoor places where one feels the powerful why of the good life.

Camping in Montana in wildfire season is not a dreamscape. It's hard on the lungs, hot. But a couple of nights out here in Missoula had to happen, for the sake of the camping trips of the past. And for all the mountain life and beach life I wanted to live and did not.

Driving up through Wyoming into a heat dome, breathing heavy wildfire air, José and I are not talking about "climate"—maybe we should be. But it's cliché to drop the term "climate" unless a specific point is to be made, and I don't have one. What we're talking about is "Montucky," the whiteness problem. José and I start to get paranoid about white supremacy. We stay at a low-budget place in Deer Lodge, and the woman who checks me in hasn't seen him. She mentions that some of the guests aren't the best—they play "music too loud." That's the code I am meant to receive, one white person to another, as she nods toward two young African American men wearing muscle shirts walking across the baking parking lot. I can't figure out in the moment how not to collude with this racial pact. Should I mention the exchange to José and make him jumpier?

We carry our luggage and the cooler up two flights of stairs past a couple of rough-looking white guys, also wearing muscle shirts. They are grilling meat atop a hibachi on the sweltering motel balcony. We are jangled and wondering about other places to call, to see if we can stay in the next town. The white guys make us nervous. They aren't flying a Confederate flag but it feels like they could. Finally we say, forget it. We came to this place to hole up a couple days, rest, not spend money. I need to catch up on the blog. José is teaching a summer film class on Zoom, in the midst of the travel. He needs to get out his notes. We keep the shades down and eat out of the cooler.

As a teenager there was a moment when I did not want to hear stories anymore from my father about places he skied during the Korean War. He had memories. I was to understand, from certain looks on his face, they had been "significant," and it made me angry. My father needed a hearing and I was not going to give it to him. As much as he seemed to have it all, he was restless and reckless. With whatever judgment I had at fifteen, I sensed it was a bad idea for him to want to make friends with my friends. Come out to the front lawn at night to smoke dope, for instance. He was on a grand jury for the county at the time, as foreman. But worries about whether either of us would get "reputations" did not preoccupy him then, or later, when we returned to review what had gone wrong between us.

I remember maybe another ten years later, after the election of Reagan, one of the Christmas holidays in Steamboat. My parents had been back in the mountains for a while, my three youngest sisters were living at home. In his late forties, my father was now semi-retired, trading a bit in the stock market. He built a magnificent lodge house with new friends, young local builder buddies. It was the family's most wonderful house yet, with a guestroom designed on the hut-hopping ideal of the German *Matratzenlager*. For a while I moved to Steamboat with my boyfriend and we set up house, with the dogs, at the base of the ski mountain. We were escaping some trouble he had found, putting our beach life on hold. No one asked to see my bad fake ID, and I got a job on the mountain as a cocktail waitress. I created a much better job in town after I found a glass greenhouse in disarray and convinced the shop owner to let me get it in order.

What I remember from living in Steamboat that was good was walking home after closing the bar in the dark quiet of the snow under a blush of stars. I remember the warm glass greenhouse in wintertime and us running the dogs behind my boyfriend's little truck. They loped at the bumper as we creeped along a dirt road that ran astride the Yampa River. There was skiing. My mother had gotten the girls touring skis and the Steamboat country club plowed a cross-country track. I remember one time, with somebody's boyfriend who fought backcountry fires in Whitefish, doing telemark turns all the way down the soft shoulder of the ski mountain.

But I did not live to ski. There was too much drinking. My youngest sisters were young, and I was anxious about the goings-on at my parents' home. I had political opinions now officially, and my parents had voted for Reagan and before him, Nixon. My father, retired before fifty, lectured me about the value of hard work—it was the American way, people who got ahead worked hard, and so forth. I received these lectures with no patience or respect, and after too many times getting his feelings hurt, he gave them up, saying he couldn't argue a point as well as I did. My mother started a paying job and began complaints about my father she'd never allowed herself before. In Steamboat she found Didion's *Slouching Towards Bethlehem*. My mother had been insulated and quite determined to believe the center was holding. Now she was waking up. What my father loved best of all was to ski to the lift line from the first floor of the house, absolutely a narrative detail belonging to the dreamscape. It *was* the dream come true for him, as real and beautiful as any other part of that time.

I had been away a good many more years when José and I returned to Pueblo for my father's funeral in 1993. He died young, from cancer.

Services were held at the Adrian Comer Funeral Home. By then there had been a shakedown of my westernness, a decade and more of finding other ways to understand the dreamscape and myself in it. In graduate school I was reading the New Western History. I read *Big Rock Candy Mountain*, Wallace Stegner's breakout novel, and realized its Bo Mason figure spoke to me of my father. My mother, ever the reader, saw similarities herself. I wrote to Wallace Stegner to ask his thoughts about women's literary history. He responded with kindness, skepticism, and affectionate chiding, saying he would offer his patriarchal blessing to my work if he were a Mormon. I attended the WLA conference for a first and then a second time, and submitted material related to Joan Didion and what I called the "category of Western." I was questioning Stegner's famous claim of the West as the landscape of hope. Stegner set his compass by the hopefulness of the West, and most WLA people did too.

I was assigned to a panel entitled "the Anti-West." Me, child of the dreamscape, the anti-West?

At my father's funeral, I remembered him to those gathered as a man who yodeled out to the mountains from his bedroom deck in Steamboat. The mountains yodeled back. We didn't always get along, I said, but I remember his infectious joy. When my father was happy, all the world was beautiful. Sandy Buchanan, after the funeral, told me she felt I got it right, the sense of his spirit. And that pleased me because Sandy, like Drew Wills, is family. They had stayed in the *Matratzenlager*, skied with my father. They saw the Steamboat life from the complicated inside. Sandy and Drew are dreamscape people—they get it.

One of the great reckonings of Stegner's life was his disavowal of the West as "hope's native home."[1] At the end, Stegner knew better. He'd seen enough boom/bust economies, wildernesses compromised. He had begun to face Indigenous genocide. In his later years Stegner lived part of the year away from his idyllic perch in the Palo Alto hills where he'd written the "Wilderness Letter," preferring Vermont. He assessed California as parochial, self-absorbed. Living in the Golden Land made Californians complacent, even smug, about what lay beyond its borders.

The day after my father's funeral, we all drove up to Pueblo to spread my father's ashes. My mother and sisters, José and I. Sandy's partner, Tommy Wood, got us a hand-gliding permit so we could drive off-road to a place Tommy knew. We bounced back country in his pickup over a decent fire trail until we got to a spot with an overlook. My mother shook some of the gravely powder loose from the remains box and kept some of it to spread later in other places. They'd had, she mused, a lot of adventures.

It's interesting to think that Stegner was never labeled "anti-West," though he reckoned with settler colonialism, Indigenous genocide, the perils for community-making of too much self-reliance, the perils of capitalism for people and planet. What is the tipping point that earns the term? Might feminism be a tipping point? Here I don't mean feminism as being a "strong woman," since being a "western woman" or a settler is, historically speaking, and in popular culture too, to be strong. Liz Chaney and Barbara Stanwyck of *The Big Valley* are strong. Strong women are admired in the West, Westerns are full of them. Ranchers, riders, cattle drivers. Tough. Not to be trifled with. But strong women are not by definition feminists. Feminists have ideas for why things are—they bring an understanding. For instance, feminists bring an understanding to Stegner's plagiarism of the work of the writer and illustrator Mary Hallock Foote, his source for *Angle of Repose*.[2] Feminists (as he refused to do) hold sexism to account.

Ah, the work of the killjoy, spreading good tidings to the tune of John Denver.

One falls into these memories, furies, gets pulled in and under, and emerges.

Tucked into our tent in the Missoula KOA, in July 2021, surrounded by the night sounds of this campground, it's good to notice the "anti-West" messenger is not getting blamed for anything tonight! She's had a quiet evening campside, fallen into a force field of remembering and been pulled through to real time by a nice dinner and quiet talk with her sweetheart. The two of them have opened the box of heart Montana cookies given by Randi Tanglen. After a while the smoky smell fades. Rest.

Finding Community through Transcription, with Zainab Abdali (Guest Post)

9:00 a.m. in Houston. I sit down at my desk with a cup of coffee, open up my laptop, and put my headphones on. I hit play. The conversation that I listen to is wide-ranging. It covers settler colonialism, motherhood, birdwatching, generational trauma, academia, and many other topics. The conversation is taking place in Texas or New Mexico or Montana or Colorado or Utah or Idaho—other than Texas, all states I have never been to. I know the person asking questions—my internship supervisor and professor Krista Comer—but not the people being interviewed, who are feminist scholars and colleagues of Dr. Comer's and with whom I've communicated only via email to collect release forms and writing samples.

But as I transcribe these conversations, I feel connected to each of the people being interviewed. One reason for this is that transcription requires close listening. You have to pay attention to every word. Zoning out for even a few seconds means having to go back and replay the audio. Even if I am listening carefully, sometimes I can't understand what is said, and need to rewind a word or a sentence multiple times to figure it out. When they name someone or some place, I spend some time googling to make sure I got the spellings right. Having had my own name misspelled and mispronounced by everyone from baristas to professors for years, I am very particular about getting names right. I am using an AI program to auto-transcribe, but the software often misspells or misinterprets certain words, especially those in Spanish. It doesn't catch a word or phrase said in a softer tone, and does not transcribe sounds at all. Birds chirping. Plane flying overhead. Car driving by. Kids playing in the background. Dog barking. Krista and interviewee laughing. I write these down in parentheses so that the transcription is a fuller record of the interview, paying attention to more than just the words—paying attention to the sounds of the place where the conversation is happening.

By the time I am done transcribing an interview, I have spent hours listening to a person's voice, and I've come to recognize their speech patterns, the particular cadence of their speech. But the sense of familiarity I feel with them is due to more than just carefully listening. It is also because of *what* they say. Many of the women being interviewed discuss their complicated relationship to the word "feminism," especially the women of color, for whom feminism was not something arrived at easily in a sudden moment of revelation, but something that took years of negotiation to claim and reclaim. Many point to college and certain college courses as an important step in their journey to feminism. Some discuss how their feminism is tied to having a strong community of women around them who support them. Some discuss their complicated connection to "home" or a home place. Again and again, I am struck by how closely I can relate to the experiences of these women whom I have never met and who have vastly different backgrounds than my own.

When I was a junior in college, I remember excitedly telling my advisor and mentor, Carol Fadda, who is an Arab American professor of English at Syracuse,[1] that while doing research for my undergraduate thesis, I had started reading *this bridge we call home*.[2] I told her how exhilarating it was to be reading this collection of writings by primarily women of color feminist scholars, including Muslim and Arab American feminists. I felt like I was reading my own experiences within its pages—a rare feeling for me, since at that time I hadn't come across many feminist texts that centered women of color or that I felt I could relate to. And I remember Carol growing emotional as well, telling me that it was moving for her to see me find this book and these essays, because she herself could remember first coming across this book and the original collection (*This Bridge Called My Back*) and feeling that same sort of excitement, the comfort of knowing you are not alone.[3] Several of the contributors to *this bridge we call home*, published in 2002, also mention what the original collection, published in 1981, meant to them when they first encountered it. Renée M. Martínez refers to it as having the impact of a mother, a sister, a *compañera*. One of the editors, AnaLouise Keating, writes of her first encounter with *This Bridge Called My Back* as a kind of coming home.

To me, this is one of the most powerful aspects of feminist scholarship, and this is what the *Living West as Feminists* project is fundamentally about—creating a space for feminists to come home to by talking, reading, and writing about our complex relationships to feminism and to place, and reflecting on our relationships with each other. Creating feminist rest areas, to use the term Dr. Comer has used in this book.

Before I started this internship early in the summer of 2021, I had been nervous about spending two months working entirely from home, just sitting in front of my computer. I started my PhD in fall 2020, so I was already exhausted from having done a whole year, my very first year of graduate studies, fully online, without the kind of in-person community of peers that had been so important for me in my undergraduate years. And now, here I was, about to start an internship where my tasks were primarily transcribing interviews, sending emails, organizing files, and website management—all done from home.

What I've come to realize as summer draws to a close is that *Living West as Feminists* has been able to cultivate a community of its own. Rather than feeling isolated during this summer, I found myself a part of a network of feminist scholars who are willing to connect their academic or professional work to their lived experiences, who approach concepts like feminism, settler colonialism, migration, and borders as not only theoretical or academic topics, but as frameworks that tangibly shape or have shaped their lives.

As much as we talk about lived experience in academia, it's still difficult to move away from the idea that *real* expertise somehow requires an impersonal, unbiased, objective approach to the theoretical concepts we study. But in the feminist rest area that all of us involved in *Living West as Feminists* have collectively created, the personal stakes of feminist theory and settler colonialism studies are made clear, and relationality, not some kind of distanced objectivity, is the defining feature of the project. Going into the second year of my graduate studies with all the surrounding uncertainty about how "normal" the academic year will be, not to mention the ever-present realization about the dire state of the job market and the humanities in general, it is communities like the one we have collectively built this summer through LWAF that provide me with a sense of comfort, and convince me of the possibility of creating a space that people can come home to.

A Rendezvous, with Melody Graulich

The one and only Melody Graulich! We meet in Swan Valley, Idaho, set up at Camp Rendezvous, a small mom-and-pop shop with no tent campers but us. Melody had planned to throw her bag down under the stars, but late-day rain and her dog, who she thinks might bark tonight, change the plan. After several nights in smokey Missoula, then two smokier nights in Deer Lodge at a so-so motel, we are glad to have been on the road again, coming down Interstate 15 to Highway 26 where we turn east. José and I wonder if we're headed in the right direction until the Snake River and change to greener land communicate that, yes, this is right. Rain on the horizon is okay if it helps clean smoke from the air.

Melody and I go back a long way, to my time as a graduate student at Brown University. I drove up to meet her for one long afternoon when she was a junior faculty at the University of New Hampshire. Was it 1993, '94? Immediately I knew I had a friend. I don't remember the specifics of what we hashed through. But the visit in New Hampshire involved a lot of talking (me), a lot of listening (her), and a bond born out of understanding ourselves as feminists raised in California who wrote about women's issues and the U.S. West.

Over almost thirty years of Western Literature Association conferences, literary readings, panels, late night drinks, Friday Awards banquets, and Saturday field trips, Melody has been a fixture of my life at WLA. *Many people's lives. She served a long tenure as editor of* Western American Literature *(1997–2013) and continues to serve in new capacities on the* WLA *Executive Council. She has authored and coauthored numerous books and some thirty-five essays, and these days is writing literary fiction including short stories and a couple of novels in progress.*[1] *Melody's creative work shows the hallmarks of someone who knows literary and cultural history and has a hankering for extraordinary women artists who buck convention. She sends me a chapter from one novel. I want to read more! The source material is drawn from the historical life of the painter Abby Williams Hill.*

The Where of Here: Swan Valley, Idaho

Krista: Here we are! We've had a rain come through and gone into the van and listened to it patter. And we have Ziggy with us, your daughter Larkin's dog, who became your dog. We've been chatting about travel ventures and traveling you've done solo, and camping alone as a woman. This is fun, to see you here!

Melody: Yep. Thank you for inviting me.

Krista: It's three hours or so for you from home, Logan (Utah). And you drove up here even though your daughter, Larkin, is coming home day after tomorrow. You haven't seen here since before the pandemic. You've also just been to Croatia. You get around! [Both laugh]

Melody: I try.

Krista: We are in Swan Valley, Idaho. Camp Rendezvous. But the where of here is the associations you bring. Why is this place significant to you?

Melody: We're looking at the west side of the Tetons. And we're here partly because the east side of the Tetons was already totally booked at the time we thought about going there. One of my favorite places in the West is Jackson Hole. For a variety of reasons. I love the Tetons. My daughter was a figure skater. Every March, she had a figure skating competition in Jackson Hole from the time she was maybe seven or eight. We would come up. While she was figure skating, I went to her performances. But when she was practicing, we would go and ski in the park. And there's a great, lovely cross-country ski to Jenny Lake that we did for many years, every year. I came to really love Jackson. When you asked to meet someplace that was important to me in the West, I thought that would be a good place. We're on the west side, instead of the east side.

Krista: So the where of here is a place that's beautiful, that calls to mind "the West" and also the memories of your daughter and raising your daughter and skiing.

Melody: And my son, who always longed for the skiing. And then, this will be of interest to you: The year that Utah State University in Logan defunded *Western American Literature*, I decided to do a trip to commemorate my work with Sabine Barcatta. Fifteen-plus years! She was the managing editor of the journal, and today is director of operations for the Western Literature Association. She and I went to a place called Jenny Lake Lodge, the most expensive place you can go in a national park because to get a cabin, you have to order three-course, all-inclusive meals, from their gourmet menu.

Sabine and I had a very good time together. We went hiking and we went swimming in Jenny Lake. A nice commemorative moment. In my mostly positive TripAdvisor review of the Jenny Lake Lodge, the headline is "National Parks Should Not Be Only for the Wealthy." It's quite nice, but it's silly to have a five-star-restaurant requirement to be able to go to a National Park.

Since then, I've gone to a couple of writing conferences in Jackson, which they have every summer. I have a lot of good associations with Jackson. I have a favorite place to stay. I have a favorite restaurant, the Blue Parrot.

Krista: You feel you belong there?

Melody: I belong there in a vacationing sense, not in the sense that I could ever live there. Partly because it's so expensive and partly because it's relatively remote. To get good health care, you have to go to Salt Lake, to get specialized good health care. Of course, there's a hospital there.

Let me say one more thing about Jackson Hole. My daughter originally played ice hockey. But the padding was so constrictive that she couldn't skate well. We called her Skates Like the Wind. It was unfortunate that I let her get into figure skating, because it's a very elitist, privileged kind of sport and most of her teammates were very wealthy. So it turned out not to have been the smartest thing to do. And one of my ironic memories about it is my now ex-husband made perhaps one of his most obnoxious comments ever, about the figure skating contest in Jackson Hole, which was that it was a fantasy for pedophiles. Creepy, isn't it? But he wasn't all wrong.

So, in terms of feminist associations to Jackson Hole, I regret that I let my daughter become a figure skater, though she was going to do what she was going to do. I wasn't going to try to stop her. She really wanted to do it.

Krista: It goes to the heart of what's complicated about being in the West and being feminist. Embodying ways of being that we understand to be feminist can be at odds with being "western." One has to check one's feminism at the door at times.

Melody: Another paradox is that part of the reason I could go ski, seven miles into Jenny Lake, a long ski and a really wonderful ski where we saw moose and elk and we once saw an ermine, was that there were all these other mothers of her teammates. I would assume that they would take care of my daughter, while I went off and did my feminist stuff. And they did. So I was pleasing myself on the backs of other women, who were in fact more privileged than I am, so it wasn't like I was exploiting anybody. But in a way, the more traditional mothers were enabling my feminist activities.

Krista: Let's pursue this conversation about outdoor sport, and the feminist moment it was for you to engage in that kind of activity.

Melody: I never framed it that way at the time, but I associate feminism with liberation, and cross-country skiing is one of the most liberating things I do. Your heart rate gets up. You feel an incredible amount of energy and endorphin rush. It's outdoors. Looking at the Tetons is really inspiring. It's beautiful. You're likely to see wildlife. It's very free.

Krista: So what makes that a feminist activity versus the activity of women who are athletic? There's something about it that you're identifying as feminist. Is it because you're already a feminist, and see it through some kind of feminist lens?

Melody: I don't think I would have applied the term "feminist" except in this conversation. When I talk about my daughter and figure skating, I should say she feels that figure skating is freeing—she feels that on ice. As I said, she skates like the wind. It was the construct around figure skating that made it an anti-feminist activity. Also, the expectations put on her. Like the first number she did was one of the songs from *Pocahontas*. There was even wind in the song, as I remember it.

But my daughter is South Korean. Putting her hair in a braid and having her play a certain role that fit in with her physicality and what she looked like. That was inappropriate. She was not American Indian. But she could play American Indian, according to her coach. Later, she skated to Mulan. She felt empowered by the skating. One of the things I would associate with cross-country skiing that's liberating is speed. And Larkin is a really talented speedy skater. I think that she would probably associate a lot of the physicality and freedom that I associate with cross-country skiing, with figure skating—although she is a good skier too, so she might associate with that too.

Krista: Continuing to pursue this, the idea of freedom implies a flip side, right? Maybe you could say what it pushed away? I'm not digging for personal details, but what's on the other side of that?

Melody: Why do you associate freedom with pushing away?

Krista: Well, you don't?

Melody: I don't think so. Maybe I could go there by thinking about: what is the opposite to freedom?

Krista: That's what I was meaning, the unfree.

Melody: Which would be restriction and constraint, enclosure, lack of movement, being on a leash. Things like that.

Krista: All of which, that kind of skiing, and the outdoors, was not about.

Melody: I'm trying to think about the title of my first book that I never finished. It had "liberation" in it. It wasn't the liberated self but it was the West as a place of liberation. And I definitely associate that with feminism and with the West. Maybe I have a blinkered, pre-framed way of thinking about women moving west as a way of liberating themselves from social constrictions.

I'm not naive. I've read enough women's history to know that it was not true for ordinary working-class women that the West was a place of liberation. But the kind of women that I've tended to write about who were artists and writers, privileged women—like Mary Austin, or currently Abby Williams Hill, or even Mary Hallock Foote—to a large degree, I think, experienced the West as a place to trade a corset for pantaloons. A debutante ball for a Snake Dance: Katy Cory is a woman who did that. I have tended to write about those women who came West as a place of opportunity for them to not have to lead traditional women's lives. And again, I want to reiterate that I well know that that was not true for the women who were forced to follow their husband on a quest for gold in the Gold Rush or to get land. And there is *Old Jules*, chronicled by Mari Sandoz, who abused all his wives. There was plenty of constriction and abuse, and lack of freedom, in women's lives in the West.

I feel somewhat guilty about that I always chose to write about the ones who had the good life.

Krista: What might a liberation program look like, for you, in your work on women artists, versus a project about women writers? Those would seem to be separate thinking-forward projects. Would you say more about this "liberation project" we are talking about, or your feminism as linked to liberation?

Melody: These largely successful women who liberated themselves in the West—whether they used the term "feminist" or not, though many of them did—had feminist ideas about how they were going to live their lives. I have been invested in telling that history. I wanted to challenge the idea that history goes like this—linear. Women who successfully broke away from conventional roles often encouraged other women to do so.

I'm thinking of an anecdote about the woman I'm writing about in my fictional work, Abby Williams Hill, who was the first woman who was hired by the Northern Pacific Railroad to paint promotional paintings of Yellowstone. When she first came West in the 1880s, with her husband, who was a doctor and was establishing a practice in Tacoma, she stopped wearing her corset. And her husband, who was quite liberated himself, said, "You know, Abby, people are talking about you. I'm trying to start a practice and, you know, can't you sort of fit in a bit more?" She said, "You wear a corset for a day." And he did. He came back and said, "I see what you mean."

So that was just one example of her rebelling against social conventions. Eventually, she adopted three daughters and encouraged them to make some of the same choices in their lives, join the Audubon Society, because women were encouraging people to kill birds for fancy feathers in their hats. There are lots of concrete details of women breaking the rules and getting away with it.

Krista: I am struck by the corset example as another about embodiment and refusing certain embodiments. Different embodiments as a possibility or foundation for a liberation project for women who come from east to west. And the alternative terms of maternity, and intergenerational passings-on of a different kind of womanhood, and livelihood (painting) as well as advocacy for creatures, that is, birds can be more than feathers for somebody's hat. These might be of a piece, suggestive of a feminist liberation project or feminist liberation vision. When did you start to think about "the West?" You grew up in California, in Salinas.

Melody: One of the things that immediately comes to mind is when I applied for colleges. My parents did not go to college. The only colleges in the East I'd heard of were Columbia and Harvard. It became clear to me that I did not know enough about the East to think about going to college there. I'm glad I didn't. It's not a regret, but I certainly had an awareness by then of East and West and how ignorant I was. My parents also didn't travel. At that point, when I was applying to college, I think the only place I had been out of state was Reno, because my parents liked to gamble.

I lived in the same community in Salinas until I was eighteen, and I was deeply attached to place. I lived out in the country, in the canyons local boy John Steinbeck called "The Pastures of Heaven." I spent a lot of my time in nature. I'm an only child and I spent a lot of time alone in the natural landscape and I still have a deep attachment to the foothills of California where I grew up. I was aware of that as a Western space. I don't think I thought of it as California, I thought of it as "the West."

I did a lot of hiking. I had a dog. And my grandfather did a lot of hiking with me while I was growing up. They lived next door. My grandparents were part of my childhood. I liked to be outside. One summer my parents moved my bed outside, and I slept outside all summer. You could do that in California, because it almost never rained in the summer.

The other thing I would say is that the only Western woman, historical woman, that I knew about was the singer and Hollywood star Dale Evans—married to the singing cowboy Roy Rogers. Until the *Big Valley* came on, sometime late in my high school years. Then Barbara Stanwyck and her fictional daughter Audra, who was played by Linda Evans, became my embodiment of wonderful, heroic Western women. And I watched the series again a few years ago, parts of it, and I still think that they're very satisfying portrayals of Western women historically.

Krista: Place theory teaches us that early ontologies of place, basic orientations, are established so young. There's a draw, a pull, a calling of certain places to people. You have a combination of the outdoor world, then Big Valley, and the emergent, televisual world of "the West" and strong women in the West.

Melody: I've always thought, and have no idea if this is true, but that I was encouraged to do physical sports, and to be a physical being as a girl more than other women of my generation, because I grew up in California.

Fig. 13. Melody with her grandfather, George, San Benancio Canyon, 1953. Melody discusses the photo in the essay "Prepositional Spaces." Photo by Gloria Graulich. Courtesy Melody Graulich.

Krista: One thing that I have been wondering is, since you're now emeritus, what do you think about your feminism now? I'm assuming there's never a moment for "retirement" from feminist thought or feminist behavior.

Melody: A lot of my feminism today is associated with thinking about my daughter, who is twenty-seven. She declares herself a feminist and is very proud that I'm a feminist. So feminism enhances my relationship with my daughter.

Now that I'm not teaching, I don't influence students. But I write lots of letters to the editor. The most recent one was about Critical Race Theory. The Utah legislature passed a law against Critical Race Theory while admitting that they didn't know what it meant. And our State Board of Education supported them. I wrote a letter to every member of the State Board of Education saying that it didn't represent my views. And I could be said to teach Critical Race Theory at some times in my life, and I certainly wouldn't stop.

I also have a lot of friends from playing bridge who are older women, several in their eighties. I think of myself as sandwiched between them and Larkin. I think about how cool they are, how they are feminists, and how to be there for them in their lives. Many of them are single, and I think about being there to help them.

Krista: So feminism is about relationships and relationality and reaching for a broader public.

Melody: For some years I have fretted about how academic writing is so ingrown, inward-directed to other academics. Historians manage to write books for both academic and general audiences. But literary critics, not really. I have written a number of essays I consider "narrative scholarship," using personal stories, memoir, within them.[2] They still ended up in academic venues, read by small audiences. Now I am writing about place(s), often the West, in fiction with feminist slants, hoping to reach nonacademic women readers, to let them know that women living a hundred, a hundred fifty years ago lived feminist lives, stubbornly stuck to their dreams. My current dream is to have my historical novel based on Abby Williams Hill's life show up in national park bookstores with one of her paintings as the cover.

A Fighting Zapotec Feminism, with
Lourdes "Lulu" Alberto

*We begin with Lulu's garden in Salt Lake City and with Lulu interviewing me!
"Why do you think the idea of the West persists for us, in North America? From
a Mexican perspective, a child of a migrant," Lulu asks. "The other orientation
was north, right? I find it so interesting that being here in the Intermountain
West, being from California, the idea of the West is also in me. I feel it very
much. There are other orientations, like* el norte, *right? Why does the West
matter so much to us?"*

*I talk, but when I read the transcript later, I find that Lulu's query about
why it matters so much falls out of my answer. I say what is predictable perhaps about the fact that the east-to-west migration is cemented in imagination
because it's the victory story where majority white settlers search out and find
"free land." Anglo-American empire defeats Spanish empire while overcom-
ing Indigenous resistance, so the east-to-west story reigns—it's the founding
tale of America. But why does the West matter to the "we" of the project? The
question goes to the heart of things, doesn't it?*

*The sense Lulu makes of "feminist Wests" is that we're shifting starting
points, and it makes her think of other starting points, of herself as an Indigenous person, part of an Indigenous diaspora. Her people do not have starting
points in the east, or in today's United States. They have traveled a different
migration route. "Indigenous people are really savvy," Lulu says, "about how
to own and remake a thing so it works for them." What she means by that is
the ability to reinvent the bad words, like* mestizaje, *of settler colonialism.
At the time of our conversation, she's just published an essay that takes up
those complexities—"Mestizaje desde Abajo: Zapotec Visual Cultures and
Decolonial Mestizaje in the Photography of Citlali Fabián."[1] Lulu entertains
that term because if she rejects the concept entirely, she does not get a full view
of Indigenous people.*

*"We can remake the world that belongs to us," she muses. "I'm thinking
specifically about Indigenous communities but more broadly, relationality."*

This musing is fitting for our project's hopes. Lulu has us thinking about how we recreate, remake a world together that has justice at its center. She references Daniel Heath Justice's Why Indigenous Literatures Matter, *which José and I have been listening to on tape in the van. We don't need diversity and inclusion, Lulu paraphrases him. We need justice, kinship.*

As the afternoon cools into evening, Lulu talks about her garden, her mother's love of Yellowstone, the complexities of migration and mestizaje for Indigenous people, fighting feminism, and how the West is remade by her Zapotecan communities.

It's a lovely long day with Ian King (Lulu's husband) and their children Roma and Fausto, and a gathering toward evening with the family in a big city park that José and I happily attend, a Zapotecan Guelaguetza. We are living the concepts of transborder traveling communities we talk about.

The Where of Here: Lulu's Garden

Krista: We have arrived into your Salt Lake City neighborhood and world through your garden—it's beautiful! You and Ian built raised beds so everything spills out. We have heard about Fausto planting sugar baby watermelon. There are so many flowers and a pear tree, key parts of relations to place, land, to history, to memory, to feminism and feminist care ethics.

Lulu: The garden is a conduit for me, to Indigenous memory. My family, we're Zapotec, from Yalalag, Oaxaca. Mexico. We always had something growing in the garden. Always herbs, lots of fruit trees. We're in California, right, so lots of citrus, peaches, plums, and items brought back from Oaxaca.

Krista: We are talking about the Zapotec community in diaspora, in Southern California.

Lulu: Yeah. I remember, as a child in California, in LA, you're in a densely urban place. And yet, the backyard felt wild. We always had chickens. Everything was really tall, that's how it felt as a little kid. Grass was tall. There were things to climb and chickens to chase around, and mud to make. It was the playful place. As I got older, my grandmother and I spent a lot of time in the kitchen. That is where she taught me about healing, about medicine, about memories of Yalalag—by asking me to go fetch herbs in the garden. Inevitably, I always came back with the wrong thing, right? And she would say, "Okay, now you know. Smell this, it smells like this. The other one, the one you're looking for, actually has a leaf like this."

Krista: Memories of what leaf we're talking about?

Lulu: Oh, it was always cilantro and *perejil*. Cilantro and parsley. As a little kid, three or four, really young—my mom went back to work at six weeks after I was born, and she quite literally handed me to my grandmother—it was a lot of running out and running back in, and is this the right thing? Is that the right thing? Checking for ripeness.

My mom was also an avid gardener. It's one of the gifts she left me. I didn't realize how deeply it had become a part of who I am until she died. For me the garden is a site where I'll be working on something. I'll remember, "Oh yeah, my grandfather told me to do this to the chile." It is a place of healing and absolute wonder. You know when the [Mormon] missionaries come through the neighborhood, they'll point to the garden. They'll say, "How can you not believe in God? Who do you think made all of this?" And I'll say, "I did? I'm the gardener here!"

Krista: Not in an individualistic way or the Protestant way of "my hard work made this"?

Lulu: No, no, no. I'm a part of an ecosystem. Yeah. And there is not one hand here, because that's a narrative of God, right? This hand that's creating this magical space, there is nothing "natural" about this garden because it's all been worked by me. But there's an ecosystem that I am entering into, that I would want to support.

The other thing about a garden is it is absolutely a process of hope. It is hard for me to feel hopeful with the political times being what they are, and COVID, and I live with my mom's recent passing very actively. She had a very rare disease—ALS, Lou Gehrig's disease, rare in Latino communities. The garden is a place where I channel her because I think how she instilled in us a love of the outdoors. Her dream, her absolute dream, the whole time we were growing up was: "When I retire." That was how she began every sentence. "When I retire, when I retire, I'm gonna buy an RV and go to every National Forest, National Park, in the West. Before I die I wanna go to Yellowstone."

Krista: Her "rest area" of the future, thinking about spaces we create of security along the road, so to speak, imagining rest areas now and of the future.

Lulu: Yes, exactly. But she got sick, and there was no time. Nobody expects to die. I didn't expect that she was going to die, it caught us off guard. We all had this feeling that we're going to run out of time, ALS is 100 percent fatal. If you are diagnosed, there is nothing that will slow it or change the course of it. To live with that impending death.

When I got tenure, I told my family "I don't want a tenure party," because everybody wanted to celebrate in the community. I said, "No, all I want is to rent cars and we're going to drive to Yellowstone. That is going to be the culmination for our family." So that's what we did. My mother was in a wheelchair, completely immobile at that point, but we drove her to Yellowstone. And she couldn't speak anymore.

I remember, that's all she talked about when we were children, Yellowstone.

When I look at a garden, it is a place where I feel nothing but hope, because you plant a seed. And that seed has so much potential. And you are hoping that in a season, or in a year, or two years, it will be bountiful. We can theorize it, in fancier terms, right, because it makes me cognizant about water in the West, and our ecology, what plants do well, the movement to go back to native plants versus, you know, most of what you find at Home Depot, Lowe's, usually native to China. It would mean honestly like 90 percent of the stuff that we have here is native to Asia. So that sort of return back to the coneflowers, Echinacea.

Krista: Plants you have in your garden. Lavender and the little orange. . . .

Lulu: Mallow and beardtongue. Tickseed, artichokes like the thistles—it's part of the thistle family. Just anything that's hardy. And there's a movement here in Salt Lake to go back to native plants. That's important to me. When I think of the garden, I think of hope. It is a place, a site of absolute hope. It is a site of community because it is a magnet for people.

Krista: There are so many bees in your garden, speaking of creaturely community.

Lulu: So many bees. There are over two hundred species of bees. I love to sit there and observe and enjoy them and talk to them and thank them for visiting my garden. It gives me a sense of awe that I rarely experience anywhere else. There's also the vegetable part of it, right? To reduce my consumerism and to have it be a grounding for my children, because you can learn about everything, soil structure, water, animals, life cycles. Fausto wanted to plant a seed and see it germinate. It becomes a learning place, a healing place. It's my babysitter—they're always out in the garden.

Krista: You said it was guilt free.

Lulu: It is absolutely.

Krista: I don't know what your sources of guilt are, not to pry. But presumably guilts have to do with whatever you're not doing you're supposed to do. Work?

Lulu: Yeah. You know my colleagues will ask me, "Oh, so, what did you do this summer?" I say, "I gardened." And to some ears, that feels very out of place. It feels like a waste of time. It feels too indulgent. One colleague said to me, "Oh, I could never spend that much time doing something that was not productive." I thought, "Wow, how sad. We are not our productivity. That is not what is happening for me in the garden."

Yes, it's a bountiful garden. Gardening creates an amazing community, people who I would not have otherwise talked to, little old white Mormon women who are walking by who also garden. We share recipes, [and say,] "What variety of this are you growing?" "Oh, my peas aren't doing well." A garden is a magnet of exchange, gardening is generous. Nobody plants a garden to be impoverished. They plant a garden to have too much. And so that exchange, it feeds me. One of the things that's on my to-do list is to have a seed exchange. We have the little libraries, the little neighborhood library movement—it's a book exchange, and we have some book pantries sprinkled around the neighborhood.

But we need a seed exchange. I'm going to build, at some point this summer, a seed library, because gardening expenses or money should not be the thing that keeps you from gardening. Seeds are expensive— they're precious. They're thought of as a luxury. If someone can grow a little patch of lettuce, or radishes or some peas, that's the kind of community that I want to create, a little spot for extra vegetables that I'm not going to eat from the garden, and then a couple of flower seeds. Let the momentum of that take over and bring people from the neighborhood. I live in a great neighborhood. Everybody is very interconnected. Yeah. If I can talk to you about gardening, I can— I can talk about it forever.

Krista: The question about the garden is a question about place, and how many places travel through the garden. Places in Oaxaca, in Southern

California, the place of here, memory, futurities. Would you think aloud with us about whatever you would call your feminism? We are asking everyone to send a visual that represents to them "feminist Wests," and you sent a picture of you that your mother took. José and I love it. We noticed it's on your profile picture on Facebook. We posted it to the blog. How do you think about feminist Wests or your own feminism or Indigenous feminism? What image comes to mind for you? A lot of times people have to wade through a lot of images that they don't think respond to how they understand feminism.

Lulu: When I think about feminism, I think about a fighting feminism. I didn't realize this until we were sitting at the kitchen table inside a bit ago, that story I was telling about Mormon missionaries coming to the front door, to evangelize Roma and Fausto! I told them, "No! You can't come up to our door. Leave." [Laughs.] My daughter loves it when I stand up for her, or when I stand up to things. She loves those kinds of stories.

Krista: Yeah, she wanted you to tell that story for a half an hour. She waited patiently sitting there to have you tell that story.

Lulu: Yeah. On the one hand, the story is about Mom making her feel safe about people coming to the front door. But also, for me, I always remind myself that I am raising an Indigenous woman, I think very purposefully. What can I leave to her that will help her be an Indigenous woman now? What do I teach her that will serve her in ten, fifteen years? I learned a lot from the women in my community. When I think of feminism, I think about those women who quite literally fought. In my community, there's a practice of arranged marriages. Everyone before my parents' generation had an arranged marriage, and they would perform arranged—

Krista: In Southern California, it traveled?

Lulu: No, in Yalalag. You would readily recognize these as arranged marriages, parents negotiate a dowry, and suitors. There's a protocol about which families are good families to marry into. And the age of the girl. The girl will have veto power—she can say no. But she has to be open to meeting suitors. And the expectation is that she will eventually say yes.

So my grandmother was married at fourteen. My grandfather was twenty-eight. That was typical. My grandmothers on both my parents' sides had a marriage like that, at fourteen and fifteen, with a much older man who could provide. Was he a good farmer? Did he have a good harvest? Did the family hold on to ancestral lands? There was always migration, in and out of Yalalag. As you know my family were leaders, and we have our ancestral lands in Yalalag, we have a home, and land. Land is important.

My grandmother on my dad's side had ten children. Seven died, three lived. My grandmother on my mom's side had nine. One died. Growing up, my grandmother, because I spent so much time with her, had a lot to say about arranged marriages, about childbirth.

Krista: Would you want to give examples?

Lulu: So, okay, so this is totally women's talk, right? In part, it's graphic. But when I think of feminism, my grandmother was arming me with information. It was information meant to protect me, bodily, physically. And to be aware. If I were to use recognizable terms to us, she was arming me to be aware of how patriarchy functioned. And to figure out ways to get around it. What fascinates me about my grandmother . . .

Krista: What is her name?

Lulu: Elvira Montellano. She was married at fourteen. She had her first baby at fifteen. My grandfather's twenty-eight. And from that point to the time that she died, she became the matriarch of the family. It was her counsel that everyone came to find—it was her permission, her blessing. When people were newly arrived in LA, they came to see her, to bring gifts. So I was always curious. She was a tough, tough lady. And I wonder, how do you get from fourteen and married, married off, to matriarch at seventy-three?

Krista: Yes, how?!

Lulu: It's funny because I was sitting in on a book proposal workshop of an Indigenous scholar, and she brings a feminist lens to her work. And she said, in passing: "This feminism feels so foreign. It feels like I'm imposing something." And then I thought, "No! We have a fighting feminism, right?" Part of how my grandmother transformed things is she quite literally, physically fought.

I was telling my friend that there are two stories where my grandmother held a knife to someone's throat, at sixteen, in order to own her place in the house. It was the moment where she took over as the mother in the house. My grandfather's sisters were also living in the house. And there was always conflict because they had been the women of the house. And now she, as the married woman, was saying she should occupy that status, as the head of household. Those moments are the kind of feminism that I have inherited, that I was brought into, a fighting feminism.

It's funny, I never put two and two together that Roma loves the fighting feminism. I tell her, "Even if you're afraid, you have to stand up." I'm thinking about the vulnerabilities of children, their bodies, both of Roma and Fausto's bodies. I'm constantly reiterating that you have to get mad, if you're scared, get mad, you can yell. It's so funny, because thinking now, that's exactly what my grandmother used to say. She wanted to forewarn me, because she would say, "On the night that you get married, something is going to happen to you. Right?" And I'm just thinking now, her as a fourteen-year-old girl, can you imagine? Something is going to happen.

Krista: I can, unfortunately.

Lulu: I'm paraphrasing, but she was implying, or what I took away from it was, "If you can survive that, you can survive anything."

Krista: She was unprepared by her own mother?

Lulu: Oh, yeah. Oh, yeah. Yeah.

Krista: I have questions about the imposition of "feminism" and whether there is a time for you in which that term or that whole language or discourse can be utilized so that it isn't "the imposition"? Because I think what you're describing in Yalalag is, you called it, in conventional terms, "patriarchal." How otherwise would you understand it? You quote María Lugones, "The Coloniality of Gender" essay, in your own piece, "Desde Abajo." Lugones talks about the historical imposition of colonial gender norms onto Indigenous communities. I don't know how you understand what was happening in Yalalag? Then they get transferred intergenerationally, in diaspora? And does a memory of those gender problems from the old gendered social order move to new places?

Lulu. I think "the patriarchy" is too limiting. It doesn't capture the exchanges between the two genders in Yalalag, and the places that women occupy that could be seen as feminist. Also, women themselves would never use those terms to describe their kinship structures. They would not describe them as "natural." My grandmother used to talk about duties.

Krista: *Comunalidad*. We were talking before on this topic.

Lulu: Yeah, comunalidad, and the "*techio*." The other duties that they participate in, offering resources. These are really impoverished communities, right? My grandparents grew up with no shoes. My parents grew up with no shoes. They didn't get electricity until the 1950s, maybe early 1960s. They don't have running water, right? These are super subsistence communities even though they participate in global commercial trade at the same time.

Krista: Things for sale, you mean?

Lulu: Import and export, yeah. But techio is about sharing resources. Within that structure, different groups of people have different roles, and they are gendered, not exclusively, but you will never see a man making tortillas. That would be offensive.

Techio is the service structure of Indigenous pueblos. Every male in the family has to give two years of service to the pueblo. That's civil service. Building roads, digging wells, digging ditches if there's a mudslide, giving sort of a night watch service. Service is the thing that makes you belong to the pueblo, in addition to bloodlines, and genealogy, this is how you maintain your status in the pueblo.

In diaspora, we don't have that. In the early years of immigration, people would go back to Yalalag to do their techio, and then return to the United States. I remember my grandmother talking about it, saying, "That person is back home for a year or two years," or "They sent their son," or "They're having their cousin do it for them because they can't cross the border." But in the United States, techio is transformed. One, there is no homeland to do that techio in. So how does that affect comunalidad? Because comunalidad is that exchange, that thing that bonds all of us, and that's tied very specifically to land. But if you take that land element out of it, then what is the thing that bonds us?

One of my good friends, Brenda Nicolas, is working on a concept called transborder comunalidad.[2] She is working with Lynn Stephen's ethnographic work on transborder identities.[3] Stephen has worked with Oaxacan Indigenous communities, and she talks about the sort of transformations of Indigenous identity that happen when you cross the border.

As I have been saying in my work, the border is just stop three, or stop four, right? "The border" is not where Indigenous transformation begins. The departure changes your sense of existing in the world and reconfigures your Indigeneity. It happens in very documented ways at the U.S.-Mexico border. But it happens in Oaxaca City, in Mexico City, it happens in Tijuana, it happens in LA, for those of us who never crossed the border, right.

Krista: What do you mean, who never crossed the border?

Lulu: Like me, I was born in the United States, so I never crossed the border.

I've been working with the concept of comunalidad viajera, which de-emphasizes the border. I first heard the term from a community organizer. That process of travel speaks to me because I think of myself as an academic migrant. You know, as a first-gen college student, first-gen PhD student, first-gen faculty member, first-gen tenured faculty member, right? I always feel I'm coming up against a world not made for me. I'm always aching for California. I'm always longing to be in my community. I'm always longing to hear the music, to hear Zapoteco spoken.

When I moved to Texas for graduate school at Rice, my mom was really upset. "I can't believe you're leaving," she said. She was upset that I was going to be gone. "You're never going to come back," she said. She knew. Yeah.

Krista: And you say, "Oh, I will, I will, I will," but all along it's not happening.

Lulu: Yeah. I promise. "Of course, I'm coming back, everybody returns." But they don't, right? This is what we know about the migrant experience. They make home somewhere else.

Krista: [Long pause.] Can we return to the conversation about feminism in your essay about the photographer? The "Desde Abajo" essay on decolonial mestizaje.

You talk in the piece about the method, the wet plate processing, that allows her to speak back to a colonial archive, to locate Indigenous presence in the archive. In your view it's a way to create Indigenous presence going forward, to make a future and a vision of a futurity. You wind that around to a discussion about the ways, in her photographs and the community that's created in the photographs, that those moments become the decolonial moments. And it's a feminist decolonial. Mixed in there is the deep relations the photographer has with other people, which can avoid or unsettle a settler gaze. I wondered if you would think about the feminist imaginary of the piece? Your idea is that through this process of taking these photographs, she creates communities outside of ones that exist, communities for people in diaspora like yourself.

Lulu: I like the term "feminism" because it forces ties that might not otherwise be present. And for me, that's really important because of the sort of context that Indigenous people occupy, which is, we're always invisible, right? And for me, in particular, in my community, because we are migrants from Mexico. And we are racialized as border crossers, as Mexican American, and the Indigeneity always falls out.

So it's against that invisibility that feminism comes in. I don't think of them as separate things. I feel like the labor of women, the culture-making of women, the political activism of women, is what actually makes our Indigenous communities visible. In the United States a lot of the labor that has been done to advance comunalidad here, the fundraising that happens to send money back to Yalalag to pay for workers who can do the infrastructure work that would otherwise be done by the men there. It's the women who do that organizing. It's the women who are producing all of that connective tissue. For me, while the communities themselves might not use "feminism"—meaning the older generation, the 1970s generations, my parents' generation, the younger generations are absolutely using those terms.

They're going through the school system, right, and they're taking our classes. They're also women of color in the United States going through the #MeToo movement, going through racial uprisings and awakenings, much like I did through the Rodney King racial uprisings in 1992. We're very American. Our politics are— I won't say Americanized, but we're being racialized. We're coming into our awakening through the racial politics. There is a possibility to imagine things that, in the past, might not have felt like they belonged to us, to find new languages and new practices so that we can own them. Because though I'm not comfortable with the term "mestizaje," I would never identify as a mestiza, I find something moving about Citlali's work and her usage of "mestizaje."[4]

Krista: And when she misuses it, that's the point. That's when it becomes used on behalf of Indigenous worldmaking.

Lulu: Yeah, yes. I guess that captures ways we can misuse feminism, have a fighting feminism, so that we do open up a space of possibility.

Oh, man, this is really fueling my own thinking. Because it usually just exists up here. And I never say it out loud, you know? I'm busy with kids. [Laughs.] It's just when I'm gardening, that's when I'm thinking about all this stuff. And I think, "Okay, when I have some time, I'll write notes. I'll write that article."

Krista: Now you have notes, you have the notes to do so. Last thoughts?

Lulu: Thank you for that. Oh my gosh, this is so awesome.

POSTSCRIPT: *IN THE SUMMER OF 2023, LULU ALBERTO GOT HER wish to return home to Los Angeles. She is now the first director of American Indian Studies at Cal State University Los Angeles. Though she misses her friends and colleagues, the students at the University of Utah, her garden, and the mountains, her Oaxacan California family rejoices!*

Colville Women, Always in Charge,
with Dina Gilio-Whitaker

Before Dina and I knew one another, we were connected through Panhe—*"the place by the water" in the Acjachemen language. I had written about Panhe in my* Surfer Girls *book. Dina wrote a master's thesis in Native studies showing its significance as a sacred site to the coalitions that stopped a major toll road and "Saved Trestles," a renowned surf spot.[1] Panhe was a presence linking us; water as a form of relationality was already there.*

Dina and I met in 2014 through gatherings of the Institute for Women Surfers, a feminist political education project open to surfing activists. In this not-university context of surf activists and a few professors, Dina quickly became a needed leader. She offered workshops on "American Settler Colonialism 101"[2] and tied settler behaviors to surf territoriality and localism, rooting it in masculine settler claims on land. This perspective was a turning point for Institute purposes and community because participants connected the seemingly unrelated dots between Native American history, surf culture, master social narratives about "discovery" in surf tourism, and territorialism in surfing. What people took away was a sense of the ways surf culture simultaneously benefits from, and is complicit in, colonial power inequities that keep Native peoples separated from their lands.

As the Institute Director, I urged us to put feminist forms of relationality first, to hold our relations as more important than any outcomes of the IWS project. Women's relationships as feminists have a history of implosion and to prioritize relationships over politics was to found the Institute on more secure ground. Indigenous relationality transformed that perspective in decolonial directions and took the stakes of our relations to place and one another toward it with implications for accountability of us all to Indigenous people and sovereignty claims.

Since the early days of our IWS meetings, Dina and I have done scholarly and nonscholarly events together, and written a forthcoming essay about a legislated land acknowledgment in California (AB 1782) that centers Indigenous/settler surfeminist collaborations. We think this land acknowledgment is the first of its kind. I wanted Dina to be part of the Living West as Feminists *project to continue conversations about feminism and being good neighbors.*

When we get to San Clemente, Dina has José and me over for dinner with her husband, Tom Whitaker. We hang out in San Clemente a few days. Dina and I go to lunch. We have time at Panhe. I feel a coming of full circle in our relations—as someone from the U.S. West, California, a counterculturalist, a feminist intellectual, a writer. For all our differences, we have a lot in common.

The Where of Here: Panhe

Krista: We're at the San Mateo Creek Campground, that's one name for where we are. Panhe is the Acjachemen name. Historically this was among the largest Acjachemen villages, eight thousand years old, and remains a ceremonial, cultural, and sacred burial site.

Dina: This is an important place for Acjachemen people, and for me personally it began here—strands of my work around environmental justice that eventually became the book *As Long as Grass Grows*, and the surf work. It's the site that shapes my thinking as it evolves, how I'm writing about it, and how I hope to convey a message to other people about accountability, what accountability means, and my own personal accountability, because that's the story. And it is a story.

It began in 2010. I had just reconnected with Tom and we were moving forward with our relationship. I had come here to San Clemente to visit. There was an event that happens every year called Earth Day at Panhe. It started after the "Save Trestles" toll road battle. A coalition of diverse groups fought the building of this toll road which would have come literally right here—we would be in the path of that highway. Just imagine a six-lane highway coming directly down this watershed and creek bed through the campground right next to the burial ground! That's what people were up in arms against. It was going to disrupt the creek bed so badly that it would have likely ruined the wave quality at Trestles. Trestles was the surfers' concern, the ecosystem the environmentalists' concern, which was spearheaded by the Sierra Club. Native people came in toward the end.

There is a story about how these interests converged into a campaign. But first it was the environmentalists, then the surfers. When Native people came in, it was not even the tribal council. It was a Native

Panhe (San Onofre)

This is Indian Country

Fig. 14. Public Service Announcement: Decolonizing Settler Surf Culture.
Courtesy Dina Gilo-Whitaker.

grassroots group led by two women. Angela Mooney D'Arcy and Rebecca
Robles, called the United Coalition to Protect Panhe. They got funding to
do a one-day event, a festival, to celebrate the saving of this place from
the toll road. It's a lovely event, the community comes out, hundreds of
people come just right down there [pointing]. There's a big, open area;
they have vendor booths, dancing, exhibits. Tom and I came to that event.
I didn't know anything about the Save Trestles story. When I learned about
the story, it was so interesting. I needed a topic for a master's thesis, and
I knew immediately this was it. That history is what I am going to study.
How did it happen that this Native sacred site was able to get saved even
though it's not a reservation and the tribe is not federally recognized?
There are all these strikes against them.

Krista: Part of the story has to do with the California Coastal
Commission?

Dina: It's all about the Coastal Commission. Because they had jurisdiction to deny the final construction permit. What I looked at was: how
much did the fact of this being a sacred site factor into their decision?

It was pretty major. But the coalition activists didn't acknowledge that. To this day. That was what was so frustrating. Surfrider Foundation didn't acknowledge it. Environmental groups didn't acknowledge it. But Native people did. There was the testimony from one particular commissioner who nailed it: Mary Schallenberger. She understood that for Native people the concept of sacred is different. You can't move a sacred site like you can move a church—that was one of her statements.

Krista: When you think of Panhe as a place of accountability for you . . . Would you talk about ways you are thinking about accountability? Perhaps as a Colville person, or as a surfer?

Dina: It began with my relationship with Rebecca. Me being somebody who's Indigenous, who comes out of Native American studies and was trained in Indigenous research methodologies, accountability is rule number one. I wasn't doing a research project with human subjects. I wasn't interviewing tribal people. I wasn't here to extract information. I was interested in the dynamics of coalition building and how the Native piece factored into this much larger story. But I relied on and made friends with Rebecca. I introduced myself because Rebecca and Angela *were* the United Coalition to Protect Panhe. So I made friends with both of them. And I took an ethic of accountability into my relationship with them, because I needed them. I needed to understand their position and how the work that they did contributed to the research. I became friends with especially Rebecca. She fed me all the documents. It was a combined effort, but Rebecca had the documents. Literally she handed everything over to me, all kinds of stuff, and it allowed me to dig into that piece of it. It was important for me to be transparent with them, throughout the process.

One of the things that came out of the Save Trestles campaign was the San Onofre Parks Foundation (SOPF).[3] Rebecca was one of its founders, with Steve Long. You know who he is, Krista—the father of Greg Long, who is a very well-known big wave surfer. They are a San Clemente family. Steve was a veteran lifeguard for thirty years down here. He was a State Park Ranger and lifeguard, total water man, and highly, highly respected. Steve and a handful of other people started SOPF, which is a cooperative association, and Rebecca was an early board member.

There are networks of these cooperative associations in the state parks, as the state parks have lost funding over the years to do their interpretive and educational functions. Losing funding gave rise to a need for these cooperative associations that work in partnership with the state parks to provide services. They got major grant funding from another foundation, which allowed them to form the San Onofre Parks Foundation.

In 2016 Rebecca decided to move to Hawaii. And she asked me if I would take her seat on the board. I felt so honored, and I felt it was the least I could do as a way to be accountable for how she worked with me and helped the research. She's a tribal elder, older than I am. Her mother was a very respected tribal elder. For my own personal sense of accountability, the least I could do was accept. The organization sees itself as stewards of the land, and for Rebecca, this is her ancestral land. To ask me, as a non-Acjachemen person, felt huge, that she would entrust me with that responsibility.

Krista: I wonder if we could talk about your early relations to place and land, when you were small. Sometimes conversations people are having with themselves and me end up thinking back to early relations to land and outlines of them show up later, in unexpected ways.

Dina: For somebody like me who is a Native person but who was born and raised far from my tribal community—our reservation, our homelands, are up in Washington and Canada—I knew, we knew our bigger family. But we only went there a couple of times when I was a kid. My sisters and I were born and raised in LA, east LA. I'm the oldest of three daughters.

I'm fully an urban Indian. But I didn't have a way of understanding that growing up. It took me going into Native American studies to really contextualize myself.

Krista: When you were growing up in east LA, what would you say was your relation to that place, or was your family's relation to that place? Your sisters' or your friends'?

Dina: I don't know. I didn't know how to think about it.

My dad built us a house. He had bought a lot. He built us a house, because he was a builder. He was a plumbing contractor and then he got his contractor's license and built us this house, on a hill. There were very few houses. We were the only one on the hill, and we were surrounded by open space. I loved walking in the hills. It was mostly dry grass. I always felt connected to nature. And it was spiritual for me to walk the land, to be out there by myself and connected to it.

My father was Sicilian. He's first-generation, born in the United States. My mother came to LA from Washington in the fifties and met my dad in a bar during the Indian relocation period. If she were alive, there would be so many questions I would ask her about that time.

You know the film *The Exiles*?[4] A UCLA film student made the film. He followed around these Indians from the Southwest pueblos, during one twenty-four-hour period. It was in black and white, and it's just raw. Intense. I couldn't watch it the first time because my mother was a barfly. My mother was full on, a severe alcoholic. She had a lot of trauma.

There was boarding school trauma that was handed down from my grandmother, and this is how I understand myself today. My mother got scapegoated in our family because of her alcoholism. I understand it much differently now, in terms of intergenerational trauma. I know now that my mother also had trauma from having a child taken from her during what's called the pre-ICWA (Indian Child Welfare Act) scoop. That's another long story, but I recently reconnected to three other siblings, children of my mom's from before I was born. The information the oldest one provided confirmed that one sibling was taken without her consent. I'm writing about that now in a new book.[5]

Krista: Wow. When you were a child, you would move between east LA to see your mom's family in Washington?

Dina: We didn't move back and forth but we did visit a couple of times. Once when I was a baby, and I don't remember it. Once in 1970, when I was twelve years old, and we took this epic road trip. Driving from LA to the Colville reservation is a long ass way with three rowdy kids. I don't know how my parents did it. [laughing] All of us in the family car.

It was a turning point in my life, I was twelve. All the stuff that was happening in 1970 in LA. The civil rights movement, Black Power and Red Power. Alcatraz, we drove through San Francisco during the Alcatraz Island occupation. Hippies were really interesting to me, and I clicked with it. The music of the time, it was a great time to be a kid in LA, to be a teenager, to be coming of age. The world was on fire with the cultural revolution. Driving through San Francisco, the hippies and the tie-dye and the head shops, all the stores. I knew I was born in the wrong town! [Both laugh.] I was seeing the Alcatraz Occupation on the news at night.

Krista: And did you identify with that cause as someone Indigenous?

Dina: Oh, totally. I always knew I was an Indian and was raised being told to be proud to be Indian. It was not a luxury my mother had in her generation, but the world was changing for the better!

Krista: So your mom would talk about that?

Dina: Yeah. Oh, yeah. Plus, we are Colvilles. The Colvilles were going through a termination battle. The federal government was targeting our reservation for termination, trying to get them to give up, to move. Our termination battle lasted twenty years. It's a case study.[6] When people study termination, they look at the Colvilles because for twenty years, our tribe fought it and we fought each other. A lot of people thought it was a good idea.

At our dinner table, we had those conversations. Terminating the reservation was being put as a vote to the tribal membership and my mom was an enrolled tribal member. My parents would talk about should my mom vote for it or not? During the fifties and sixties, a lot of people said we should do it, because we're modern people. They believed the hype of the federal government about releasing them from the "yoke of federal supervision." That's literally the language they used to sell it. Becoming "free from federal domination." The tribes were like, "Yeah, we don't want to continue to be seen as 'backwards savages.' We're modern people. And we don't want to be saddled by the federal government."

It seemed a good idea to stand on their own. So it was tempting for them to vote for it, especially because there was money. Nobody knew exactly how much, but I distinctly remember $40,000 or $50,000 per tribal member. In the late sixties, think about how much money that was—it was a fortune. You can see why it would be appealing.

But then the tide shifted, and the elders said we should never sell our land. If we sell our land, we are no longer Colvilles. That's literally how they put it. In the end, I think our mother voted against it. So I grew up with these conversations, knowing I was Colville. We went to the land, we hunted, we hung out with our cousins and our aunts and uncles and it was rough, because there was a lot of drinking. It was rough. The alcohol really impacted our family.

Krista: Did you have a sense of being part of the "U.S. West"? You are growing up in LA, and loving San Francisco, knowing about what's going on at Alcatraz, traveling to Colville lands in Washington. Anything you'd like to talk about related the U.S. West, or how you saw that idea later?

Dina: I can't say that I had any particular consciousness about it being "the West." I was just within it. In all these different kinds of ways, it shows up and is expressed, manifests. The fishbowl analogy comes to mind. You're in the middle of it, but you don't know it. Because it's the waters that you swim in and the air that you breathe.

Krista: What comes to mind for you?

Dina: The predominant historical narratives—pioneers, covered wagons, the Wild West, settlement. But I think of all these other ways that the West has shaped the U.S., especially around the Cultural Revolution in the 1960s and the 1970s. That's a very particular way that we can talk about the West.

Krista: We've talked about accountability a lot here, and outside this conversation. Here you mention research ethics, friendship, how Rebecca entrusts you with documents, and then offers you a role in the San Onofre Parks Foundation. Being honored by that, and wanting to be reciprocal, you agree. You give back.

You and I have other projects we're doing about accountabilities, the "Climates of Violence, Feminist Accountability" symposium that was in the works and then paused with COVID. And our collaborative work about surfeminism and California AB 1782, surfing as the state sport.[7]

How does feminism for you engage a conversation about accountability? Or can you think about a story of how feminism is expressed in relation to land or to place?

Dina: Yeah, you know, feminism isn't for me like it was for you. Like you come into this very explicit feminist consciousness in the early eighties.

Krista: Seventies. [Laughs.]

Dina: Seventies. Oh! I was reading in the blog about you going to the West Coast Music Festival in the early 1980s.

Krista: Right, by the 1980s, I'm ready to go places with it. But before that, it's happening. Yeah.

Dina: For me, I would not have known the word "feminist." I could not have related to feminism. But I would learn later from other Colville women, they would tell me, "Colville women were always in charge." Colville women, including my mother, were never subservient to men.

And even my mother, who was so crippled by her own trauma, would never succumb to my Sicilian father's attempts to dominate her. She modeled that for me, I understand that now. You could say that's a lived Indigenous feminism for Colville women. But once I look back on it, I was being it.

Krista: This looser sense is what our conversations have been teasing out. I don't know that I used that term, "feminist," in the 1970s. But I know that I was oriented in that direction. And I wasn't taking no for an answer.

Dina: Right. That's how I was—not taking no for an answer. Here is a story: the way that showed up for me was in high school, and I was a majorette. I grew up being a majorette from the time I was seven. I was a really good baton twirler. I always had a dream that I was going to be the majorette for my high school. So I get there, and I'm really good. But our school had never had a majorette. I tried to find out how could I be that? I go to the drill team, well known in LA for how good it was. The drill team instructor was like, "No, no, no, no, no, I don't want a three-ring circus out there in the halftime shows on the football field." Shut me down. I was so mad. But I'm not taking no for an answer. And who does that? Like, who shuts down a kid's dream like that?

I went to the school principal, Miss Avant. I told her what Miss Most [the drill team instructor] had said. The principal could appreciate it because she had been a majorette. She was very cool about it, diplomatic. She says to go see Mr. Rinaldo, the band director. See what he says. So Mr. Rinaldo, it's his jazz band. Eagle Rock High School was known for its jazz band. It was the best high school jazz band in the state. Mr. Rinaldo, he hated marching band. He hated that he had to do marching band. And he said, "I don't care what you do, just don't get me in trouble with Miss Most." In other words, I figured out how to subvert the drill team instructor without getting Mr. Rinaldo in trouble, since it was his jurisdiction.

I had to follow certain parameters after that, but I made it happen. I was the high school majorette for three years. I'm not going to let somebody freaking shut me down and accept no for an answer. And that was the kind of sensibility that I brought into surfing, maybe eight years later.

And my mother, we come from a tribal culture that was gender equitable. Most Native cultures are matrilineal and if not, at least matriarchal. Women have power. Our tribe was that way, even though my mother never would have said it in those terms. And she was so dysfunctional. She caught so much dysfunction, but she embodied the power. She fought with our father. All the years I was growing up, he was the quintessential patriarchal Sicilian father, saying: You're going to get married and have kids and if you want a job, be a secretary, a hairdresser, because that's what the women in that family did.

I was like, no fucking way. And my mom always said you can be whatever you want to be, you do what you want to do. You be an individual, you figure out who you are. That's how she raised us and she had to fight our father about it.

This clash of cultures within our family is really how I understand it now. She would not capitulate to him. She had to fight with him a lot and the message came through loud and clear for me and my sisters. My younger sister became the first in our high school to be on the guys' gymnastics team. Nothing like that had happened before. She was so good, too good for the girls' team, so they let her be on the guys' team. She has been breaking barriers as an athlete all her life.

Krista: This is the one that also surfs?

Dina: Right. She surfs, and races cars. She's a level-three ski instructor. She's radical. She's a radical jock, jockette. Our other sister is an amazing musician. And an athlete. We all three of us did things none of the other women in our family were doing. We didn't recognize limits. By 1980 when I moved to Hawaii . . .

Krista: Pipeline seemed possible?

Dina: Yeah. Women don't surf Pipeline, but why not? Why can't I? Like, who's going to say no?

Krista: I assume some people said no.

Dina: Well, the guys didn't like it, but more to the point, they didn't take me seriously. And it's testosterone hell, a place like that. And I will send you this photo to post to the blog—it's the only time I was in *Surfer Magazine*, '81, or '82. The back cover. They took a photograph of the crowd, the Pipeline littered with people. I'm the only girl in the crowd, documentary evidence that it's true. Probably thirty people in the frame, and me, the only girl with all the guys scrapping for waves. Wearing a red bathing suit. And I'm just watching them go by.

Krista: Sitting on the shoulder? Hoping? [Laughs.] Trying to keep your wits about you?

Dina: Pretty much, pretty much.

Krista: Wow! Fast-forwarding to now, how would you express feminist thought? You and I have had many conversations about this over some years. I'm not looking for a set thing. But there is being a "strong woman," as an individual, then there's having a feminist framework to understand structures or relationships. One might feed the other, but they aren't the same thing. You can't stage an argument by being a strong woman. You can if you're out surfing, but in terms of a way to think about a liberation project?

Dina: Yeah. It's about reclaiming women's power, as a Native person, on a cultural level, like being told that Colville women have always been in charge, which has stuck with me so much. Despite the way it looks, the way that it's come to look in Indian country during the Red Power movement when the men had the mic and there was a lot of abuse in those movements. We all know that American Indian men have internalized a lot of patriarchal behavior. But Colville women have always resisted that. For me, hearing that was so empowering. My mother was not empowered, at least outwardly, but when I really think about it, her whole life was about resisting colonial-patriarchal abuse—though she raised us to be individuals, she was so dysfunctional, and there was just so much trauma. It's so interesting how your perspective about the things that shaped your life can change so much as you mature.

To get to the framework of feminism as a project, like an intellectual project, is useful because it gives us a common language. That's what's so attractive.

Krista: Right. And ideally, a community, a relational project, you know, not an abstract kind of idea.

Dina: Yeah that common language. I never took a class in feminism, ever. The classes were there, especially in grad school, but for whatever reason, it didn't compel me. It wasn't until I was out of school that I became more aware of Indigenous feminist thought.

This common language allows us as women to talk to each other across difference. And that's why it's so important to understand various kinds of feminist projects, you know, white feminism, and black feminism and queer feminism, Indigenous feminism. The ways feminisms show up in these particularities. Because they're different. You felt like your identity was really as a feminist, right? That was core to your identity. My core identity was being Indigenous. I had to figure out who I was in the context of that, before I could get to who I was as a woman. If that makes sense.

Krista: I hear a lot of women of color say that and a lot of Indigenous women say that. Yeah.

For me, being a girl, a woman, was the core identity. I have four younger sisters. We were known as "the Comer girls." Five girls, it was a thing. I would not have called myself a white girl. I was a girl, boys came after me a lot, and my feminism in those days was some kind of attitude or fury about weird behavior, what I'd call today sexual violence, which I didn't understand at that time and thought was my fault. And the need for autonomy. I did not intend to be like my mother, to conform to what she accepted. She took us camping, she was trying to figure out her life, but she did not stand up to my father, that I could see. I had to do that. She was very ambivalent about behaviors out of the box. "Abortion rights" were not in my mind. I cared about being independent, about survival without being attached to my parents or a man.

None of my friends were so outspoken, and I didn't even know where it came from. That was what caused the trouble and why boys got mad—I smoked and drank and all that, but the trouble really was the fact I had a mind and it did not occur to me not to say what I thought. I was always challenging stuff—parents, boys, teachers.

Dina: I like this *Living West* project as an interactive way of talking about feminism that keeps it alive for regular women. So it doesn't get bogged down. Because if you're not studying feminism, in an academic way, it seems that either you are a feminist or you're anti-feminist. In the world, "feminist" is a dirty word for a lot of people.

Krista: Or feminism is "equal pay." Getting a piece of the pie, Sheryl Sandberg and "leaning in" and being able to show up for "careers" and balance it all. That's a feminist.

Dina: Yeah, it's a narrow way of seeing things. I think humanity is always trying to give birth to something new. And it's revolutionary because life as we know it in a Eurocentric society is steeped in oppression, all kinds of oppression. Like, that's what patriarchal colonialism does.

As we try to give birth to something that transcends these multiple oppressions, it's going to be women that are going to change the world, women and Indigenous people, and other people of color. That's where it has to go. That's what it means to shed or transcend oppressions. To be a woman with a public platform is no small thing. And I take pride in that. From not being willing to accept no for an answer and being a majorette to just calling it like it is, to talking about colonialism on the pages of *Sierra Magazine* or other non-Indigenous publications.[8]

Krista: Yeah, those recent pieces of yours are great. They hit hard. They "school" audiences. Whether people can tolerate it's a different matter.

Dina: This is what I do, though, in Zoom rooms and classrooms and big rooms of scientists and lawyers and conservationists. I tend to be pretty uncensored, and I'm constantly surprised about not having a lot of pushback. People are ready to hear.

ROAD FINDS
Slowing Down for Home

In early August we get rumblings from our children. "When did you say you were coming home?" I've said the date a few times, written it down, but there is surprise. Neither of our boys is used to us being gone. In a contest between hoverers and benign-neglect parents, we are people who are around. My older son has a flight to DC soon—he will be leaving Houston for graduate school. Both of them say no, we don't need you to come home, to assist with rides or moving or boxes or storage. We want you to have fun! It's good, Mom and Dad, it's good. It's fine. We've got it.

José and I look at each other doubtfully.

We get on the road with the goal of arriving in Houston before our oldest leaves town.

It's been a lot of miles between Salt Lake City to St. George, Utah (home of the Best Western Coral Hills—love that place and its pool), and on to Los Angeles. High winds, rain, open skies, and traffic. On the outskirts of Las Vegas, we get turned around looking for a Starbucks, then head on toward water. In San Clemente, we see Dina. Then we spend a night with my sister Lee in San Diego. With Lee, we have a swim at Ocean Beach. It's a dog-friendly beach where a jetty divides the surf break from a marina, a horizon of waves and sailboats, and a lot of happy dogs running. Then the straightaways of I-10. It's a blistering, baking border drive through very conservative country. I am listening to a book about militiamen who take it on themselves to "interview" border migrants. We feel the West trailing out behind us as we head south, then east, trekking the Sun Belt, eventually closing in on Houston.

Living West at the intersection of the Gulf Coast South—hurricane country, majority-minority country.

I tell José, "Hey, this trip has been easy. I'm liking this life in the van."

"Easy?!" he says. "You're working. A lot!"

"But you're doing everything else," I tell him. "I just get in the van and we go, until the next stop."

Our sons are young men in their early and midtwenties. Running their own lives, capable. They don't need us in the way they once did. But we see what we see. It's good we arrive when we do. Not because the house is burning, but because when our older son leaves town the next day, we have witnessed the boxes and memories he sorts, the friends he meets late in the evening for a last drink. We have blessed, in person, this life that is his. José drives him to the airport, we see him off one more time because it is a series of these partings and well-wishings that reassure young people the world is good, they can go forward.

My younger son moves out of his apartment ten days later for a job in San Francisco. We get a rental van. José wants to drive. He's got some fuel in his tank still for covering miles, especially if it's for one of the kids. I go over to the apartment my son is leaving with a tub of cleaning supplies and write a note on something I wrap up so he will unwrap it in the city. We watch him do goodbyes, all his bonded guy friends separating and not concerned to hide their feelings. These moves are big now, not summers away but life next-stages. Some two thousand miles hence, José parks on the street in Haight Ashbury to unload couches, a bed, two leather chairs, boxes. Jesse gets invitations the first night to a party up on Stinson Beach, and then another, and immediately he enters a new circle of friends, ecstatic to be blocks from Golden Gate Park. José returns the van across the Bay in Oakland, stays overnight with one of my sisters, flies home, and begins teaching for the fall semester.

We are here together, José and I, in our home we love, with one other.

This is the "I" writing, who is living West as a feminist, trying to slow down, now officially with an empty nest. There have been gap years before in Brazil and Ecuador, study abroad trips to Turkey, Cuba, Spain. Family times in San Francisco, Pueblo, and Monterrey, Mexico. There have been graduations and words spoken around a circle that were solid and honored us and carry us forward.

But this time is different.

Here we are, José and I, fifty miles from Galveston and the Gulf, with our bamboo trees in the back, the pond with goldfish in the front. The cat our son rescued during Hurricane Harvey.

It's quiet long enough to do laundry, put away camping gear, feel out the changes. Then the buzz starts. The dashing, the choices between walking or writing or sacrificing both to prepare for class. I have department duties. I've had them all summer, but they ramp up.

I am good at being a grown up, the oldest child, the mother who balances, the university citizen. Too good. It's time to figure out an alternative that is not a Band-Aid, figure out something real. Because you realize at some point the balancing act will always be an act. No amount of planning or negotiation or yoga or "support" will satisfy the impossibility of juggling all the balls at once. Students, faculty, staff, everybody is speeding, demanding more of our bodies, our relationships, our time. On bucolic campuses like ours, the grind culture of late capitalism thrives.

I try to take stock in the idea of slow and the concept of "slow scholarship" as a feminist research politics.[1] I try to be mindful of slowing down my own scholarship as an ethics of research and the relations sustaining knowledge. Slowing down is about working conditions in universities, our structures of power, and who does the institutional work of caring. In other words, slow scholarship is a program for remaking the university. I try to think about how to create feminist rest areas in my home institution where I actually walk the talk. As I update the blog and get teaching notes in order, I mull over that, talking real talk here, there's no way I could or should have taken "slow" advice as a junior faculty. I likely will need to retire to take that advice now. If I am serious about slowing down, and writing what I have to write, retirement seems to be the only way. Still, we read a lot of theory work that helps us to aspire, that pushes back, and in the small gap of possibility that opens, I try to imagine feminist rest areas ahead.

Retracing the Western Black Family in Whitehouse, Texas, with Kalenda Eaton

An unseasonal snowstorm flurries around us in Whitehouse. Big dry flakes spiraling from the sky. Kalenda has flown in from Norman to talk to us about her family homestead, and only José, who by chance wore a jacket, is dressed for cold. Kalenda smartly pulls a just-bought sweatshirt hood over her head and we laugh about this weather spectacle. We thought spring was on the way!

As Kalenda and I have talked over the last year about doing this interview together, I've come to learn why she offers such a unique leadership perspective as director of the Black Homesteader's Project, a collaboration between the National Park Service, the University of Oklahoma, which is Kalenda's home institution, and the Center for Great Plains Studies at the University of Nebraska at Lincoln.[1] Born and raised in Northern California, Kalenda's grandmaternal ties are in East Texas and Oklahoma, including the family land in east Texas where we do our interview. Every other year, the larger family returns for a reunion to this land, some hundred people commemorating family legacies. When we talk about opening up a conversation about the West and feminism, her work and family legacy teaches us how.

"Land ties tend to be more real than the personal ties in my family," she reflects. The land where we meet has been in the family well over a century. As a legacy of place and space, what a rarity in African American history. "To be able to point to a place and say, 'My people have been here for this long,'" she pauses looking around us on this snowy day. "It's significant."

Our conversations take place across three distinct sites.

The first site is the land, the homestead, and hearing about communities it built and supports today. Kalenda is the family historian, its djeli *or storyteller.[2] We talk about Freedom Colonies through Texas, and how they fashioned autonomous spaces for Black life, as did the all-Black towns, for instance, in Oklahoma. Whitehouse was not a Freedom Colony, though. Its ethnic histories were mixed. The second site is the hilltop Antioch Cemetery, affiliated with the Whitehouse Church of God and Christ, the family's church over generations. We pass under a lovely archway of wrought iron and, from the hilly mound, take a walking tour of the cemetery to pay respects to family and to visit headstones and tended graves surrounded by pine trees. The third site is conducted in lawnchairs set up in the back of the van, heaters on full blast, shutting out the flurries. There Kalenda reflects on womanism, feminism, and being from the West.*

"Behind the piney curtain" was a phrase I conjured, before we met up with Kalenda in Whitehouse, a popular sentiment for this part of Texas. The phrase refers to the curtains or stands of pine woods distinguishing the bioregion but also its reputation as an enclave of white supremacy, a transition space into the Deep South. Many white students come to Rice from places like Tyler, which is close to Whitehouse, and they talk about "escaping."

Until today, José too, born in Houston, has had this popularized sense of where we are.

Listening to Kalenda's family histories radically reorients the cultural geography. Her family, she tells us, especially its women, understood themselves to be inside of the West and the West to be inside of them. Being raised close to the land allowed for their wonderful "willfulness." If one is thinking this place of Whitehouse is only behind the piney curtain, think again.

The Where of Here, Part One: The Land

Kalenda: We are in Whitehouse, Texas, on a portion of the land that my great-great-grandfather owned and passed down to one of his daughters, Amanda. Eventually it came to her daughter, and other children. Pauline, Cousin Polly, was my grandmother's first cousin and now it is in the hands of Cousin Pauline's children. This portion of the land, and the house, is in front of the tracks that are governed by my branch of the family.

The clearing, behind cousin Polly's house and now Cousin Carol's house, used to be all woods. Our branch of the family tree has thirty-some acres of forest remaining. It was passed down from Papa George and Georgia Ann to Hazel, who was their first child, to Clara and Annabelle and Gordon. And then once Annabelle and Gordon passed away, it was passed down to Clara, who was my grandmother. And then she passed it down to her four children, and those children are passing it down to us.

The land we're standing on has been in our family since the 1890s. I've always felt it to be very significant. Probably because I am a scholar of African American history and culture, but even aside from that, to be able to point to a place and say, "My people have been here for this long," it is so significant. It's much easier to do in Native American histories, right? And Chicanx and Latinx histories. But when it comes to African Americans—because of the history of slavery in the United States and also because of predatory lending, redlining, and land taken away due to gentrification—not many people can say, "This is property that we've had for so many years."

I also think about space and place as it relates to Indigenous stories. Especially because as a descendant of people who were able to take advantage of land, right? Not the same sort of term that they use in Oklahoma, "free land," but land that was not originally their own. I always think about those connections.

I remember a story my grandmother told me about when she was very young, growing up down here. Every summer, the Indians would come to the land, she told me. And Papa George, her grandfather, would let them do their ceremonies on the land. She remembered growing up and watching, seeing from afar. Papa George made sure that they had access to the land. She didn't know at the time what was going on. It was probably a powwow. But that story stayed with me. There was an understanding and connection that he had, in terms of the importance of this land and the sacred nature of the land and space.

Papa George was allegedly affiliated with the Choctaw. Maybe a freedman? And there is a family picture with my great-great-grandmother wearing textiles attributable to a Native tribe, but the stories diverge. Whether or not he actually was a Choctaw freedman, we don't know. Even so, there was no question that Indigenous people could come back to the space. Wherever it was. He owned a lot of land around here.

We are on a very community-based space. Cousin Carol has cameras on the trees now because no one was living here for a long time. She lives in Houston. Before her nephew moved in, people were squatting on the land. So she has surveillance.

During its heyday, the space provided for the building of the town Whitehouse. You saw the sign, George Taylor Road. Papa George was an important contributor to the growth and development of Whitehouse. In 1900 he donated some of his acreage to build Mt. Elam Baptist Church, which used to be out here in the "country" but moved within the White-house city limits in 1983. A lot of farmers helped build Whitehouse and he was one of them. It's interesting to think about this fact in terms of the land and all the Freedom Colonies throughout Texas. The Freedom Colonies and communities throughout southern, central, and northern Texas were able to fashion some sense of civic autonomy. In the same way that you have the all-Black towns in Oklahoma. You have several Freedom Colonies that are around, and in Smith County. We're in Smith County now.

But Whitehouse itself wasn't one, as far as I know. It was mixed in terms of ethnic groups. But several around here were all Black, with churches and schools and what have you.

Krista: Professionalized.

Kalenda: Right, exactly. They worked with people who were farming in the area, and were major contributors to development, progress, and growth. Attempting to establish confidence among the next generation, right, but also a legacy.

I think about George Taylor related to building the local community. He was instrumental in starting a community school for local Black children. In his own family, he was very focused on making sure that all of his children, and especially the girls, were educated. He made sure that everyone had an equal distribution of land, of opportunities. I won't say never, but he was not known to put restrictions on his daughters. They became these willful and adventurous, phenomenal women. Coming out of an environment where they had not been made to feel as if they could not do whatever it was that they would like to do. If we think about the heart of feminism, he definitely was a feminist of his day.

Ok, I will show you the cemetery. Are you okay being at a cemetery? Some people don't like to go to cemeteries.

José: I'm okay. For sure.

Krista: I'm familiar.

The Where of Here, Part Two: Antioch Cemetery
Kalenda: I just wanted to show you something. I didn't have a plan.

Krista: Tell us where we are.

Fig. 15. Two generations of women in the early twentieth-century West; Eaton's great-grandmother and grandmother ca. 1930s. Courtesy Kalenda Eaton.

Kalenda: [chuckling] Every time you ask me the question, I feel like it's *This American Life*. [Kalenda and Krista laughing.] Where are we? I'm trying not to fall in a hole here, Krista, that's my main goal. [laughing]

Okay, we're at the Antioch Cemetery, where all of my family on my mother's side, the majority of them, are buried. This cemetery is affiliated with the Whitehouse Church of God and Christ. A lot of the members and families who live in Whitehouse and attend that church are buried here as well.

Krista: It's a hilltop cemetery. Surrounded by pines and you come through a beautiful wrought iron archway that says "The Antioch Cemetery."

Kalenda: Yes. The land that we just left, the family property, belonged to Pauline Pettigrew [gesturing to gravestone]—right there. Cousin Polly. And her husband.

Krista: 1916 to 2004. A long life.

Kalenda: Quite a long time. [gesturing] The large pieces here, these belong to the infamous George and Georgia Ann Taylor.

This is Gordon Ervin, my grandmother's brother, who was killed in a motorcycle accident. My uncle Gordon is named after him. Aunt Annie is our lovely wild one, who eventually lived in Los Angeles. That's her over there. Annie Burrell, and her brother Daniel Culberson. He had several children.

This here is my grandmother's sister, Annabelle. And her husband Henry. She met Uncle Henry in Oklahoma and they moved to Los Angeles.

I'm trying to find Hazel. Where'd she go? Hazel's here somewhere. She was the first daughter and the first child. She was very important. You see these last names like Ervin. My grandmother's maiden name is Ervin. The Ervins live out in this area, the Pettigrews, all people who are relatives by marriage. There are people who live in the community, the Ervins, the Pettigrews, the Smiths. I'm still trying to find the headstone. Her children are here.

Where'd you go, Hazel?

I have a picture of her headstone. When it's not muddy, you can see it clearly. Our cousins take care of the cemetery and clean off the headstones.

I have it. [Laughs.] Here it is with the flowers. Born in 1888. This is my great-grandmother, Hazel Taylor *Chavez*, if you notice.

José: [Admiring.] Yeah.

Kalenda: As I said, several of the women were married more than once. My aunt Cassie was married five times. My great-grandmother married three times. Yes, number three was a Mexican laborer living in Tulsa. So, Hazel Taylor is the maiden name. But she was Hazel Taylor Ervin. That's my grandmother's father, Mitchell Ervin. And then Hazel Taylor Robinson. That was Mr. Robinson, husband number two. Mr. Jack as they called him, from Oklahoma. And finally, Hazel Taylor Chavez. She was married to Macedonia Chavez when she passed away, yes.

You learn so much with [chuckles] gravestones. I never knew that George Taylor was a mason. Until you see the gravestone and you come to the cemetery. There are other relatives out here. My aunt Cassie Brooks should be out here. But these are the ones relevant to my lineage.

The Where of Here, Part Three: In the Van, Antioch Cemetery

Krista: We're so happy to be warmed up, around the heat!

We've been taking a journey to various parts of your family history and your relationship to place and to land, and you've told us a fair amount about the way in which the legacies of George Taylor were very favorable to his women-children. Let's talk about the terms of your relation to place and to land and feminism or womanism—a term you use in your scholarship, and feminist theory, Black feminist theory.[3] It doesn't have to be a "theoretical conversation," but is the journey we've just made a womanist journey?

Kalenda: "Womanism" is a distinguished term, and what it means for those who still use the term—a lot of people don't still use the term, but I use the term in scholarship. I do not walk around saying "I am a womanist," but I will use the term when I am speaking about the ways women of color, or specifically African American women, are empowering not only themselves but also the entire community.

That's not to say that feminist politics are not community focused, but when we think about feminism, whether it be Black feminism or any type of feminism, it is focused on inequality and the rights of women, empowering women, making sure that women's voices are at the fore. When we think about womanism, it is all of those things. But I use it to mean the ways that both men and women and children and whomever else, elders, can be uplifted, protected, loved, cared for, through a very female-driven or woman-driven politics, not necessarily woman-centered. Women are central and important, and are key figures in this longer story, and as it relates to place, they are defined by their feminism. I would say that.

All the people that I've introduced you to, whether it be their final resting place, or stories about them, their actions, these wonderful narratives are connected to how they saw themselves outside of restrictions that might have been placed upon them as women. They saw themselves outside of the traditional role of wife, right? We joke in our family a lot about that Aunt So-and-So was married five times. This aunt was married three times. This one married four times. If we think about the late nineteenth and early twentieth century, to be divorced, and the stigma of divorce, and then to get married again, and then divorced again. Or marry whoever you want to marry across ethnic lines. There was a lot of female-driven action that these women were taking, in a classic feminist way, when we think about the definition of feminism.

Krista: As focused on women's liberation, women-centered liberation?

Kalenda: Yes.

Krista: So the legacy isn't "respectability?"

Kalenda: No. It's funny. It's not respectability in the way in which we think today about "respectability politics," or not allowing for willful women. But definitely respectability in terms of rules about how a proper woman should act outside of their marital situation. For example, my grandmother tells stories all the time about how her mother would never let her go to the school dances. She couldn't do any of that, right. The church was very important and very central to the family. If you had any kind of social time, it was in church. At the same time, you had contradictions. Not in the definition of "loose women." But respectability is not associated with not being a divorcée.

Respectability was looking a certain way, acting a certain way, carrying yourself in a particular way, being cultured. That was a part of these women's lives even as they were numbers runners, and doing all sorts of things [laughs]. I like that because it brings us to all the nuances and diversity of womanhood, of women's experiences and women's histories. It's not just respectability politics versus "the blues women." Or church women, or club women, right? You have bits and pieces of that making up these women's experiences.

Krista: Can you talk about the West? Your sense of how having a western history or identity was influential in the kind of women they were?

Kalenda: Going back to how you have a little bit of this, a little bit of that and it is still okay, I always identified that "diversity" as resulting from being Western women. The understood role of women during these periods tended to be aligned within a particular binary. You're either one or the other type, right? The West as a space, of course we theorize this, as contested space, fractured borders, but if we generalize or popularize it, the West as a contentious space doesn't fit easily into our understanding of American history. Those who don't include Mexican American history, don't include Native American history, don't include African American history, Asian American history, when they're talking about the early West. They would like it to fit neatly into a very static Manifest Destiny idea of frontierism, even still today when we know better. But if we're going to get into the weeds into what the West actually is, it's anti-American in terms of that popular American narrative of territorial conquest.

The sorts of liberties Black women who were living free in the West could take, those liberties can be almost endless. That doesn't mean there's not racism, doesn't mean there's no gender discrimination. We know that there's a long-standing history of enslavement in the western spaces, right. But there are also other realities, other narratives that can be told and ways in which people live their lives, sometimes in spite of and other times as a result of their surroundings.

When we're talking about the women in my family, or I think about Black womanhood in western spaces, I am always thinking that people are able to do certain things because of what I would say is a narrative that fits outside of "America's" definition of exceptionalism.

Krista: So where do you think these women got it, where did they get "the West"? Was it popular culture? A way of talking about things? Did they read dime novels? Was it a form of "Go West Young Man," in the air, and everybody had that feeling about the West as a space of alternative social order?

Kalenda: It was part and parcel of who they were from birth. They were, they are, from the soil. From the 1880s-on generation, they were people who were born and came from the space. It's very different than those African Americans who have emigrated in, from the South, right. Or those who are emigrating into Oklahoma Territory, or who were freedmen living in Indian Territory after being emancipated by the tribes. That's a different conceptualization of the West.

Krista: They were inside it.

Kalenda: They were inside it and it was inside of them. And that allows for the willfulness, this is all they knew, right? This open space, land that you see around you, that's all they knew. Running out barefoot into the grass, it's a cliché, but you know what I mean. Yeah, the horses and the cows, which doesn't necessarily mean it's West—that may just mean rural. But the space is how they came into being, how they knew themselves. That story, and not just in my own family, often gets missed, right? Because it's usually, "we're people who came in from other places in the United States and then tried to make our way." And then they become a part of their environments over time. Or thinking about Stegner, who says, "No, they never do settle, they just move through," you know, are always nomadic. What I am saying about my family is very different than that.

Krista: Can you think about living your womanism, or feminism in relation to place? Maybe as a kid, some precursor story to who you became?

Kalenda: Especially as it relates to place consciousness, I would move us outside of Texas to Vallejo, and the San Francisco Bay Area. I am from Northern California, as you know. I think of the Redwoods and Sonoma County. I think about Carolyn Finney's *Black Faces, White Spaces*, and she talks about this contentious relationship between African Americans and the natural environment. There are other different essays that have popped up over the years about people of color not feeling welcome in National Parks.

I always had a totally different experience. The opposite experience. My mother was very good about us hiking in the woods, skiing in Tahoe, or falling, I should say, when we skied at Lake Tahoe! We were always out and about in nature. Or in very specific western landscapes. Redwood trees. Muir Woods. Those are my childhood memories. Being very close to the land, but also in the ways in which I could see my little, small self as a speck in the great expanse of a wonderful natural environment.

We didn't have to go into the woods, we could just go to hike, we had a waterfront, in the city where I grew up, with the naval base across the way. We would go out to the waterfront and go walking. If I think about my grandmother, she's coming from this space in the southern Plains, but always outside, outdoors. She did a lot of baking and other things indoors, but she had beautiful vegetable gardens and rose gardens. My hands were always dirty and in the mud. I think about my childhood, and me laying in the grass. I thought the lawn was so large, playing with little dandelions or whatever little things.

Krista: You didn't feel Other. You felt: "This is mine. I belong here."

Kalenda: There was never any moment to make me feel otherwise. I never had an experience early on where it was like, "Oh, this is not your space." "Of course!" I thought. We were always going out into these spaces! That's not the same experience that a lot of people have.

Krista: How does that link to womanism or feminism for you, however you would define that?

Kalenda: It relates definitely to women's space and to women understanding or taking on this natural space as their own. The women were the ones taking me to the spaces, and taking our cousins and other people. It's not like I was going hiking with my uncles. And so, without trying, without sounding like I'm being essentialist, like "Oh, women in nature and Mother Nature," there really was, in my experience, a strong connection between an appreciation of land and landscape, nature and environment, that came through the eyes and actions of the women around me. One could argue that might be a feminism unto itself.

Krista: Would you argue that?

Kalenda: Why not?

Krista: So, your early memories of being embodied with other women outdoors are a foundation of your western identity.

Kalenda: Yeah, we would go walking. My grandmother, myself, my mother, it would be multigenerational. In the state parks, go for drives in Napa Valley. Going up and down, just to be out there. I mean we weren't going anywhere in particular.

José: One thing that strikes me as different is the various geographic locations of your family story, and you as a family storyteller. The maintenance of different geographies, but the sameness of family. Something like that. Things seem to be so networked.

I'm making more of a commentary. I don't know if you want to do anything with that? But it seems unusual—it's not just that it's rich. I haven't come across that kind of formulation.

Kalenda: A lot of it is tied to a national story of Black migration, movement. Migration and settlement. I won't use the word "peripatetic." But it's movement that's intentional, and not a result necessarily of displacement. This is kind of another story, right? You have, of course, the pushing out and the exile, whatever you're running from, racial terrorism and what have you. But then you have these other stories of people who are just saying, you know: "Let's venture out, let's see."

Agency, a form of agency. When we're thinking about western spaces and the network you are speaking of, there really was a network of people who went from Texas to Los Angeles, or from Texas to Oklahoma, to other parts of California. Whether as a result of the war and working in the shipyards, there was always a call for people to come work in the shipyards. All of this, whether or not they actually did work in shipyards, was connected back to other parts of the Western space. When I was growing up as an only child, and for most of my childhood into teenage years, the youngest grandchild, I was always at my grandparents' house. My grandmother was very active and all of her friends were from all of these other places. My friends, their aunts and uncles and grandparents, were from other parts of California or Texas or, again, Oklahoma. There was a sense of them being in both places at once, where we were and where they had come from.

Krista: It was normative, this transregional sense.

Kalenda: Right, yeah, and of course, you'd have those connections to the deeper, deep, Deep South too. But that understanding and feeling of what it meant to be a part of the region was something that was normal. And it wasn't until I went to college in the South, Deep South, Dillard University in New Orleans, that I understood that this was something different. That what I was used to was not necessarily what everyone was used to, in terms of how one defines themselves regionally.

Krista: When you think of being from Texas, you don't think of being from the South, you think of being from the West. Is that right?

Kalenda: Yes. That's always the [laughs]— the debate with Texans, because it's like Southwest, West, South, you know.

Krista: Right, but I'm thinking of you.

Kalenda: I definitely associate Whitehouse with being more Western, I think because it's not Houston. The people I know from Houston, and my friends and others that I know, identify themselves as southerners in ways that people from other parts of North Texas don't.

Krista: What triggered the question was the New Orleans link. Because Texas is a slave state. It's the only state in the West.

Kalenda: Well, do you not count Oklahoma? It's a larger comment on how we define "southern" and do we define "southern" only in terms of enslavement? Because if that's the case, then Delaware is southern, right? People were enslaved in Delaware. They were enslaved in Massachusetts. We can still be Western and be a slave state. Both can exist. Just like you can be Northern and be a slave state, right.

Krista: I'm absorbing this. It goes against the grain so much.

Kalenda: That's everything I've been trying to say! What I do in my work is troubling the line not for the sake of being controversial. But because I find that there's a very narrow way of thinking about these experiences. Because it makes it easier, right? To say, "Oh, well, this is what's happening here. This is what's happening there. These are the experiences of these people." What do you do about all these others here? What do you do about those who fit outside of this geography? Or who fit inside geographically, and fit inside in terms of scholarly definitions, but fit outside in terms of the way that American history wants to define things? What do you do with that group? Are they no longer western?

José: It depends who's writing the story, right? If it's Governor Abbott in Texas, and he wants everybody to forget Texas was a slave state, then you don't want to forget that. Right. But if you're trying to tell a story like you're telling, your story of emigration with an "e" not an "i" is the one that is counter to a typical Anglo-American emigration where the movement is always West to some finite point. If you have to go back, return, there's something wrong. But in your story, in your community's story, maintaining the homes, and the "back homes," it's not a problem, right? Because they're alive, "back homes" are alive. But in typical Anglo-American westernness, those back homes are left behind for something "better."

Kalenda: When you first mentioned the project and described it, Krista, what popped in my mind were these women that we've been talking about today. It wasn't necessarily myself, right? It was these women, and the ways in which I've regarded them as prime examples of what feminism looks like, in a western context.

To answer your question of what I would like the project to be? First of all, what it is already, what you're doing is phenomenal. What I would like it to be: a way to open that conversation up more. That's what you're doing with different perspectives and narratives. You start to redefine, or maybe define, what the theoretical framework is, and what it could be. If it's the latter, I think that's beneficial not only to scholarship but to the public in terms of public history and in capturing these oral narratives and voices.

PART 2

SUMMER 2022

Launching in the Time of Family, with Krista Comer

We have launched round two of interviews! Summer 2022 is rolling. Last summer our travels focused on doing interviews, connecting with people, and writing the blogs more or less as they came. We had one winter interview with Kalenda Eaton, keeping the project alive amid flurries of snow. Otherwise, not much research or writing time 'til teaching and meetings adjourned.

This summer, life has put extended family events into the mix of our *Living West* travels. Two graduations and a family memorial land squarely on the map. What that means is that for me there's a different relationality and feeling to this summer's trip. Far more inside the ebb and flow of the family into which I was born.

In the first week of June, we head north from Houston. This time the route runs through Lubbock, then to Santa Fe. We are lucky José's sister Laura is house-sitting and cat-sitting for Amiga. Laura is so good to us! Zainab Abdali has been funded for a second summer of public humanities research assistance, and she stands ready to manage logistics and collaborate. With both Laura and Zainab as foundations, José and I travel up Highway 6, past College Station and Texas A&M, Aggieland. Very green, rolling hills, big trucks. Fast.

We wonder aloud: how very many guns are traveling the roads with us? The Uvalde shootings at Robb Elementary feel fresh and personal, and the fact that Uvalde is a Latino/a Trump town engaged in what looks to be a police cover-up confounds the grief.

The summer plan is to finish what we've begun. We have four interviews, though we travel more miles to meet up in places that are outliers on the map of last summer's journey. José and I interview Audrey Goodman first in Santa Fe under the trees of the Georgia O'Keeffe Research Center Gardens. In a summer of family, Audrey anchors us in our project. There's the bonus of staying at the Silver Saddle Motel near Elena Valdez and her daughter, Zeni, and husband, Matt. I send my mom a picture of the Silver Saddle sign, which reminds her of motels from the 1940s when she traveled from Pueblo to Southern California for summers with her grandmother.

José and I drive two long days from Santa Fe to the Bay Area for back-to-back graduations and a cluster of parties with the various Comer women and attending entourage. A graduation of Olivia Argosino-Comer from the Katherine Delmar Burke school, top-of-the-line all-girls K–8 education in San Francisco. There is Sophie Griffing Comer's University of California, Santa Cruz college graduation, our family's first scientist. She is headed to nursing school. José and I come dressed up, bearing gifts, and I show both nieces their official presence on the *Living West* timeline.

Family events have a way of spreading. We get to the Bay Area and around my sisters, and my time-containment strategies go mushy. Do I have a calendar? Days blend into nighttime with lunches, dinners. There is drink, cannabis, music, dessert, and what all. We are a lot of people. Five sisters, their partners, my mother, her brother (my uncle), nieces and nephews, cousins, the friends spending the night. We are an intense crew *before* the cancer IV diagnoses of two of the sisters, who live past them. A guy friend of mine taking pictures of us once remarked that we were a moving wave of women falling in and out of love with one another about fifty times a day.

In the temporality of my family, there must be room to talk, listen, interrupt, digress—to get lost, upset, and reoriented. Someone goes on a walk, checks out the sunset, loses her phone or another sister's phone or that daughter's phone or her friend's phone. Ideally there is time to hang out in the pool, which my family does well.

We spend a few days with three party rooms at the Seaside Resort in Aptos, a resort space looking over the Pacific. We go later to Alameda, home of Sophie's parents, Mike Griffing and Corinne Comer, each with work lives dedicated to trade unionism for the California Nurses Association, and now one of their sons and his partner are organizers with the National Nurses Association.

In that mayhem of energy and movement, we cross the Bay Bridge to see our son Jesse for quieter heart-to-hearts. One year after graduating from Rice, he has landed on his feet with a new job in San Francisco, still living in Haight-Ashbury, and thoroughly enchanted with city life. We see him five times for three lunches and two dinners and at least ten miles of walking. That kid loves to walk.

Eventually José and I will venture north again, to interview Susan Bernardin in Corvallis, another anchor for the project. After Corvallis, we will head east over the Cascades to Bend, to a memorial family gathering for my cousin Beau Houston.

We have a few thousand miles ahead of us to meet up with Victoria Lamont on her sheep farm in St. Agatha, Ontario, and then a visit with Margaret Jacobs in Lincoln. I've been reading Margaret's recent *After One Hundred Winters*, about instances of settler and Indigenous reconciliation. With Margaret's thoughts and my own recent writing and thinking about feminist accountabilities in mind, José and I decide to punctuate our trip toward the sheep farm and Victoria in Canada with a visit to Mesa Verde National Park.

The Archives of Gardens, with Audrey Goodman

It's serendipity that Audrey is in Santa Fe the very same week that we pass through on this summer's Living West tour. She is doing advance work as the president of the Western Literature Association (WLA) in 2022 with her co-president, Lisa Tatonetti. We find Audrey in the gardens of the Georgia O'Keeffe Research Center. It's Monday, the Center is closed to the public, but Audrey has arranged for us to be there in the midst of all else she is doing! The gardens will change in the next few years, some of the trees will come down, and Audrey tells us to soak up the grounds as they are while we can.

After our time in the gardens, and in keeping with Audrey's sense of place as tied to food cultures and local cuisine, we walk to the Santa Fe Teahouse for lunch. The Teahouse spreads its pleasures over several split-level dining areas, some indoors, some out. I remember Audrey's burrata, heirloom tomato, and basil salad. For the table we ordered the cold avocado cucumber soup. I took home a warm scone of pear and sliced almonds. José was already happy and then he saw Wes Studi having lunch with a friend and looking, as José said, very much like himself.

I am mindful, reviewing these words later, that the time in Santa Fe preceded the U.S. Supreme Court Dobbs decision, which overturned women's constitutional right to an abortion. The Women's March organizers had dubbed it a "Summer of Rage." But the only public rage we saw was on billboards decrying abortion. If I didn't plug in to news or social media, little along the way told a story about the end of an era of women's civil rights.

Audrey's and my conversation is interestingly back-and-forth. Her questions about the project become an occasion to reflect on where we are in the midst of things, in process.

The Where of Here: O'Keeffe Research Center, Santa Fe

Audrey: We are in the garden of the O'Keeffe Research Center. It is a place that has many layers of complicated history that certainly preceded me but also provided a ground for scholarly exploration, for personal

147

exploration. I picked it because it's a powerful Indigenous space, Tewa land, the White Shell Water Place originally. That's not really visible except in the greenery, perhaps, and in the lushness of this environment. I think about this place through Indigenous lands and the range of sovereignties that are not always visible in Santa Fe. At the same time, being here is an opportunity to reflect on those histories and find places and ways to make lots of stories visible.

That's a process that I've been engaged in throughout my work, but especially in this place, and in this building, where I had my favorite office ever. It was on the second floor, in the front. I got to come here every day and do my work and think—and come out in this garden. It's a generative place for me, in terms of my thinking, in terms of giving me an opportunity to expand my knowledge of living in place and to work collaboratively with other scholars.

Krista: Do you have a first memory of knowing about Georgia O'Keeffe? Or beholding her work, having it speak to you?

Audrey: Her landscapes in northern New Mexico, of Abiquiu: I loved the way that she would paint a place many times. There would be: The Black Place I, The Black Place II, The Black Place III. Apprehending her work over time, and seeing how she found her places, and how her art and her vision led her to pick the places where she wanted to work, was a powerful model for me.

I came here, though, because one of my colleagues, my department chair, had put in my mailbox a notice for Research Center Fellowship applications. I wasn't writing about O'Keeffe in that book. But this Center, under the vision of the previous director, Barbara Lynes, was a place to bring together scholars in American modernism. That gave me an opportunity to come here with my work in literature and photography and be in conversation with not only what O'Keeffe was doing, but with her role as a pioneering modernist, and a pioneering woman in terms of her lived experience in the West.

O'Keeffe was a model of how to work in the West and how to create a vocabulary for "re-visioning place in the U.S. West," as I say in my essay for Routledge's *Gender and the West*.[1] And how to live in a place, and develop a relation through everyday observation. How to find the places that, I won't say she made her own, but that became significant through her representation of them. You see it in the ways that she will look at the interior of a flower, at a city view from one window. She's an artist who is very conscious of her perspective and the scale in which she works, in how she develops her way of seeing. She continued that practice until the end of her life. She was persistent.

Krista: As someone educated at Columbia, from the East Coast, interested in modernism, how did you come to work on the West? Not that the West "belongs" to people who are raised in the West because the West travels. I'm thinking of Neil Campbell's important notion of west-ness and how the West moves and is created at its outsides and borders.[2] How did "the West" begin to speak to you?

Audrey: It spoke to me through the writers. My introduction to the West primarily was through novelists and poets and powerful photographers and artists who shared their way of seeing and working through their relations to place in a way that resonated with work that I'd done previously. When I was a college student, I was drawn to feminist poets, to the work of Elizabeth Bishop, and Sylvia Plath, and Marianne Moore, poets who were intensely aware of their own place, and of the language that they wanted to use to claim their identities in relation to lots of different places. They moved around and were very much itinerant modernists.

When I was in graduate school, and I was thinking about local knowledges, I was drawn to poets of the early twentieth century, but also to writers like Cather, Mary Austin, who contended with the languages and the feelings of everyday places. Those places were in the West. These writers were responding at a historical moment of tremendous economic change and cultural change. Their work was responding to and creating a sense of . . . I don't know . . . it was kind of messy work. But work trying to articulate what it was to be connected to the West, or what it was to be a white woman in this area of the Southwest. We see that in the writings of Austin.

I was interested in their language, and in their process of trying to figure things out, through lots of different forms. Cather's fiction is complicated. Through its effort to work with archival materials, different kinds of family memories, different kinds of environmental histories, and to integrate them. It's also complicated formally, in the way that she composes the different sections and juxtaposes points of view. I was interested in Austin's work for those reasons as well. That seemed different to me than the emerging genre of the popular Western, very narrative driven, but at the same time a genre that had all these crazy disruptions and representations of landscape, and all kinds of gender trouble. Popular Westerns were a lot of fun to work with.

As I started to explore different genres that were contending with the complexity of western spaces, I started to think about regionality, from a literary point of view, but also as something that is composed, that's invented, that is problematic. I started to think about regionality generally.

Krista: Of the questions I shared with you for today, are there any that you wanted to answer? Sometimes questions speak to us in a way that suggest something we'd like to talk about.

Audrey: One question was about where people feel at home.

Krista: Yes, what are "your places," or "your people's places?"

Audrey: For me, the places are offices and libraries and workspaces. Like this office at the O'Keeffe Center. I loved working in wonderful archives at the Center for Creative Photography in Tucson too. For me, being in the archive, then being able to go out and walk in the canyons, like Sabino Canyon outside of Tucson, having read and thought about Silko's *Almanac of the Dead*. Then to go back into the archives. That conversation, one that I am trying to make visible between literary texts and visual texts and archival materials, is something that an archive enables.

Krista: They are workspaces and they're also spaces in which intellectual women, and ideas, can be centered.

Audrey: Yes.

Krista: A close friend, Rosemary Hennessy, has just completed *In the Company of Radical Women Writers*, about writers of the 1930s. One way perhaps to become feminist is through the company of other thinkers and writers?

Audrey: Institutions are important too. They're difficult places, but important feminist work happens there. You can say the Huntington Library, with a very complicated colonial history, also gives an opportunity to get to texts, like the manuscript I looked at with all of the notes taken by Charis Wilson when she was with the photographer Edward Weston.[3] They were doing their *California and the West* book. I was able to be in that library, looking at Charis Wilson's notes of their day-to-day life, what contributions she made, what her transcriptions contributed to that book. Recognizing the value of those institutions, whether they're universities or libraries' collections, as places that give space to tell stories about the West.

Other places where I'm at home are in the offices and studies that I've created for myself. My favorite study was my house in Albuquerque where I had a beautiful white desk and the windows open and nothing fluttering.

Krista: A bit like the visual that you shared of Georgia O'Keeffe's. A representation of "feminist Wests."

Audrey: Her working space. I'm interested in her vision, but also what her daily life was like. What created the conditions for her to do that work? Of course, she was privileged to do that work. But she also created that.

Thinking about other places, I love being in and living in Atlanta. In the West and elsewhere, I've looked for the places where I feel connected to the local culture, and for me that's often through taste and food. One of my favorite places is in Albuquerque, Duran Central Pharmacy—have you been there?

Krista: I don't know. What would you eat if we were sitting there?

Audrey: I'd eat a bowl of green chile. It's the purest. I love green chile in all forms, but there it is served in a bowl, and you can get beans in it, you can get chicken. But I don't need those things.

Krista: All you need is the chile?

Audrey: Just the chile! I might have an egg on the side. They make flour tortillas that are bigger than anyone should eat in one sitting, but sometimes you can't help it. [Krista and José laugh.] There are women who make the tortillas and you sit at the counter or you sit out in the little patio. I've been going to Duran's since my first visit to New Mexico as a graduate student. Staying at an inn, going to the photo archives at the Museum of New Mexico, carving out a week to do dissertation research. Somehow it always begins at Duran's. Have the green chile, then you can move on and do other things.

Being up here in Santa Fe, when I was working at the O'Keeffe and living in Nambé, on the road to Chimayó, every week we had to go to Española, to El Parasol, and have the burrito with either green or red chile, extra chile. If I didn't get that every week, I was missing out.

Krista: What kind of food did you grow up with?

Fig. 16. Laura Gilpin (1891–1979). Studio of Georgia O'Keeffe overlooking Chama Valley, 1960. Gelatin silver print. 7 ⅝ x 9 ⅝ in. Amon Carter Museum of American Art, Fort Worth, Texas. Bequest of the artist. p1979.108.469. © 1979 Amon Carter Museum of American Art.

Audrey: I grew up with lots of different kinds of food. My mother was a really committed cook. She was the kind of cook who watched Julia Child and would try anything. She learned how to make great tomato sauce from her neighbor downstairs who was an immigrant from southern Italy and always welcomed her into her house. She would make lasagna.

My mother still talks about when we spent a year in France, when I was young, because my father was on sabbatical. She would go to the markets there and buy cauliflower that when you cut it open the water is dripping out of it, it's so fresh. My mother had a real appreciation for fresh food. She was a good cook. We always enjoyed eating. But we did not eat chile!

Krista: Your father was a professor? Does that mean you grew up inside of institutional contexts related to universities?

Audrey: Loosely. He was a math professor and also a serious bassoon player and my mother was a violist, amateur. My grandfather was a pianist and piano teacher and traveled all around, trying to make a living.

Krista: Were there symphonies? Small chamber orchestras? Was there an institutional context for music? I'm thinking through the sites where we get the urge . . . for particular locations.

I grew up in a business family that was, I might say, deinstitutionalized. As a young woman, I didn't think of myself as belonging to an organization or cause. "The world" was either the beach or places I had explored or wanted to go, or the world of business. The university is a place organized around people who are committed to a mission, not around making money. Whatever you want to say about the limits of educational institutions, they are not organized around making money. That's not the formal mission. For me, university life was a move to a structure or mission from a way of living that did not have a structure or mission. Or the structure was personal, for personal gain.

But it sounds to me like you grew up around structures of many kinds.

Audrey: Yeah. My family was not in business. We were teachers, artists. One grandfather was a surgeon. Another grandfather was a pianist. There were lawyers, professional people who were dedicated to causes. One, generations back, was a congressman. Another was an early trustee of the University of Chicago. One grandmother studied art at Cooper Union and played harp; her grandmother was also an artist and musician who settled in Wabaunsee County, Kansas. And there were writers. People dedicated to their work and associated with institutions, not part of a firm or business organization. Business is foreign to me.

But you know, necessary, to be familiar with and [Krista laughs] you know, to manage in the world.

Krista: Are you one of these children like Marilynne Robinson, *When I Was a Child I Read Books*?

Audrey: I read a lot of books.

Krista: Did you have a favorite? Did you have like a little study in your room? A special place?

Audrey: I had my own room. I don't have any siblings. If I wasn't going to be reading, I had to find another way to entertain myself. Reading was a big part of my life. I loved a lot of classic novels. I read all the Louisa

May Alcott books many times. I read the *Little House on the Prairie* series. I would start at the beginning and read them all through several times. I read the Brontes. In high school, I had a wonderful poetry teacher. I read lots of poets: Whitman. I read Dickinson, I read Stevens, I came to love Tennessee Williams and Eugene O'Neill. I had great teachers.

Krista: Shall we talk about feminism? In this project, everyone is dedicated to place studies or western studies. We work through different feminist frameworks. You've worked explicitly through feminist points of departure—the new piece in Susan Bernardin's book[4] for instance. But unless we specifically ask ourselves how we embody "feminism" in relation to place, land, the question often seems to slip away, elude us.

Audrey: My way of thinking through feminism comes from poets and artists. From Adrienne Rich, who was such an important poet for me early on. I studied poetry, I wrote poetry. And her statements, about locational poetics and what it is to be located in a body, in a family, in a sexuality, working through that in the language of poetry. And Gloria Anzaldúa's writings, which are enacted. Her feminism is put into action through her poetry but also is theorized and a matter of reflection. That's a model for feminist action through writing.

I also had powerful teachers, professors, advisors, and now colleagues. But not through feminist theory on its own terms.

Krista: Is there a conversation you'd like to have that we haven't touched on?

Audrey: I'm interested in how this project has shifted in the process of doing the interviews. What had you imagined and wanted it to be when you started, and how have the people you've brought in, and the conversations you've had, fulfilled that or shifted your sense of what it's going to be?

Krista: I didn't have a grand picture of what it would be, coming in. I missed people, because of COVID. One of my sisters liquidated a retirement account during COVID. She said, "I'm going to spend some of this money." I was like, "Well, she's got a lot more money than I do. But I'm going to liquidate something too." So we bought this van. We needed a reason to use it.

Audrey: It's a COVID van.

Krista: Yeah! And my children don't live at home anymore, so we had that new liberty. What has happened I wouldn't say it's been . . . happenstance. Because I have taken care with the structure of things, and the tone. But something has come about by unconscious design. Right out of the gate, our relations with people were so heartening. We are meeting outside of departments or conference contexts. The project opened something different. It has produced well-being, for me and for others.

Audrey: One of the things I love about WLA and the people who keep coming back is that there's this desire to recognize the value of our institutional work but also work outside of it. We are all interested in being in that in-between space. As you say, doing academic work is weirdly disembodied, because of where you have to be.

Krista: All of the institutions we are in are struggling to define why humanities should be funded. We are trying to convert what we know to share with people who are not going to have conversations in a way we would as scholars. And not sacrifice the sophistication of concepts as a way to engage the public, but rethink how we talk about what we do. Can we say things about ourselves, use personal narrative, for instance?

Look at writers. I'm with a lot of writers at Rice and elsewhere. They talk a lot about themselves in relation to their work, and their work in relation to their lives. They're trained to talk about themselves, and they know how to do it. It's not shooting from the hip. It's curated.

Audrey: Sure, absolutely.

Krista: I would like scholars to be able to do that better. One of the things that I could imagine for our project is having a follow-up symposium where we could talk about writing across genres, which makes everybody nervous. If we don't know what we're doing, this should make us nervous. We shouldn't talk off the cuff about things we're not prepared to stand up and say. I've done that at WLA, when I wasn't prepared for the feelings that came up. I don't think that kind of overvulnerability does anyone any good. Writers do have that experience happen to them, overvulnerability. They also handle it well, actually.

Audrey: I've just come to Sante Fe from San Marcos, Texas, where I was part of a group of contributors to a scholarly volume about the writing of Sandra Cisneros. In San Marcos we were talking about the difference that Cisneros had in mind between the author, the public persona, versus the self that comes through in the writing. As scholars, I think we move between those kinds of identifications.

The questions of our personal investments become entwined with the work we do, with the institutional work we do, and also with what we publish, and what we choose to put out there. The question of the personal becomes a little more complicated. A lot of it goes into the work and gets translated into forms that are scholarly. In some cases, the forms have to do with institutional work. I've learned a lot from Susan Stanford Friedman who talks about how academic situations matter. What difference are you making in access to knowledge, or providing a structure that is equitable for women, and scholars of color and students who are first-generation students? That work matters, and it gives a space for transformation of knowledge and transformation of fields that's beyond the reach of an individual writer or an individual scholar.

Krista: I'm thinking about Stephanie LeMenager, in *Living Oil*, and her sense of that book's origin in the archives that aren't apparent—in her family mythologies and history in oil.[5] These unapparent archives seem fruitful places for us to push on.

With some of the creative writers in my department, I'm learning how to write out of a more expansive sense of archive. I'm teaching students to do it too. We are learning to write differently, to make pitches, *not* arguments. The pitch is something we as scholars don't learn.

Audrey: It's not promotion. It's like an enticement. Inviting someone to listen and be interested and want to hear more.

Krista: Yes! And it's appropriate to a general-public audience. That's how you pitch nonfiction to a trade book editor. I've been taking that seriously and training my students to not craft arguments which their parents will never understand.

Audrey: Right. They ask, "Who are you arguing with? What are you arguing against?" And then you say, "Well, it's very complicated, it's a scholarly thing." But then no one really cares outside of academia.

Krista: Taking seriously the crisis of the humanities, the need to not cordon off the knowledges we have for some small group of people. And to train students in ways that take seriously that we have things to offer. Can we cross the town/gown divide? What skills does it take to do so? It seems to me it takes skills of not restraining ourselves in such disciplined ways.

At the end, can I ask about an early memory of something "feminist?"

Audrey: An early memory. I think of my family of strong women and unconventional women, and women who have chosen not to conform in lots of ways. That was definitely true of my mother, who cared about music and who wore Levi's and a chamois shirt every day of her life. She ran marathons. More than anything she loved her time in New Hampshire on Lake Winnipesaukee and the freedom of skinny-dipping in the lake and playing music and doing what she wanted to do.

That was a deep part of my childhood.

My thinking and feeling about my mother and her independence changed when I was a teenager. She suffered a serious injury from a bike accident that required brain surgery. It took a few years for her to recover as fully as she could, but she was not the same person afterwards. Would she have become conscious of her feminism and acted on it if she hadn't been injured? How would she have exercised her independence as an older woman? Hard to know.

The question of her feminism, and that of my grandmothers, aunts, cousins, and other female ancestors, is complicated. I see patterns of independent placemaking, in the West and elsewhere, as well as the need to adapt to the demands of husbands and children and to move accordingly. For some, the combination of economic privilege and choice of how to live afforded great freedom—true of some women of my mother's generation and younger who became language teachers, or went back to the land in Maine and built a yurt and then left their male partner for a female partner. Or lived alone and traveled the world, or created new homes for themselves in Puerto Rico or Fiji. For others, there never seemed to be enough money for either stability or such freedoms; their mobilities were not of their choosing.

My grandmother had a very independent life, and her mother actually grew up in Denver and then came back to Boston. I have other relatives who came from the West and moved around and came back. It's a pattern that goes back many generations. On every side of my family, we moved. We were in Nebraska, Colorado, Kansas, Oklahoma—and Massachusetts, Connecticut, New York, New Jersey, Florida.

An early memory of feminism is the women who were both creating the conditions for their lives and ready to move. Because of their marriages and their families, they had to be ready to create new attachments. That's deep in my lived experience of my family, and something that I felt I had the power to learn from and shape for myself.

The Both/And, with Susan Bernardin

We meet at a café on a rainy day in Corvallis, then find a dry place in Susan's office to set up. Since 2017, Susan has been director of the School of Language, Culture, and Society, at Oregon State University. Today the campus is closed in observance of Juneteenth. Otherwise, Susan had chosen Peavy Hall, in the recently redesigned College of Forestry facility. She wanted to show us Marys Peak, the highest in the Oregon coastal range, and an installation by the Wakanim Artist Collaborative, "Things Remembered in the Flood." Wakanim translates as "many canoes." In the role of Director of the School, Susan facilitated several major hires to bring Indigenous scholars to the university.[1]

Susan and I have known one another now nearly thirty years. Family, children, health, love of Santa Cruz, job issues, and discussion of our respective fields in Indigenous and feminist studies—all source materials for commiseration. In 2018 we coedited a special issue of Western American Literature *to commemorate the fiftieth anniversary of the Western Literature Association (WLA) and think forward with hopes for the future.[2] Susan's new major undertaking* Gender and the American West *is about to appear at thirty-five essays strong.[3] No editor that is not Susan Bernardin could have brought together such disparate fields and people and then held space for coexistences as vulnerable. She is a right person to talk with about doing our work in the heart of legacies of conflict and mistrust and the need for one another as base for change.*

I have come ready to listen, but also to listen for openings that don't lead us in directions we both know too well. Susan is practiced at thinking and living some of the Living West *project's most vexed issues—issues of settler whiteness and the ways whiteness can take over a room even as one tries to displace it. Issues related to feminism and the ways so many women of color and Indigenous women remain aloof to the term and its presumed politics. And then there is "West."*

On a rainy Juneteenth in Corvallis, we talk. We talk about the Marlboro Man and Virginia Slims—you've come a long way, baby! How can it be that

cigarette ads were signposts of young white feminists coming into conscious-
ness? About the difficulty of making space for reflection, and the efficiency
culture baked into our lives.

The refrain of "both/and" emerges as a way to express how Susan lives being
a non-Indigenous person who works in Indigenous studies. Thinking about the
West ... it's impossible not to carry popular culture with you, that Marlboro
Man mythos and iconic history. It's always a both/and scenario.

"Trump's administration showed the way in which the West has its pull,
you know." Susan is talking in broad strokes. "I think about that line from
The Brief and Wondrous Life of Oscar Wao, *'No matter what you believe,*
the fukú [curse] believes in you.'"

She says: "You may not believe in the West, but the West believes in you.
It's got that gravitational pull."

"Ah, Junot Díaz," she sighs, "Another author I can't teach anymore."

The Where of Here: Oregon State University, Corvallis

Krista: Thank you, thank you—you go to Hawaiʻi in a couple days with
your family and you still made time to see us! You and I were texting a
bit before our meeting today. Any chance you want to comment on it?

Susan: It's that there's a lot of deep-seated stuff around the West, that
doesn't work its way out, maybe consciously. Then the other part of it
is thinking about what it means to be a feminist academic, a scholarly
writer of my age and generation. You're coming to terms with the very
real day-to-day efforts to carve out space.

You asked me before about an early sense of "feminism." What did I
tell you? About my mother and a friend having disagreements over the
Equal Rights Amendment. And me at ten or eleven walking the long way
home from school to evade this creepy boy on my block. On that same
street, at a different time, I was run off the road and followed into a field
by two white men in a pickup truck. One of them grinned as he tried to
run me down. I was terrified. We talked about a literary memory of a children's book I got out of the library in the third grade. The boys "gender
up" to solve the mystery at the end, and the girls are told to bake cookies.
I remember the anger.

I was remembering other instances we have talked about that seeded
my path as an academic. Some we laughed over, like the egregious

Fig. 17. "This is Kalapuyan Land" is the brainchild of Grand Ronde/Kalapuya curator-artist Steph Littlebird Fogel. Oregon State University, 2021. From Five Oaks Museum, "This is Kalapuyan Land," exhibit, September 28, 2020. Courtesy Julia Bradshaw.

Modern Language Association hotel bedroom interviews that were part of the culture. At what point did folks in the profession say, "Are you out of your fucking mind? What is this?" Instead of like, "Okay, interviews are done in hotel rooms, and you wait in the hallway till it's your turn. You go and sit in someone's bedroom and have a professional interview."

And the way in which you made that okay, in your head, as also happened when starting graduate school. The Whisper Network was "stay away from this professor and that professor," and what I wanted to do as a graduate student got circumscribed. I look back, and I'm like, "Why weren't we extending our activism that way?" We were unionizing. We were marching in the streets about the invasion of Kuwait. There was political activism among the graduate students in Santa Cruz in the early nineties. But it didn't extend in that way.

To think back and say, "Well, what was I doing to not make that happen?" For our conversation, I have been wrestling with the violences in academia, however minor they may be comparatively, and the way in which I worry I've participated in my own diminishment as a feminist academic working in these particular structures.

But not always, right? I think of becoming a tenure-track academic at University of Minnesota-Morris, finding out I was being paid less than a male colleague hired at the same time. I went to the dean, and they changed it. At Oneonta, my next appointment, the provost decided all incoming faculty would not get credited time and I had already been a tenure-track faculty for five years at Minnesota. I filed a grievance, because the dean had made a different agreement with me when I came in to the job, and I won. But at what cost to myself? In spite of that, I did not receive the same salary increases, or get the awards that male colleagues received, bestowed by all-senior-male-faculty. I could go on.

Then alongside that, not wanting to, in turn, practice harm myself on others, and the kind of inescapability of all of that together.

We don't typically afford ourselves time to reflect in this way, Krista, right? We give talks and go to conferences. But it's a sense of reckoning with oneself, reckoning with choices made and not made. And reckoning with the wreck of this Western world, where the lands are burning, the trees are dying, the oceans are warming, and the sea level is rising. Students in my Women and Natural Resources class are writing their final projects on what it means to be their age and their generation, looking to a future that is not feeling very certain. There's a reckoning around that generationally as well. That's just heavy stuff.

And I very much am aware that the *Roe v. Wade* decision is going to come out any day. And it's weighing on me in a visceral, existential way. It's another hinge moment in our country.

Krista: I appreciate everything you're saying. I want to pause on your statement about an opportunity to reflect. We are in fields [feminist and Indigenous studies] that would invite you to do that, right, supposedly. And yet, perhaps we don't do it very much.

Susan: The oppressiveness of this efficiency culture, where we're constantly going! We are in meetings, and supposed to be producing. I've virtually no time to read and write. That's, of course, self-inflicted. I'm in an administrative position that is extremely time-consuming and demanding. It's also a way I can pay it forward by taking up administrative tasks as a way for other faculty to focus on writing and teaching. But we inhabit a culture that is hell-bent on keeping us from reflecting. It's baked into mainstream U.S. culture: drive-through, go-go, don't take vacation. And that productivity model has led us to this reckoning moment that we're in.

Krista: Let's talk about the where of here, have a conversation about place, where we belong and where we don't. Where are we?

Susan: Academics are a weird lot. Our jobs routinely take us to locations that we do not have generational connections to because of the vagaries and challenges of finding positions. The question is: How do you become related to a particular place that you may, now, have no connection to? This is on top of: What does it mean to live the complexities of life in a settler colonial nation, premised on white supremacy, called the United States? How do we live in relation to land that you do not carry ancestral and cultural relationships with? How to center Indigenous ways of being in relation to place, without centering whiteness or co-opting?

This is very important work for white people because so often we end up recentering ourselves. Corvallis is a place I've lived in for under five years. I reflect a lot on this place. And it's not just because I am always thinking about land acknowledgments, about how you live those land acknowledgments. These are Kalapuya homelands. Our new colleague David Lewis is the first tenure-track Kalapuya faculty member at Oregon State. Descendants of the peoples forcibly removed from what is now called Corvallis are still here of course, and descendants are members of the Confederated Tribes of Siletz Indians whose reservation is by the coast, and the Confederated Tribes of Grand Ronde, whose reservation is located west of Salem.

I live those questions, I would say every day, in my life and in my work. What does that mean, to live in a place, a different iteration of "the West," which is the Willamette Valley, and the particular histories of the Willamette Valley? Of course, Oregon's histories of anti-Blackness and anti-Indigeneity flow through the state's history, from its founding as an explicitly white state, through the termination era of the 1950s. Reckoning with those histories, it's always on my mind.

We are meeting in my office here in the School of Language, Culture, and Society because it is raining and cold. It is Juneteenth Celebration; the buildings are locked. I had wanted to bring you to the Peavy Forestry Building—it's both an inside and outside space, a stunning architectural work. The design offers amazing views of Marys Peak, the highest peak in the coastal range. It's become a site of collaboration between the Grand Ronde and local environmental groups to rename waterways and other landmarks through their original Kalapuya names.[4] There is a great video about it with David Harrelson, Cultural Resources Department Manager at the Confederated Tribes of Grand Ronde.[5]

I'm still very much learning how to orient myself. There's just so many Wests in the one. To me, it always begins with the homelands that you're working or residing on, and reflecting on what that means and how you practice relationality. That's the where of here, and of the West, in terms of how I live, and work, and where I'm trying to make a bit of a difference.

The practice of "positionality," a cornerstone of feminism, means trying to be accountable to the histories that have made my being in this place possible, and how to be an accountable ally, colleague, community member.

Krista: Can you talk about places you feel you belong, or are at home, or do not feel at home? I acknowledge the layers of this question for people so aware that our lives are conducted in lands that are previously inhabited, inhabited now, and, in any case, stolen. With those acknowledgments in play, I want to hear more about you growing up near the New Hampshire coast and about "the rock." We have talked about the meaning of this rock to you, ways the rock came back to you. Because it records a child's moment in which there isn't an awareness of other inhabitations, or other accountabilities. One inhabits it as though the world is as it should be.

I wondered if you would talk about that rock in New Hampshire, the history of it.

Susan: I didn't grow up in New Hampshire. I grew up in Massachusetts, but I spent summers in New Hampshire and I still go to this beach, Rye Beach. New Hampshire has only eighteen miles of Atlantic coastline, not what you think of as "coast" in New England, like Maine or the Cape.

My story of the rock is about continuity and change, the paradox of continuity through change, and change through continuity. As someone who descends from immigrants, from Ireland and French Canadians, who have a more complex ancestry, I would say that the only place that I have experienced intergenerational continuity is that beach, Rye Beach. Because my mother and father both grew up going there beginning in the 1930s (for my father) and the 1940s (for my mother), without knowing each other. There'd be big family groups coming from the French Canadian side who came down from Quebec in the end of the nineteenth century and settled in those French Canadian communities of Lawrence.

I'm struck by the continuity of the place. Only in recent years, before and following the death of my father, I've seen it in all these old family photographs I've found. The houses. The beach is instantly recognizable, at eighty to a hundred-plus years' remove. Minute in geologic time and lived history in this settler place. Photographs tell me that my paternal great-grandfather's large French Canadian family came up to New Hampshire from the Lawrence area for beach visits. That tradition must have been carried on by my paternal grandfather, Eugene, too, because family photographs of my father and his siblings, usually with dogs, show many summers in the 1930s onward at the beach.

It's the same beach, and it's fascinating to me, because it looks the same. Even some of the houses are still there. It's immediately recognizable. The land, the rocks, and the shape of the beach. And that large rock—it's striking the large rock is still there. Also, it's not very large. Even though we call it "big rock."

I remember playing there as a child, falling, scraping my knee on its barnacles, and taking my daughters down there to play in the sea water trapped around it at low tide. A great rock for sitting on, despite the barnacles.

When my older daughter was four and my younger daughter a year and a half, I went back to that rock on a much-dreamed visit the summer of my "chemo year." I had spent months before that so weak and wracked by pain that I would meditate for hours on Rye Beach and that rock.

It's an anchor, pun intended, a memory anchor for me. I've always loved the ocean, in all its myriad and endless iterations of shape, smell, location, and being. I think that's just deep-seated stuff. I love the ocean. Anywhere I go, it's always where I want to be.

Krista: [Big breath.] Wow. Thank you. Thank you for that.

I hoped to think a minute with you about another place I've heard you talk about. And about people, who live on and near the Salmon and Klamath Rivers. It was a discussion of places we don't belong, where we know we don't belong, and how is it for us to be in those places.

Susan: Yes. Karuk Tribe homelands. Specifically the center of the Karuk world, at the confluence of the Salmon and Klamath Rivers, are very special. I've been there many times, and it's inspirited, you can feel it. It's beautiful.

Phone lines weren't even in till the 1970s. It's a two-hour drive from Yreka and two-hour drive from Eureka, on the coast. You have to know how to take care of yourself up there because it's so far to get to stores and whatever else. Auntie Violet Super, a fluent elder whom I was fortunate to spend time with over a period of years, told me that once you go in the Salmon River, you always have to come back. That area attracted white hippies in the 1960s, who had a commune. There's a number of organic farms and the area has attracted a lot of cannabis operations, unfortunately, that are messing with the Klamath River.

And of course, the Klamath River has been extremely challenged by damming—the most visible sign is the collapse of the salmon population in the river, catastrophic for Klamath River tribes' well-being and livelihoods. The final steps in the restoration of the river through un-damming are happening now, the result of decades of advocacy and coalition-building.[6] That will be transformative, it should really improve water quality, reduce fish disease, reopen spawning habitat. Right now, it's a really struggling river.

I feel a strong sense of kinship to that place. And a recognition that I'm not from that place, nor do I belong to that place.

Krista: Can we talk about what those feelings are, beyond—if it's possible—our practiced "aware" ways of thinking? How it is to be in place, as white feminists, or as white people, however you might characterize the outsider-ness? Maybe you wouldn't use those terms. How it is to be asked, for instance, as you were as a young woman, to attend ceremony?

Susan: As a companion and to help take some elders to the ceremony, my position is I wouldn't say no, if I'm asked, but I try to avoid situations where there's a sense that I am asking to be present.

I wouldn't want to overthink this. This isn't some existential thing. It happened when I was much younger, and some elders were alive who I was spending time with. I was spending more time in that community. How one feels in one's twenties and how one feels now are different. Back then, I don't think I had the toolkit I have now to sit with that feeling of betweenness. I have it much better now.

I am who I am. Back then, it was the fear of being misunderstood as someone who was being a prying interloper. Because of the history of outsiders coming in, the history of academic extractive colonialism and the very subjects I was writing about, the fear was there might be a way I was replicating those relations. I was doing a new introduction to *In the Land of the Grasshopper Song*, first published in 1957, by two field matrons who spent two years on the Klamath River in 1908 and 1909, promoting Bureau of Indian Affairs policies of assimilation.[7] In the late 1990s and early 2000s, when I spent a lot of time there, sometimes I was referred to as "that grasshopper song lady," referencing the field matrons who wrote that book, and whose work I was writing about. I thought it was hilarious. You know, it's like, the schoolmarm! You got to have a really good sense of humor about yourself. Don't take things too seriously.

But yeah, you announce yourself. I am "out," you know, in my otherness and difference, in spaces like that. And given how violent that history has been, I am not wanting, in any way intentionally or inadvertently or otherwise, to make people uncomfortable. There is a balance and the worry, as an outsider coming in, that you are changing the molecules in the room by your very presence. You mitigate harm, as much as you can.

The question is what does it mean to be not just implicated but to be agents, as the field matrons were, of cultural genocide? And yet, in that space, trying to make shifts. If you are situating them in a form of messy relationality, are you trying to justify or overly contextualize the matrons being there? Really, at the end of the day, they shouldn't have been there.

I have thought about this question for decades. The field matrons were there because of federal Indian policy and programs. They were there specifically to advance cultural genocide through assimilation. Yet, the book they produced documented and affirmed that Karuk people had survived genocide across Northern California in the 1800s, and were carrying on and through despite ongoing assaults. Boarding schools, land and water dispossession, mining despoilation.

In related ways, Indigenous communities and tribal nations across California have used recordings and field notes to reconstruct and reawaken ceremonies, technologies like canoes, and languages. You have all these sound recordings from anthropologists in California, from which Indigenous communities have been resuscitating sleeping languages, languages considered extinct. So is the fact that that book *In the Land of the Grasshopper Song*, which is full of treasured family stories, right? It's gossipy and juicy, it's valuable. But what's the trade-off? Which is also that constitutive question of whether you undo systemic structures from within the institution, the university? Or are you simply doing service work? I am always inhabiting the contradictions.

Krista: One of the questions that you ask about the field matrons, as agents of cultural genocide, and that we could ask about positions inside of institutions that are compromised in so many ways, is: what is the possibility of relationality? Can there be hope in relations so implicated in genocidal histories? Is there anything recoverable?

Susan: I've always been interested in relationships across difference— and I have to believe it's possible. I do think about the question of recuperability or repairability, and I think it is a "both/and." Consider an example of "both/and" from my workplace. Oregon State is Oregon's land grant institution. It was purchased with funds from expropriated (aka stolen) Indigenous homelands in southern Oregon. The university has adopted a land acknowledgment and that's a step towards relationality— some would say performative relationality. But what follows from that? What about land back? OSU is forty-five minutes from the Indian boarding school Chemawa, which is still operating!

The horror and violence of these histories, their ongoing impacts of gendered colonialism on Indigenous communities, must be reckoned with, which is why I keep going back to the story of the grasshopper book and its afterlives. Maybe I keep reckoning with irresolvability. But I must hold on to the imperative of relationality as an ongoing set of commitments that shift. Being hyperaware of my positionality can be a tool—also it can be a trap, sliding into recentering whiteness.

One can practice stealth feminist anti-racist advocacy in certain spaces, right? That's really important. There's just not a lot of Indigenous folks in the academy, right? Or BIPOC faculty more broadly. So what's the role of allies? Where can you make moves and shift, either via stealth or confrontationally, in different kinds of spaces? Where do you step back, and where do you step in?

A cluster hire we just did, three new Indigenous faculty—I sent you the announcement.[8] We will have an Indigenous studies minor. But I am often in all-white spaces in administrative meetings. I'm hyperaware of that. I'm not always sure other folks in the meeting are as hyperaware, because we don't discuss it. It's bumpy as hell. You will have limited capacities to make shifts. But I'm mindful that I have a responsibility in those spaces, to advance institutional transformation.

ROAD FINDS
Falling Rocks

On the summit of Mesa Verde's flat-top mountains, a great hum of life governs the skies and land. José and I hold hands and walk about quietly, looking out one mesa past another in a receding horizon of mesas. We read that Mesa Verde, as ancestral home, is visited by the twenty-six Affiliated Tribes of Mesa Verde.[1] Among them are the Southern Ute and the Ute Mountain Ute, who, along with the Arapahoe and Comanche, came to make lives in lands that were colonized and renamed Pueblo, Colorado, where I was born.

Then the news breaks of the *Dobbs* decision. *Roe v. Wade* has been overturned.

It is June 24, morning. I am in Far Lodge on the bottom floor where there is internet capacity. I grab the edge of a heavy worktable. I hear reports later from a stunned Cecile Richards, former president of Planned Parenthood and a fellow Texas feminist. No amount of expecting *Roe* to be overturned and preparing others for danger ahead safeguards this moment when rocks finally crash down the mountain. José and I have a colleague's workshop lined up and plan to go, and after, to walk about Mesa Verde's historic cliff dwellings. The workshop leader changes opening remarks to address what is officially a post-*Roe* moment. Reeling, furious, I think about the *Living West* project as we move toward the last few interviews.

José encourages me to write my thoughts down now.

We have entered an emergency for women's health, economic viability, safety, psychological well-being, and futures. It's *been* an emergency for many women, many people, now it's worse. Every part of women's and girls' lives have relations to reproductive processes because being raised female in this country requires navigating expectations imposed by all the institutions enforcing gender norms. The most vulnerable of women, by race, class, age, and geography, will suffer the worst of targeting. Impacts on Native American women, and women living in tribal lands who already face barriers to access, accelerate colonial attacks on Indigenous women's bodies and sovereignty.[2] Families and men and nonbinary people and trans men are affected. But women and girls are 99 percent of the constituency whose bodies are direct targets of state and federal policing forces. White women's access to whiteness as a source of social currency will not disappear because of *Dobbs*, though other factors—education, economic status, religion, existing family responsibilities, and again geography (region, rurality/urbanity)—inflect how whiteness will be lived under it.

Amid calls to follow new leadership at the helm of the Women's Marches, and amid white women's complacency and/or fraught reckonings with whiteness, can white feminists keep our wits about us, not become paralyzed by histories of our blind spots and by what we know will be uneven impacts? Can we carry our own water, so to speak, shoulder our thinking in the liberation fights of now while also taking leadership from people we are trained to second-guess?

This moment of *Dobbs*, as I see it, needs widespread consciousness-raising about the economic and patriarchal stakes of controlling women's reproductive lives. Isn't it obvious by now there is a need to take seriously the history of reproductive labor as a foundation of wealth accumulation for capitalism?[3] Too often structural analyses neglect women's reproductive labor as historical sources of amassing wealth. Not to homogenize "women's reproductive labor" as a universally exploitable group. No. Reproductive capacities are exploitable in disgustingly myriad ways. Capitalism profits from hierarchies of race and *Dobbs* is underwritten by a Supreme Court and particular state leaders whose patriarchal politics mesh with those profits and with ethnonationalist white supremacy.

White supremacy would have us forget histories of enslaved women whose children create wealth for enslavers. Or forget involuntary sterilizations of African American, Native, and Latinx women. White feminists have needed to learn, and keep remembering, the distinction between rights and justice. Reproductive justice is about far more than being "pro-choice."[4] But the divisiveness of the politics of abortion has occluded and confused the distinction. I remember the moment I first learned this distinction, in Nicaragua, from Nicaraguan women. It was 1985 but this is not a one-time lesson. I have needed to learn again, and learn more about where settler wealth in this country comes from. Indigenous land theft, labor theft, and slavery. *And* the exploitation of women's reproductive capacity. Because settler colonialism is a family affair. It spreads by reproducing majority white settler populations, supplanting Indigenous often matrilineal kin systems with heteropatriarchal law. The figure of the "pioneer" white woman in a poke bonnet raising hearty frontier offspring is a stealth engine propelling Manifest Destiny.

White heteropatriarchy, like settler colonialism, is a structure, not an event.

In my own family history, on my mother's side, the Renfrows from Scotland, then Kentucky and then Missouri, tell of a family of brothers who, one after another, come further West and are, the notebooks say, "killed by the Indians." Likely the brothers had womenfolk with them trekking West, family. Who were these women? Would they have become like my grandmother, no-nonsense, raised in an orphanage, business-minded, tirelessly upwardly mobile? I have more digging to do to find out. Accounting for our histories as white women means not taking up the racial privilege to look away.

For much of the 1990s and into 2000s, I remember many white women using this phrase: "I'm just a white girl." "Oh, I'm a white girl." The phrase meant: I have no history, I'm bland, "white bread." It implied my legacy is not worthwhile, I renounce it, or, perhaps, I don't know my history. It was a disclaimer I heard delivered from the podium at academic conferences; it was half-humor, half-apology. I had a couple of graduate school friends who said, "Oh, I'm a white girl," then shrugged. The attempt was to decenter whiteness and white women in discussions about non-white racial oppression and colonial histories. I did not like women speaking about themselves in miniaturized girly form—though what was being reduced, it was understood, was the "white" part. Was the shrug about shame, a mandate to shut up attached to the decentering of whiteness? Was it a feeble effort to signal "I support women of color" and a willingness to give the spotlight to "them"? Half-humor likely masked an awkward cluelessness about how else to represent or even betray the racial situation one has inhabited, still inhabits. I remember being inarticulate about my discomfort, I didn't know how else to speak about myself, and wouldn't talk about my history anyway. Every hard thing that went into not wanting to speak about where I came from was also something that needed figuring out.

Today I see better how attention to place and placemaking helps deconstruct the settler unconscious of the United States and redirect what colonialism has put in motion. José and I have repeatedly said to one another as we drive around, "Everywhere we go is Indian country," because the fact sinks in again and again. Place-based methodology offers everyone, but especially white people and white feminists, a place to start and a method to uncover our histories to ourselves. By locating ourselves in place, across places, digging into history and memory, we stop expunging what we need to find out to grapple with the specificities of settler life and behavior. We find details that tell us about the where, the when, the who and how. Placing ourselves goes against the invisibilities and forgetting of whiteness and the way it lives without having awareness. If privilege is an ability to not look, not learn, not ask, not remember, placemaking acts as interventionist pedagogy where one interrupts the privilege of unconsciousness, the taken-for-grantedness of settler presence and mobility.

Since leaving Oregon and our time with Susan Bernardin, and leaving the memorial for my cousin Beau in Bend whose children, I find out, are enrolled members of Tolowa Dee-Ni' nation, I have felt more personally than ever my implication in the violence of settler history. Why am I only now coming to know this about Beau's children? There is more to learn about them and also my old friend Tom Richmond, who talks about himself today as Tututni and who I knew well years ago when I lived with him and his mother across the Umpqua River.[5] Such reserve about Indigeneity governed those earlier moments, it seems, though their connections to the land and water was so obviously different and appealing than anything I had been around before. It showed me a way to be that has never left me.

On the day of the *Dobbs* decision, we walk into ancient cliff dwellings, marveling. We eat dinner looking out on the mesas. I feel so many histories of this land. In this high place where human voices are small, it's tempting to feel outside of history. It makes no sense to feel outside of history since Mesa Verde is devoted to Indigenous histories and all of the national parks are monuments to settler history. Perhaps this feeling is a ghostly trace of whiteness, and of white ideas about nature as "natural" and/or wilderness?

The night of the *Dobbs* decision, the moon is a waning crescent, 18 percent illumination, and the stars hang incomparably close and thick. I have never seen a "dark sky" night. Mesa Verde is the center of the darkest skies in the United States, and it feels like it! The night sky, in 2022 we read, is much like the night sky observed a thousand years ago by the ancestral Pueblo. How such a thing is possible across history is impossible to comprehend. I am again tempted by settler ghosts, this time to imagine that the night sky here links us across time to cliff dwellers. Isn't that a kind of settler science, collapsing into the interim all the centuries of history that can never add up? Perhaps it's better not to imagine us as linked. I am not them. I am here now, with José, in a place that humbles us.

Returning to Pueblo as Myself, with Krista Comer

The Sangre de Cristo Arts Center is the immediate where of here, a place mean-ingful for Pueblo and for me. We set ourselves up in front of a colorful mosaic of inlaid polished stone. Each stone names a distinguished leader or board member of the arts center's complex of galleries, performance theater, and children's museum. I come from these people up on the wall, Helen White, Kathy Farley, Bob Jackson. The stories of their lives and aspirations are part of how my family tells about our Pueblo.

Fig. 18. Donor Patrons, Sangre de Cristo Arts Center, Pueblo. Courtesy José Aranda.

This time, coming to Pueblo, I wanted to enter town not from memory but from an intention to arrive as myself today. We talk ourselves to exhaustion about what's different this visit versus last, talk in the shadow of a fallen Roe, *touching on issues of violence against women and directions for feminism right now. I am trying to take stock of settler legacies, subjecting memory to fact and that distance turns up unexpected angles for seeing the borders of a polite childhood.*

Again, José does the interviewing honors.

The Where of Here: The Sangre de Cristo Arts Center

José: Good morning. It's June 30. We've been seeing the sights and taking in what has changed for you about visiting Pueblo. I think it might be good to have you talk about the where of here, Round Two.

Krista: Thanks! We've been, and I've been on a journey within a journey since we left Bend. Right now, we are at the Sangre de Cristo Arts Center and Conference Center in front of this art piece. It commemorates leaders of Pueblo, people I knew or my parents knew when I was growing up.

We're here, basically in the heart of settler wealth. For much of my young life, I was close to Helen Thatcher White, who provided seed money for this arts center, and for other ventures in town. People called her "Sitty." I loved Sitty as a child. I loved her into my twenties when she died. She was close to my aunt Adrian. They lived together more than twenty years in a home on, yes, Comanche Road. There was a lot of whispering about them I would come to find out: what kind of living together did they do? Growing up I didn't wonder anything. I took at face value that Sitty was family. My aunt thought of her and lived with her as family. My aunt took care of her until the end, and I would come to Pueblo as a young adult to see how things were going.

I came here to the arts center because Sitty was a collector of Taos painters and art of the West. She gave a major gift to the Center that built the gallery space for the Francis King Western Art Collection. Some of its paintings include pieces from her collections. She was a Thatcher, banking money. She had been married and her husband died relatively young. Her sons, in particular the older son Butch, carried on the business, the Minnequa Banks. We are talking about empire kind of wealth—banking, railroads, utilities, ranching, mining.

I think of myself as linked to this arts center through Sitty and my aunt Adrian and their homes. They had Remingtons and Sharps hanging on the walls, all of them Sitty's paintings. Eventually they hung stuff in a colorful mountain place called "The Getaway" in Colorado City where we went to visit as kids in the summers. It has a lake and we'd take out paddleboats. Before I knew what "a Remington" or "a Sharp" was, I was schooled in the aesthetics of Western landscape, and I love them. I can't "unmix" those earlier parts of me and my history from who I am today.

José, you and I have talked about Randi Tanglen and her reflections about whiteness, and her Mennonite family homesteading on the Fort Peck Indian Reservation. Randi talks about Joanna Brooks, who writes about Mormon girlhood. And Randi's friend the poet Mandy Smoker, who she meets as an adult—from the Fort Peck tribe. Like Randi, I can't unmix the generosities and goodwill of my people from the oppressiveness. You told me it's probably better to keep looking at the mix than to turn away. That has to be right.

Last summer you and I were out on the Beulah Road, in prairie country, near the home of my grandparents when I was a child. You interviewed me and I talked about how the picture window of that gorgeous house had taught me and framed for me an aesthetic of Western landscape perception. It goes to the heart of what my work has been about as a scholar but also who I am as someone from the U.S. West. Which is to say someone with an unconscious way of looking and being that are settler ways of perceiving land and place. As a young scholar, I came to understand unpeopled landscape as a landscape ideology. Scholars weren't talking yet about settler landscapes. I made a point to have the cover of my first book, *Landscapes of the New West*, contradict the idea of a "beautiful landscape" by picturing trailer parks and urban Los Angeles. When I advertise my classes at Rice, the posters can't be "natural landscapes," removed of people. They can't be anything "exotic."

José: And here at the Sangre de Cristo Center, what are you thinking?

Krista: It's a surprise to realize how much of the arts center is a story of women's leadership and collaboration. I had such an attitude growing up about "these kinds" of women and their notions of leadership! Junior League women like my mother who "volunteered." I'm not sure, looking back, that I knew much about them. I knew my mother, but I didn't really know the other women she considered friends. The stone at the top of the mosaic recognizes Kathy Farley, the Center's founder with her friend and the other founder, Pat Kelly. Who I think was eventually her partner, after Farley divorced. In a recent video, she talks about the Center as it celebrated its fiftieth anniversary.[1] Quite an accomplishment, I see now. As a younger person, all I could see was women's focus on manners and on Charity Balls announced in the society pages of the local newspaper. Their judgments of one another. In my own family, I had to fight the organizations my mother wanted to me to join—cotillion, doing volunteer work with an organization that was society girls in training. No way was I going to do that.

Before today, what I remembered from early teen years was a scary story from my mother about a terrible assault against Kathy Farley. Her husband at the time was in Congress, and he'd been involved in a reprimand of police for using the N-word in confidential conversation and reports. The case got attention, press; at the state capitol, there were Black protests. In retribution, someone slashed the N-word into the back of Kathy's legs, knocked her out on her back porch and carved the word on her legs. I remember the story as hushed, the way my mother told it. Though it wasn't secret, as I thought it was, I looked into it and found reporting in the *New York Times*.[2] The details scared my mother. This was a very angry guy. She said the women friends also worried: had Kathy been raped? We had moved to San Francisco by the time it happened (1970). But my mom was home visiting. She went to see Kathy in the hospital. There were guards posted to the door. Afterward, my mom got a visit from the police. Had Kathy told her something? I don't think they ever got him.

Imagine living with that. But Kathy Farley didn't let herself be shut down. Imagine. Lots of women of the early 1970s era of women's liberation didn't allow themselves to be shut down. Farley was the most well-known of the women who ultimately got the Center up and running. All of them motivated each other in building projects, fundraising for these art collections, making Pueblo a "cultured place." Plus, she was raising four children!

José: That story is so provocative, and it goes to the larger stakes of this project. From battling systemic racism, to politically motivated violence against women, to high culture. I'm hearing a story about violence against women which makes me think of the unfortunate disastrous decision a week ago from the Supreme Court to dismantle the last vestiges of *Roe*. How has this news affected the way you are thinking about what's at stake as you go visit your feminist colleagues?

Krista: I've been listening to people, in our project, and generally, on the road. You say women talk to me—it's true. I never thought about it, but you noticed all kinds of women on the road just tell me stuff, like that woman owner of the motel in Colorado Springs, complaining about her husband.

In our project, it's clear everyone wants distance from "white feminism"—the women of color, Indigenous women, and white feminists. Everyone is worried about feminism being colonized by "white feminism." So that's one thing I'm thinking about as we go visit people. To keep pursuing conversations about whiteness so it doesn't sabotage us. Race is a collective question for us, a problem to navigate.

Everybody in the interviews also talks about care—not as a problem, but as a presence in their lives. Care work happens inside of family, of family relations to land. Care is done as institutional work and as reconciliation. From the white women, care has to do with a lot of worry about histories of harm and injury, not wanting to take up all the space in the room because of "whiteness molecules." Chicana and Black feminists talk about family and family histories and reproducing those histories, but aside from structures of white supremacy or Spanish settler legacies. Attention to land and to place is expressed as care work. Caring for the land and relations it holds.

But to come to the question about *Dobbs* is, I think, very tough. I can speak to maybe how I want to think about reproductive justice, which is not the same as potential action. Many of us in this project have an analysis of how wealth is built—through expropriation of labor and of personhood, you dehumanize people when you enslave them so you can use them for financial gain. So there's an analysis of wealth built into white power. There's another analysis, settler analysis, about the expropriation of land and land speculation as forms of building wealth and of making the settlers into "natives;" the elimination of or the assimilation of Native people such that the settlers become "native." This is, as you know, baseline settler colonial theory.

One of the things that *Dobbs* is making me think about in terms of public conversations is putting forward a third source of wealth building—the historical theft of reproductive labor from women by virtue of making it free, unpaid, in the realm of "private" life, or the "natural order," and therefore available without expense to capital as it was gaining momentum historically.

José: Right, we've been talking about this. This reading of where we get wealth reframes any simple notion of violence against women.

Krista: Yes! In materialist feminist analysis, the work of reproducing humanity is understood to be extremely valuable. Not only biological reproduction, but the broader work of reproducing and caring for the social order. Social reproduction. The end of *Dobbs* is a moment for an analysis of women's reproductive labor and social care as sources of wealth for capitalism and colonialism worldwide.

This is not a very public-facing conversation, maybe, but perhaps capitalism is more on the table these days? I see a lot of Black activism after the murder of George Floyd, a lot of younger people's activism, like the group SURJ (Stand Up for Racial Justice), that speak explicitly about capitalism as a draining force, predatory. Or the term "grind culture," as a way young Black activists talk about capitalist work demands. Understanding women's reproductive capacity as a wealth-source of capitalism, and putting care work more at the center of activist thought and struggle, would strengthen a collective sense of the major problems as well as the solutions they require.

Another reframe is needed, and it's controversial. To claim "women's rights" or reproductive justice for "women and girls" and not be scared off or silenced by worries that this use of "women," by definition, is transphobic or anti-trans or essentialist. Women are the bull's-eye of this assault, let's not soft-pedal the misogyny. The volatility of public opinion about claiming the problems for women, that it's politically retrograde to make the claim, is really concerning. A friend and former Rice postdoc, Carly Thomsen—you remember Carly . . .

José: Of course!

Krista: Carly has been working as a queer theorist on why LGBTQ+ reproductive justice advocates should retain "women" rather than move to "pregnant people" as a language of activist inclusion. She's just done a piece in *Ms.* magazine.[3] She shows that sex-neutral language (the language of "people") hides the sexism of abortion bans, which harms not only pregnant women but also trans men and nonbinary people. Trans men, while they may not identify as women, face discrimination because of being assigned female at birth. She draws on Loretta Ross and Rickie Solinger, both important to thinking that reframed pro-choice politics into reproductive justice.[4] Ross talks about rhetorics of "inclusion" as analogous to "color-blind" arguments about race. They sidestep consciousness about race and racism. Carly has also done an opinion piece on fake Crisis Pregnancy Centers, "CPCs," with graphs and stats, for the *New York Times*.[5] The work is public and very good.

I'm also in mind of Jia Tolentino's piece about the criminalization of pregnancy, in the recent *New Yorker*.[6] She's from Houston, by the way. Criminalizing pregnancy is part of this conversation about violence against women which works by subjecting not only pregnant women to surveillance and legal peril but also anyone who comes into contact with pregnancies that don't go "normally." So doctors, family, medical staff, pharmacies. The surveillance isolates women in medical or health trouble from allies. That's what abusers do: isolate women.

In terms of a public-facing message, the work of the project is to create conversations, share what we can of ourselves and our challenges and our sense of U.S. West feminism. To talk from our "feminist rest areas," not absent of conflict, but with confidence that women have one another's backs. We need unity, more alliances and engaged ways of being together. Again, not without differences.

José: Right, balancing the need for outcomes while honoring difference.

Krista: The way forward must be a way that can put all the pieces of the crisis of this moment together. Whether it has to do with climate, a climate emergency, because, of course, climate emergency is about histories of colonialism, it's about dispossession, it's about "mastery" of natural resources and control of animal life for profit. What is that new book by the geographer? Oh yeah, *Pollution Is Colonialism*. The moment calls for reckonings, and a broad unity.

And I think a final thing: I'm wanting to use the phrase "coming home to whiteness." I think for white feminists, we need to come home more to our whiteness. Try to get off the ledge about it. Embrace the anxiety.

That might help to change the way in which white women do not have one another's backs—the competition, the ways in which women disable one another. Not that non-white women don't do that. But for white women it's coming from a place that— ugh, it's complicated, and we just need to give it up. To go forward under different leadership, we have to. Our power is relationality, right? Of establishing bonds of trust so that we can do work that needs doing.

José, do you have anything you'd like to say at the end? Please say something.

José: I'm reminded by your blog, which this summer began with family and family relations, that those relations are expanding the project in the sense of connectivity and possibility and futurity. I think that is very hopeful.

I think that what's so disturbing about *Dobbs* is that it goes against the grain of not just family relations, ironically, but it also licenses this deep unsettledness among many communities, especially white communities, that hurtfulness and woundedness are things to project onto others, especially Others of color. I take heart in your project and my participation in the project and your making connections.

It does seem to me that we're literally driving through parts of the country where some rationale for hurtfulness as a way of being, a way of experiencing the world, has taken very deep root. I think there is a need for not just solidarity but the task of healing, healing for everybody that we encounter. And I think that dovetails with climate change as well. The need to heal so that we understand how best to live a more sustainable life. It's an emotional time. And I'm glad I'm on the road with you on these issues.

ROAD FINDS
El Pueblo Museum

I have done no homework coming to El Pueblo Museum—just getting us here and parked in the museum lot is the goal. I have not looked up the current exhibition. My mind is in the old Pueblo of going to lunch at Magpie's with my aunt, and indeed José and I do go there and for old time's sake, order a Reuben sandwich, my aunt's favorite. I have a cringey memory of how Adrian would ask for particular small things, a half cup of coffee, she would point to where she wanted it poured in the cup. Always accustomed to each small pleasure being honored, whatever was the best Pueblo had to offer, Adrian got it.

There are two women in a booth having a gossipy conversation about their women friends, and it's agitating for me, and I ask José helplessly, "Why did we come here?"

The woman who waits on us is familiar. Tall and thin under an apron gathered at the waist. I ask, "Do you remember Adrian Comer?" She smiles broadly. "Yes! What a great bunch of ladies they were, don't make them like that anymore." I take a breath. José laughs. He knew Adrian too and went through the family visits and half-cups of coffee.

Magpie's I expect, but I didn't expect the "Borderlands of Southern Colorado" exhibition at El Pueblo Museum.[1] It's been close to forty years since the New Western History blew up the collusion of U.S. West studies with histories of conquest. I had no idea the New Western History had come home to Pueblo!

The *West as America* exhibition at the National Gallery of Art that debuted in 1991 curated a new way of seeing and talking about westward expansion, western art and artifacts. It came at the exact moment I was a graduate student in the Northeast, puzzling over how to think about California and the U.S. West. I still use that landmark *West as America* exhibition book with glossy photos, curated by William Truettner and published by the Smithsonian, as a reference in my courses on the U.S. West. I bring it out when we visit Houston's Museum of Fine Arts to see the Hudson Valley painters and especially the Remingtons of the Hogg Brothers Collection.[2]

El Pueblo Museum is an impressive example of what is possible in public history. A sign hanging from the museum rafters announces: "This is your museum. Pueblo is your community." What? I mean, that's not what the Sangre de Cristo Arts Center telegraphs. I am an "insider," even so to me it says: You are about to enter a high-art venue, so mind your manners. Put on some lipstick.

El Pueblo Museum is sited at the 1842 El Pueblo trading post on the Arkansas River, which Indigenous people called Napeste and the Spanish called Rio Nepesta. The curating voice whose words bid us enter is none other than Gloria Anzaldúa. "Borderlands are created by the emotional residue of an unnatural boundary," the placards say. Imposed divisions create "volatility."

The exhibition superimposes histories of Indigenous presence over Spanish settlement and then, later, Anglo and Black freedpeople's arrivals. It shows the centrality of southern Colorado spaces, from 1450 on, to competing battles for empire. We learn that the Comanches, commanded by Tabivo Naritgant, or Cuerno Verde to the Spanish, face off in 1779 against a combined force of Spanish, Ute, and Apache. Until then, Comanches defend lands south of modern Pueblo, but they are defeated, their commander killed, and the Comanches negotiate peace with the Spanish Empire.

On display next are sections of the original 1848 Treaty of Guadalupe Hidalgo. It lays out the end of the Mexican-American War, the move of the border of the United States to the Rio Grande in a giant land expropriation that nets, to the United States, an additional one-third of national territory. Spanish Empire has now made peace with Anglo America. One of the most consequential articles of the treaty is highlighted, Article VII, noting Mexican citizens can retain property rights and become U.S. citizens, or move to the Republic of Mexico.

Then there is a section entitled "Women of the Borderlands," and I talk to the white woman working the gift shop, who tells me she is new to Pueblo and wanted to get involved so she volunteered.[3] "Isn't the museum great? Did you see the women's history section," she asks, "about the English law of coverture? Demanding Spanish and Indigenous women surrender legal claims and property rights to their Anglo husbands! They had more rights than [white] American women," she wants me to know.

José is thrilled to find "Chicano Power" T-shirts in the gift shop. He gets black shirts for himself and our sons and a Chicana power for his sister Laura, who is holding down the watering and whatever else at home in Houston with the famous cat Amiga. We talk with a couple of the young interns, who are high school students. We're still jazzed up from the contemporary art installation and its photos. There is *Chicano Political Youth* by Juan Espinoza of Pueblo, taken during the early 1970s. And other photos—one of a younger guy, close-cut hair, wearing a hoodie with the words "Mi Raza," by Juan Fuentes of Denver. A couple of paintings hold our attention: *Nuestra Señora de Guadalupe* from Carlos Sandoval of San Luis; and a *curandera* figure, *Cosmic Seamstress* by Stevon Lucero of Denver.

At the time of my parents' departure from Pueblo to San Francisco in the mid-1960s, Chicano movement activism was heating up. Famously Corky Gonzales in Denver would support students in a local high school to stage a walkout. Their demands were for history and literature classes relevant to them, and for bilingual classes in Spanish and English. Many movement historians see Denver as the starting place of Chicano activism.[4]

I think a lot about the draw of my parents to California during the Summer of Love, their move toward a city that was the headquarters of hippies and countercultural rebellion. But in contexts of this new Pueblo I encounter in this visit, it's possible to see what else, historically, they left behind. A testy borderlands, a racial contest brewing, even if it seemed emergent, on the margins. The question of white flight comes to mind, my parents' "good instincts" for when a neighborhood was about to change, "turn." In today's Pueblo, Adrian's funeral home has been repurposed as an Evangelical church, led by Rob and Sheryl Hernandez. One of my parents' places, in Oxnard, is now *El Funeraria del Angel*.

José and I find the exhibit research team plaque and identify a number of colleague friends. We know these people, what they do, why they do it. This is the world we claim, our chosen communities. Patty Limerick, who I've known a long time, and who wrote such a great endorsement for my book *Landscapes of the New West*, is on the list as expected, which prompts me to reach out to her and make a time to visit next week in Boulder. Late in the summer, Zainab Abdali and I will do a presentation from the *Living West* project for graduate students enrolled in the Center of the American West Summer Institute program in Applied History.

What a statement the museum makes about colleagues' work turned to the public! I come out of the building with a headache because I am holding back so many tears to think this is Pueblo now. I sensed it growing up, but it was a kind of shadow, at the fringes. Maybe the "new Pueblo" of El Pueblo Museum is just new to me?

Toward the end of my aunt's life, when I returned to visit Pueblo and to visit her, it was always a challenge to figure out something to do that was wholesome for me, that did not drive me crazy. Adrian had such a beautiful house, pool, olive trees shading backyard containers of impatiens. She was an elegant cook. But to go back and spend time always required a lot of phone calls home to José for support, because of the blaring FOX News, the lunches out and agitating toxic gossip. On one of the last visits my younger son was with me, and we had gotten an upgraded car at the airport. A red Mustang. I rolled back the top and one day I thought of something authentically fun that my son and I could do with Adrian. I made a lunch for us, and bundled her up in blankets, and we drove out to Rye. We got out of the car, set the wheels of the wheelchair, and had a picnic under the trees on a wooden table. It was a great day and not the last outing, but close to it. Adrian's last outing was to get her hair done before my mother arrived.

If the timing had been right and Adrian were alive during the Southern Borderlands exhibit, I could have taken us there. I could point to the placards and to the art, and the history of women, and Jesse could explain his Chicano Power T-shirt. I could say, "Yes, we'll go to Magpie's. But first, I want to show you something."

True Confessions of a Settler Scholar, with Victoria Lamont

We cross the Canadian border during the Fourth of July weekend into farm and windmill country and arrive at Victoria's sheep farm. St. Agatha, southwestern Ontario. Victoria awaits us down a wooded drive with a couple of Border Collies heeled at her side. Later we will meet Viki Kidd, her friend and partner in herding and dog training. Her partner in life, John Straube, will fix us dinner. Right now we hear him work with a tractor throttle.

A lot of us in the Western Literature Association (WLA) have heard Victoria talk about sheep and dogs and farm life. But to be here in person, a celebration! The place feels tucked away in pastoral green, a surprise given what we are under ten kilometers from the University of Waterloo, known as the "MIT of Canada," with forty thousand students. The fifteen-hundred-mile stretch to get to St. Agatha from Pueblo is the longest we've traveled to do a single interview. José wanted to make the drive; he loves the ambition of it and of finding his friend and fellow scholar of nineteenth-century studies across the border.

A roomy farmhouse spreads out, dogs frisky to have us there but they do just as Victoria tells them, the benefits of being a dog trainer. The living area doors open onto a big wooden deck with tables and chairs and flowers in pots bringing color.

The barn house is straight ahead. A "bank barn," its design is traditional to farmers in the area who excavate what they muck from the barn floor and create a mini-driveway from it to the side so machinery can be driven onto a second floor and stored with the huge rolled hay bales for wintering sheep.

Walking out into the open land, we see patches of greenspace and Victoria tells us about Bobolinks, an endangered bird species that nest in the chest high grasses. The males are black with white-streaked backs. Farming methods today cut hay early, which destroys nests. Victoria's attitudes toward haying have been radically changed by seeing the slaughter of the nesting birds. After haying she saw nothing but birds of prey, scavenger birds coming in for whatever eggs or fledglings remained. The farm space is affected by all kinds of global processes, and even if it's in just a small way, she tries to make it a habitat for

189

birds and animals that need a place to live. On your own land, it's possible to have agency, do something.

We take a video of Victoria working the dogs with the sheep, and post it to the blog. The white dogs, Maremma, stay with them year-round, protection from coyotes. We are surrounded by panting dogs, all of them doing their jobs. Elly is the exception. Her job is to get up on Victoria's lap and snuggle.

It's noon when we park the van, and by the time we leave it's close to midnight. Farm life, sheep, and dinnertime talk of the fragility of democracy. What else for the Americans over the Fourth of July but Canadian outrage about Trump!

The Where of Here: Sheep Farm in St. Agatha, Ontario

Krista: For the last hour we have been talking about the where of here. The sheep, and dogs, and various grasses. There is so much birdsong.

Victoria: I've lived here since 2008. It's 147 acres of farmland just outside of Waterloo. We are situated in some of the best farmland in the world. I've been fortunate to travel a lot. I've seen farmland in Europe. And we're lucky to be close to this incredibly fertile, beautiful farmland.

When we bought the farm in 2008, it was cash crops. And the house had been let go. We've fixed it up and shifted to raising grasses, and planting sheep pasture. We work with a partner who's also a close friend of mine with extensive knowledge of sheep husbandry, Viki Kidd. She does most of the work with the sheep but it's a partnership. She handles the sheep side of things. And my partner John handles the machinery. You saw his little "test house," where he tests building materials. He's at University too, appointed between architecture and engineering.

I like the gardens and I support Viki in looking after the sheep. I help with lambing. Viki breeds about fifty ewes a year, and lambs them in February and March. I take night shifts, to make sure that the lambs arrive safely, help them out if there needs to be intervention. That's one perspective of where we are.

Krista: Do you want to offer others?

Victoria: We are a habitat for different creatures. I'm conscious of that. There's a lot of life here. When I talk about "ownership," I understand that that is a privilege. And it's a construct; it is luck, not entitlement. I'm conscious of supporting the life that's here. Deer, coyotes, rodents, there's other critters that live here by design. That have always lived here, right? There's a lot of different birds.

I'm a bird person. I know most of the bird species that live here. We were talking earlier about supporting habitats for the grassland birds, like meadowlarks and bobolinks that nest here, which is in conflict with raising hay. We come up with compromises so that those birds still can nest. That's the other perspective of "the where of here," the kinds of life that inhabit this space.

We have a colony of barn swallows and their habitat is disappearing because modern barn styles don't support them. When you drove here from Windsor, you might have noticed little kinds of houses?

Krista: Yes.

Victoria: Those are supposed to be barn swallow habitat. When you destroy a bird habitat, since it's a threatened species, you have to replace it. But you will never see a barn swallow use those structures. They are useless. A barn swallow will not go near them. The little houses make people feel good, but it's not actually helping.

You saw in our barn a lot of barn swallows flying around, nesting. They like it here, and that's important to me.

And then a third perspective on "the where of here" is historical and colonial, right. This is the traditional territory of the Six Nations of the Grand River. Ten miles on either side of the Grand River is called the Haldimand Tract. This land specifically is not on the Haldimand Tract. But that is treaty land and that treaty has not been fulfilled. The university I work on is on that land. There is the perspective, right, that this land was inhabited by Indigenous people for thousands of years before my ancestors came here.

I'm descended from Scottish immigrants who settled here in the 1830s and the 401 Highway, actually goes right through the homestead of Alexander Lamont, my ancestor, and they settled here in the 1830s.

Their homestead, the 401 Highway, was built right through the treaty land. I've looked at old maps and figured out where it was. That was an early period of intensive settlement in this area, so there's that whole colonial history that this land is a part of.

Krista: You were raised in Edmonton, in the suburbs of Edmonton in Western Canada and Alberta.

Victoria: The way Canadian settlement worked was the mostly Scottish and Irish and English settlers of what was then Upper Canada had families who also wanted land. As western land was colonized they moved gradually West, acquiring it. My father was born in Manitoba because Alexander Lamont's descendants eventually made their way to Manitoba. On my mother's side, in the early 1900s, were Eastern European immigrants to central Ontario. They gradually migrated further west until my mother and father ended up in Alberta, bordering on Montana.

Two hundred miles north of the border is Edmonton. That's where I'm from. I grew up oriented to the outdoors. As a teenager I liked horses. I liked to hang out at farms. When I finished my PhD, I got a job at Waterloo and this is where I ended up.

Krista: We work in regional studies. Place is important to people. And yet, there is a way in which we don't talk about that, as such. We don't talk about how place is important to us personally. We talk about particular places we work on and the significance or the history or the layeredness of those places. But one of the things that's been interesting is to talk with us who have feminist commitments about the places that we are from or love or feel.

Victoria: There is probably no space I feel like I belong in more than this farm. I don't know how to describe it. But I come out here every morning and I hear the birds and I'm just so happy to be here. I love this place. That is highly fraught I know, right, because that is the product of settler discourse, telling me that I belong here. Because historically I do not.

Krista: This is the very thing we're trying to tease apart, the ways in which we love the places that we . . .

Victoria: That we don't belong, yeah. [laughs]

Krista: And yet we do belong to them somehow. So please talk a minute about what it's like in the morning, leaving aside for a minute how much of a fiction it is and the historical overlay that we become so good at talking through.

Victoria: I come out with a coffee. I putter around in the garden. I look at how the plants are doing. I love the progress of the plants. I like growing flowers.

Krista: I can tell.

Victoria: I'm too lazy to be a vegetable gardener. I putter around. I look at the flowers. I chart the progress of the birds through different, "Oh, who's nesting where?" After a storm, I look around to see if any nests have been dislodged and see if I can intervene. I work out here as long as the weather cooperates. I do a lot of writing here. I wrote a lot of the book that I'm just finishing up right now.

Krista: Have you written about this place?

Victoria: No, I haven't. I should. My academic writing is disconnected from my everyday life. It feels weird to think about writing about my everyday life. Right? I consider myself a writer but my everyday life doesn't feel like it's a subject for my writing. And the book I've just written is a biography about someone else's everyday life! It's a biography of B. M. Bower, so it's all about her everyday life [laughs].[1] Like, who wants to read about my everyday life? I haven't thought about writing about my own, but I would like to.

Krista: You've talked about belonging, with all its complications. Are there places you feel you don't belong?

Victoria: Definitely certain formal administrative places, institutional spaces. It's highly dependent and some of that is my background, a wrong-side-of-the-tracks, Alberta, blue-collar thing. Not very many in my family went to university.

I'm from a blended family. All together there were nine. Two of my brothers have passed away. I have two sisters out west. One of my sisters went to university. Oh, no, two of my sisters did.

Krista: You are first generation to go to college?

Victoria: For the most part—my mother did attend art college. Certainly spaces that are associated with authority, I'm not comfortable sitting in the dean's office, asking for resources. It doesn't feel like I belong there. I've had more practice at it as a tenured faculty member. It's not the most powerful position in the world, but it's a lot more power than a lot of people have. So I'm getting a little bit better at it. But certainly, it's not my happy place.

Krista: Well, that's important too, to know, that you understand your history to be the wrong side of the tracks, blue collar.

Victoria: Yeah.

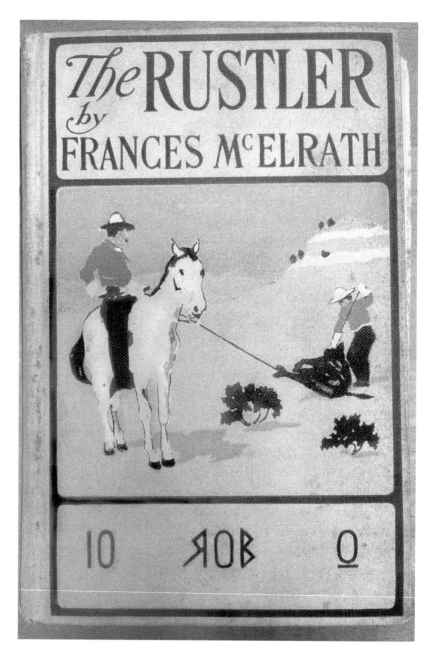

Fig. 19. Cover of Frances McElrath's 1902 novel *The Rustler*, a domestic-feminist alternative to Owen Wister's *The Virginian*. Courtesy Victoria Lamont.

Krista: I'll file that a minute and come back to it. Since you've raised B. M. Bower, and you provided that wonderful visual from Bower's *Jean of the Lazy A* for the blog, and then *The Rustler* by Francis McElrath, as book-cover examples of a "feminist West," let's talk about your developing feminist perspective. You have written as a feminist about woman suffrage memorials.[2] But here we are talking about book covers. The cover for *Jean of the Lazy A* on the blog, first. It shows a young woman with a cinched waist and western gear on the back of a bucking horse. It's a classic pulp novel visual.

Victoria: The thing about the popular feminism of that time and moving forward is it could be expressed as long as it didn't undermine the femininity of the heroine. There had to be a reassurance that she's still a girl, shaped like a girl or acting like a girl. The heroine in Frances McElrath's *The Rustler* can be powerful so long as her power comes from a maternal place. Reading some of the pulp westerns from the 1920s, the female gunfighter will come on the scene. She's wearing sort of dirty clothes, and she's doing something rough, she's roping a calf. But there will still be that moment where, "Oh, but look at how curvy she is!" Emblematic of the popular feminism of that time.

In the *Jean of the Lazy A* for the blog, the heroine is having fun on this bucking horse. She's got a lot of authority, agency. I love the colors. The vibrancy, evoking a lot of activity. It's dynamic. When people popularly think about the West as a space that empowers women, that's an image that they think about. But it's problematic, right? Because of an underlying "Oh, but she's still a woman." We have to be reassured that, oh, the gender categories are maintained.

Krista: How did you come to work on Bower? How did B. M. Bower attract feminist attention from you?

Victoria: When you asked me to interview for this project I really wanted to do it, but I wasn't sure how to situate myself. I'm different from a lot of the scholars in this field because I don't come at the West from a place of identification. When I started going to WLA regularly, I learned that I came at it as an intellectual. It was: "Look, there's this woman. She's writing Westerns. Scholars are saying women didn't write Westerns." I want to know more and came to write about it.[3] I started to work on Bower.

I wasn't interested in western American literature. I didn't read a lot of it. I started graduate school and encountered it through the scholar Christine Bold and her courses. The literature raised interesting intellectual questions for me. I started going to WLA and a lot of the scholars that I got to know were coming at it also from this place of identification with the region, which I was not conscious of in myself.

Even though I am, I was born in the West. The Canadian West. But I didn't have that sense of attachment to place driving the scholarship. Then, intellectually, "place" became more interesting as I learned more about those questions. Working on Bower, all I had were her novels. I didn't know anything about her as a person, or what places those novels were coming out of.

As I learned more about her life story, and about connections between where she was living and what she was doing, and what she was writing, questions of place really animated the work, made her writing more interesting. I did start, through this influence of the WLA, to think: "I am a Westerner." It made me look more critically at my own history, and situate myself in the history that I was learning, that I was studying.

I became aware of myself as a settler, and a part of settler culture. My family and my upbringing was influenced by settler culture in ways that were completely repressed. There is a circular movement that comes back to thinking about my own situatedness as a Westerner. But that was not something that drove my work initially. I knew I wanted to do Americanist scholarship, but I could have just as easily ended up being a Dickinson scholar, it was such an accidental thing that got me into it.

Krista: How about coming at it with a feminist approach? One recurrent conversation is about when people come of age as feminists. Those early impressions influence what we identify or disidentify with.

Victoria: I don't know. Certainly my feminism is a response to growing up with a lot of really toxic misogyny, normalized misogyny, especially in school, which was not fun for me. I realize now that a lot of what happened was just normalized misogyny. Girls were harassed constantly. And the school system just . . .

Krista: Including you.

Victoria: Yes, including me. I decided to become an academic because the space of the university felt so right. I was always a smart kid. But in junior high and high school, being smart was not an asset. I think that's a class thing. Finally, I got to this place where being smart was rewarded, valued. But certainly, first twelve years of school were not fun, right. Those experiences, at a gut level, is when I became a feminist. Because living through that was just so traumatic.

Krista: Traumatic?

Victoria: Yes. I feel a deep commitment to dismantling the conditions that put people through that. It extends to anyone experiencing any socially enabled oppression or exploitation. It extends to all beings, right, who are affected. You can't stop with sexism.

Krista: Right. But your own experience was as a blue-collar girl.

Victoria: Yeah, yes. Definitely. I connect it to blue-collar culture because that's where the males feel empowered—through dominating women. I'm not a sociologist, but that is my theory.

Krista: And in your own history?

Victoria: In my own experience, that's where they got their power. And so the school . . .

Krista: This would be guys at the school, who were all blue-collar guys?

Victoria: Yeah.

Krista: Is there an example you'd like to share? It doesn't have to be about you personally, I'm not hunting for . . .

Victoria: Oh, sure. I'll give you an example. This would be about seventh grade. There were male students who were assaulting girls, right? They were grabbing their breasts, grabbing their buttocks. This would happen in the class with a teacher there. One girl in particular, she was very tall. Her physical development was advanced for her age, and she was a target. What I heard was a teacher or some teachers took those boys aside who were involved and said to them, "Oh, yeah, we know you want to do it, but you can't do it." But they normalized it, they sort of said, "Yeah, of course you want to."

It was that kind of stuff that happened in classes with authority figures there. The girls were not safe in school. But it was completely accepted. It never occurred to anyone to go and tell their parents, "Hey, did you know that we're being assaulted?" We didn't even use the term "assault," right? Like, we have the language now to call that assault. But that's not what we called it, right? We would've called it, "Oh, you know, they're groping or they're messing around." Something that's much less violent, cleansed of the violence of what they were doing.

Krista: Do you want to talk about anything we haven't talked about or ask me something or José something?

Victoria: You've helped me think the intellectual drives behind my feminist studies, but then there's the affective, like, why am I feminist—it's a deeply felt commitment to things that are wrong with the world that should be exposed.

Krista: A feminism that includes animals.

Victoria: I'm not "an animal studies person." I've learned some things from it, but . . .

Krista: You're leading an animal studies life here. You talked about riding horses early and birds. You do sheep midwifery. I'd say that's a fairly real time "animal studies."

Victoria: I've always been oriented towards animals, whether it was cats or dogs. Early in life, if we found an animal and wanted to bring it home, the parents would say okay. [Laughs.] So we always had dogs and cats at home, and, that sense of power relations, of normalized patriarchy, of people who are enacting it and perpetrating it, you don't want to reenact that in your relationship with animals. Right? I don't want to, right. I have to remind myself.

Krista: Because people do reenact it.

Victoria: Yeah. You don't want to objectify animals the way you've been objectified. Some of these animals we have, they're our property. Right? Like, Elly is my property. But that's not what she is to me.

Sometimes you have to make tough decisions. I decide when their life ends. And when you're managing livestock, some things that you do are practical but maybe a violation. We remove the sheep tails, because they get certain diseases from flies laying eggs in their tails. When they're little, when they're not even twenty-four hours old, they get a band put on their tail, that cuts off the blood supply. I'm not going to do it and tell myself that it's just normal. Right? Like, you are causing suffering to this animal. I don't know the right words for it. When you're working with livestock, suffering can happen. Let's not pretend that it's not happening, which some farmers, that's the attitude they take, that it doesn't exist. But I can't.

I can't participate in the objectification of another creature. That does not align with my feminism.

Krista: You and I have talked about "rural femininity," and rural gender roles and culture as complicated sometimes for feminists. You choose your battles carefully.

Victoria: This is conservative country. We're adjacent to a thriving Mennonite community. We do a lot of business with them. I go and I shop at the Mennonite store. They have very different ideas about gender than I do. There is also conservative agrarian culture, southern Ontario conservatism. And how productive is it? There are mixed views in my family and John's family, which tends to be more conservative. They live nearby as dairy farmers. He was raised milking cows. I have siblings who I don't agree with politically. So in some settings, what is going to be accomplished? You have to think.

On the other hand, there's "Well, what am I doing? I should be causing friction." I feel an obligation to create friction. I can tolerate sexism more than I can tolerate racism. I feel racism is where I have to create more friction, because as a white woman I have a lot of privilege. I have to leverage my whiteness when the opportunity or when the duty is called upon. But how much effect is it going to have? That negotiation in the different spaces where I circulate, it could be a family gathering in John's hometown or a faculty meeting.

Krista: In the faculty meeting, do you come with your rural woman identity as much?

Victoria: That's interesting. [Laughs.] My department is quite progressive. Anti-racism is normalized, anti-sexism is normalized. So there's no problem. Well, I shouldn't say that. Because in situations around hiring, I have had to say, when we're creating job descriptions, "This is a recipe for a white person." Right? Because my department is better than it was, but at one time it was almost entirely white. I had to push back against that, but in other ways it's much easier to articulate feminist positions in that context.

Then there will be a family gathering where there's the racist uncle or the transphobic cousin, and I struggle. Do I say, "Okay, I'm not going to go to Christmas dinner because I know you're going to make some comment"?

Those are issues that are spatial. They're a function of this place where I am, and my profession, which puts me in more of an urban cosmopolitan framework. The faculty are from all over Canada and the United States. Students are from all over. A lot of Middle Eastern students, more and more Black and Latinx students. I'm in a cosmopolitan setting. But in terms of my personal life, situated here on a farm, we have our farming friends. Rural Ontario is incredibly white. If you go to any agricultural fair, and fairs are huge in Ontario—especially in the fall, every town has their fair—it will be a sea of white faces everywhere. Then you go to Toronto, and you're the only white person. You go on the subway, you're the only white person on the subway. Right. It's incredibly white.

Krista: How's that for you?

Victoria: Being the only white person on the subway? [Laughs.]

Krista: No, being white in a sea of white people.

Victoria: Being in a sea of white people? It's weird. Growing up, it wasn't weird. It was just the way it was.

Krista: You were always around white people?

Victoria: Well, no, but Edmonton was very segregated. And there was a lot of normalized white supremacy. Which I participated in and my family participated in. I had a close friend who actually had to leave because of the racism, and when she left, I said, "I don't understand why you're leaving." She said, "I can't stand it here. It's so racist." And I said, "I don't know—"

Krista: That was a moment of learning for you.

Victoria: No. I didn't get it. I had no clue. [Laughs.] I was so naïve.

Krista: Where was this? Where did it happen?

Victoria: This happened when we went to university together and after we both finished. She was of color and we had known each other since high school. She says, "I'll probably leave this place." And I just did not understand what she was talking about.

Krista: This is after university?

Victoria: Yeah, after we just finished university. So we were twenty-two, something like that.

Krista: Your race consciousness started to develop then?

Victoria: No. It did not. [Laughs.] I'm ashamed to say.

Krista: Well, you have company.

Victoria: I have to say there was a lot of kicking and screaming. It was as an academic and working in Western Studies. You can't call yourself a scholar of this subject matter and not engage with race—you just cannot. I came to that realization when I started engaging closely with postcolonial theory. My supervisor, Mary Chapman, pushed me to read Indigenous authors, and I didn't want to. "I can't do that," I said, "it's too thorny." And I didn't want to deal with it.

This is part of whiteness—you don't have to deal with things. I just didn't see why I would have to deal with it. It was through scholarship, actually. And through teaching, because my students are becoming more and more diverse, and I have to be more accountable to them. When I first started teaching in Waterloo, the student body was local and white, but that has changed. So it felt wrong.

True Confessions of a White Scholar.

Reconciling Feminism, with Margaret Jacobs

Our visit with Margaret Jacobs in Lincoln represents the last interview of the project. Her newly published After One Hundred Winters *has been our steady companion this summer over a lot of miles. I have a hard copy of the book in the van and also listen on Audible, so I hear the voice of the book in my mind; I trust it. The call to white settlers to learn the Indigenous histories of their homeplaces is one I take to heart with a new urgency because the book's documentary storytelling shows us ordinary people enacting land-back repatriations and practicing right relations today. Reconciliation seems more possible than I realized, not an abstraction.*

I have followed Margaret's work in comparative settler studies for many years. The outspoken feminist call to the field of U.S. West History, "What's Gender Got to Do with It?" has kept me company along what feels at times a lonely ride. I am thrilled Margaret agrees to be interviewed.

We've crossed paths along the way of scholarly lives. At Rice, she gave a lecture some years ago that I was happy to attend. We were both panelists for an important "Symposium on the Significance of the Frontier in Transnational History" at the Huntington Library in 2012, where Patrick Wolfe gave a keynote and settler studies moved to the center of U.S. western studies. We've had almost-dinner plans a couple of times at Western Literature Association meetings, which Margaret attends occasionally with Tom Lynch, her husband, a colleague who is well known in WLA *circles and former editor of* Western American Literature.

Margaret invites us to a very nice lunch place, the Hub Café. Later she will host us at her home, and Tom makes a great summertime dinner that we eat outdoors. We watch their dogs romp. Fireflies come out and the air is warm then humid. A huge storm lets down to wash the streets clean.

Since 2020, Margaret has served as director of the Center for Great Plains Studies. What an unexpected treat that José and I get to walk the museum space on the Center's first floor for the Contemporary Indigeneity exhibition.[1]

The Where of Here: Lincoln, Nebraska

Krista: We are here with the much-celebrated Margaret Jacobs [both laugh]! You have a lot of projects and major awards, and a number of new public projects.

Margaret: We're at a place called Pioneers Park—ironic, because so much of my work is about trying to question that category of the pioneer and use the term "settler" instead, and then to also scrutinize what it means to be a settler. So it's ironic to be here. But that's what living in Nebraska is like because there is such a fetishization of homesteading and of white settlers. It's an interesting place to live.

I've been here for eighteen and a half years. That's the longest I've lived anywhere. I don't think I ever imagined myself living in this place. But it suits me in a lot of ways. Lincoln itself is an extremely livable city. I feel like people have made a real commitment in the city to build a strong community. It's a refugee resettlement area; it's had a strong urban Indian community since the 1950s. And it's been a surprisingly great space to live and work, especially for the issues that I'm really interested in around Indigenous people, settlers, and immigration.

Krista: Initially you thought of doing an interview in Colorado Springs, since you were raised at least partly in Colorado Springs. You've written about Colorado Springs and the infamous Sand Creek Massacre as a way to think through what a reconciliatory or right posture of knowing one's own place might be for the work you do with Indigenous people. Instead, Lincoln ultimately was the place you chose for our time together.

Margaret: There's a disjunction in my life between where I feel most comfortable or where I would say I have a place identity, versus where I actually live. I grew up in Colorado from the time I was six to eighteen. That's always felt like home, and it's the person I was there, this very outdoorsy, tomboyish girl that feels like "the real me." That person who has an identity of living in the mountains and being a little bit rugged and being into the wilderness. But I don't live in that place anymore. And yet, that identity is one that I claim, and feel.

But to be truthful, that identity also includes a settler, a white settler identity and I'm probing that right now. I'm writing a book called *Playing Pioneer Woman*. It's a coming-of-age memoir. It's about a lot of things. It's about my mother and about my childhood, and about growing up in an area that had been the homelands of the Ute, Cheyenne, and Arapaho people, but never meeting a Ute, Cheyenne, or Arapaho person until much later. The Indigenous people had been removed from that area. I know there were many Indigenous people who lived in Colorado Springs, but they weren't visible to me as a child. And the community I grew up in is called Chipita Park. It's named for a Ute woman. I lived up Ute Pass. But there were no Utes in the area. And there were very few non-white people. We had one Jewish family, one Chinese American family, one Japanese American family, one African American family. There were a number of Mexican American families, but many of them had Anglo last names. Growing up, I didn't recognize most Mexican American families as Mexican American.

It was a very odd place to grow up. It was extremely white. And as I write this new book on *Playing Pioneer Woman*, I'm thinking about what it means to grow up in a space like that, where I was schooled in what it means to live there, schooled to believe that I was entitled to live in this place, and I was more entitled to live in that space than other people were. I'm really enjoying working on this book, because, one, it's fun to think about your childhood and where I gained a sense of a strong Rocky Mountain identity. But what comes with that is this settler privilege, this settler sense of entitlement.

Originally, I thought it would be interesting to do an interview there, because it's a place that is so close to me. Yet, I haven't lived there since I moved back to Colorado briefly in 1995. I haven't lived in Colorado for a very long time. My mom used to live there. We'd go back and visit her a lot. But Nebraska is my true home now. It's taken me a long time to get used to this place. It's so different from where I grew up. And as I was saying earlier, there's a fetishization of pioneers here.

What's been rewarding to me living here is meeting and befriending Indigenous people in the area. When we first moved here, we moved from southern New Mexico, a very diverse place. I was concerned about moving to another place that was very predominantly white, and I wanted to make sure I met people beyond that demographic. So the first thing I did was to sign up for an Omaha-language class that the university used to offer—they no longer do. It was a very interesting class. You can imagine not many people are taking this. There were about eight to ten people in the class. And we all took the class for two years together. And we met every day for the first year, five days a week. And then in the second year, we met for three or four days a week.

But I became close to my classmates, most of whom were non-Native. Our instructor who was adopted into the Omaha tribe would bring Omaha elders to class all the time and I got to know them. And it was a really formative experience to learn or to try to learn this language. I've since thought about the politics of non-Native people learning Native languages, but at the time, for me it was an opportunity to get out of a white bubble. I enjoyed that a lot. And it helped me start to get an appreciation of this area through Indigenous eyes, through the Indigenous peoples who call this place home.

More recently, I cofounded a project called the Genoa Indian School Digital Reconciliation project.[2] We wanted to do that project in a way that wasn't a bunch of academics, especially non-Native academics, "gathering information." From the beginning, we've had a council of tribal community advisors. We have people from the Santee Sioux tribe, the Omaha, Winnebago, and Ponca tribes—which are the four recognized tribes in Nebraska—plus the Pawnee, who were removed. One of the members is Pawnee. That's been a great way to meet Native people in the state. And to take direction from them about what they want the project to do. What matters to them? How do they want information made public or not?

Krista: You see it as a repatriation project?

Margaret: We're trying to get all the government documents we can for the school, which are difficult to find. They're scattered about. We see it as repatriating records, through a digital platform. What we have right now are government documents, students' applications, things government administrators wrote about the children, which are often demeaning and horrible. We're moving into a new phase, which is more oral histories with descendants about the meaning of the school to their family members. We're trying to supplement the record.

In 2018 I approached a local journalist named Kevin Abourezk, who's Rosebud, Lakota, about doing a project together that we call Reconciliation Rising.[3] And that's been incredibly satisfying and rewarding. We've been interviewing people, much like you and José are doing. We've been

Fig. 20. Margaret walks with Kevin Abourezk, her collaborator on the Reconciliation Rising multimedia project, on land newly repatriated to the Ioway Tribe of Kansas and Nebraska. Courtesy Tom Lynch.

interviewing both Natives and non-Natives who are working together in some way to confront the abuses and crimes that happened in the past. Not to just acknowledge them but do something about them. We've interviewed a lot of people who are involved in returning land to Native people, non-Native people working with Native people and deciding to give back ten acres or sixty acres or some bit of land. For example, we've spent a lot of time with a lot of Pawnee people. One of the stories we made into a podcast and a short film, *The Return of the Pawnees*, was about a German American man named Roger Welsh who returned sixty acres of land to the Pawnee people.[4]

Krista: This story is where you end *After One Hundred Winters*.

Margaret: Yeah. In Central Nebraska. We interviewed Roger Welsh, and then went down to the Pawnee Nation and interviewed dozens of people about the meaning of this land return and the meaning of coming back to Nebraska after they'd been exiled from here in the 1870s. It gave me new eyes to see the beauty and the wonder of this place. It's been so layered over with GMO corn and soy beans, and cement and asphalt and parking lots. Big stadium arenas and football stadiums. Sometimes you can't see the beauty of this place.

But hanging out with Pawnee people, and most recently, a delegation of Otoe-Missouria people who came up to Lincoln, and hanging out with them and going out into the prairies. To them, this is home. I remember talking to a young woman named Christina Faw Faw. We were up on a prairie near here, a beautiful spring morning, and she said, "Oh, gosh, I just feel so at home." It was very moving because it helped me to feel more at home here to see the beauty of this land through its original owners and occupants and stewards. It's been a slow process but I feel like I'm coming to inhabit, truly inhabit this place in a respectful, reverent manner. I still have the Rocky Mountain identity but I feel more close to this place than I used to.

Krista: Thank you, Margaret. So many things we could think about. Since we're here, in Pioneer Park, I'd love you to talk about *Playing Pioneer Woman*. I assume the title is a play on "playing Indian."

Margaret: Yeah. Well, you may know that that's a book by Phil Deloria.[5]

Krista: Yes.

Margaret: Phil and I have been friends since we were both in grad school. That's an amazing book. In part, it is a play on that. There's so much to that book. But one of the things my book is about is the role that play has in teaching us about our place in the world. I used to go down to the creek behind my house where I grew up in Colorado and play pioneer woman.

Krista: "Play pioneer woman"?

Margaret: Yeah, I'd read Laura Ingalls Wilder, like so many people. I'd go play down by the creek, and I'd pretend I was this pioneer woman. As I've been writing this book, I realized that my mom was playing pioneer woman too. My father died when I was five. And she had three young children to raise.

Krista: She was going to persevere.

Margaret: She was going to persevere but she also she never remarried. She wanted to be very independent. She had a strong sense of what I consider a Western pioneer identity, a sense that she didn't need anybody else in her life, she could do it all herself. I started to riff on that. The book looks at everything from the myth I grew up on as a child. We sang this song all the time: "If I had a wagon, I would go to Colorado, go to Colorado. If I had a wagon, I would go to the state where a man can walk a mile high."[6] I don't know if you know that song?

Krista: I do. [Both laugh.]

Margaret: That's the first chapter, "If I Had a Wagon." Then another chapter is called "Native." You remember those bumper stickers they used to have in Colorado that say "Native"? They have what looks like the license plate of Colorado, and it says "Native." I used to go around in my mom's vw bug and we'd see those signs everywhere. I was so mad that people had those because I was not a native. And by that I don't mean Native American, but I couldn't claim being a native to Colorado.

Krista: You were born elsewhere.

Margaret: Right! And I didn't like it. I felt like I was excluded. It never occurred to me how grating that would be as a Native person to see those bumper stickers that were meant to say, "Hey, I belong here and . . ." but totally erased Indigenous peoples' identity.

Krista: What would you play down by the river? How would you play pioneer woman?

Margaret: I would make a little house and a little grove. I'd stack up some rocks and pretend I was making little stews.

Krista: You would domesticate.

Margaret: Yes.

Krista: In a nuclear family kind of way?

Margaret: No, there were no men. There were no people. [Laughs.] I had a really tough time with my brothers growing up. My mom was single and so was my grandmother, my mother's mother. There were two women authority figures, no male head of household. My brothers were tyrannical with me. And often violent.

So my little domesticated space was a female space. I'd make stews, I would harvest wheat from grass stems. Sometimes I would dam up the creek, I loved to play in the water.

Krista: What would happen when you dammed the creek?

Margaret: I might wade out in it, if it was a hot day, or collect stones. I've started to write on this and it is interesting because I didn't imagine any history of this place at all as I was domesticating it and playing a pioneer woman. I never imagined Indian people there, or any people at all.

Krista: It was wilderness.

Margaret: Yeah. The book also riffs on the very strong whiteness of this place, of attitudes toward immigrants where I grew up. It has a section I'm going to call "Melodrama," which is about Cripple Creek. We used to go there all the time with visitors. I will get into some of the extractive economy in the area, the tourist economy. I'm having fun with that book.

Krista: I wanted to hear you talk about a sense of yourself as a feminist and how that came to be. Is the solo behavior, being autonomous and outdoorsy, part of it?

Margaret: My first feminist foray would be that autonomous child, very individualistic, very angry, truly, about male privilege, male freedoms that I didn't share as a child growing up. But that's not where I remained as a feminist.

Krista: No, of course not. But if we could stay here for a minute, because what I'm finding over a lot of these conversations is how formative that early moment is and how helpful it is not to hold it at bay. Speaking for myself here too. If you were willing to say a little bit more about being angry?

Margaret: Yeah. Well, I grew up in the seventies. That was an incredible moment, as a child, to grow up, as a girl. I remember the TV show—maybe you saw it?—*Free to Be . . . You and Me*.[7]

Krista: I never saw it. But I know about it.

Margaret: It was really important to me. I asked my mom to get the book that went along with it. I still have it—it's a purple book. I love that book. It had songs with it. And it was really important to me as a child. I've been looking for another book that I remember as a child called *Girls Are People Too*, but I cannot find that book anywhere.

I saw my brothers and they seemed to have so many more freedoms than I did. I felt like my mom let them do things that she wouldn't let me do. They treated me really poorly. I was angry that she didn't stop them from doing that.

Krista: Can you share anything about them, without sharing more than you want to share?

Margaret: They're probably not things that are unusual, other girls experienced it. But for example, my brothers were four and six years older than me. They were really close. We'd go out in the beautiful backyard area by the creek and they'd say, "Oh, you want to play hide and seek with us?" I was like, "Oh, yeah, I would love to." They'd say, "Well, you go hide, you go hide," and I'd go hide, and they'd never come find me [laughs]. They'd do stuff like that.

Or we had a big swing in our area down by the creek, over a marshy area. We called it the bog. We had a picnic table on one side and we would take this big rope swing and stand up on the table, and then we'd jump on the swing and go across the bog and come back. So one time one of my brothers says, "Hey, let's swing together. You jump on my lap." He stood facing the bog, and I stood with my back to it. And he said, "When I say 'three,' let's jump together on the swing." So when he said "three," I jumped, but he didn't. He just let the swing go. And I got dragged through this bog. Stuff like that.

One brother in particular was violent. He would hit me a lot, and I was so mad that my mom wouldn't do anything about this. I think feminism was a little refuge for me as a child.

Krista: As a child?

Margaret: Yeah. My mom did not identify as feminist. No women I knew as a child identified as feminist.

Krista: Did you think of that term?

Margaret: No, not at all. I don't know what term I would have used. Maybe "women's rights," or I don't know.

Krista: But you identified it as a something, a consciousness or a something.

Margaret: Yeah. Finding those two books was really helpful to me to think that it wasn't an experience that was mine alone, but it was something many women had experienced. I remember even reading Betty Friedan's *Feminine Mystique* when I was in high school.

Krista: Independently?

Margaret: Yeah. Because I was searching for a way to understand this world around me, which seemed to restrict women so much but give so many freedoms to men. I was so angry about it.

Krista: So would that have been a library book? How would you have found that book?

Margaret: It was a library book.

Krista: You were a library book reader?

Margaret: I was really into the library. Maybe that's part of it. I was a very nerdy girl. I was smart. But being a smart girl was an impediment. So, again, I was searching for some sense of affirmation or something like that.

Krista: You were both nerdy but a tomboy. Those two don't often go together. Playing pioneer woman. Can you think of an early story about yourself as a feminist? Before you become the feminist you are today?

Margaret: Well, I was thinking about this, you gave me questions in advance. To give you a bit of background, I went off to college, where I found a lot of other people, other women, who were like myself.

Krista: In the early eighties?

Margaret: In the early eighties. It was a wonderful moment because there were a lot of young women of color and I got really close to them both as friends and as activists. We published a feminist newspaper together. We took classes on women's history or women writers of color. What I mean is that, in that early period of the eighties, feminism was very multicultural, very multiracial. That was extremely important to me, a formative part of my life.

Krista: I'm a little older than you but I think our college years parallel. I went to college very young and then dropped out. Then I went back. The kind of world you're describing of education and of a women's studies that was very race-aware was the world that I encountered, absolutely, as a first "official" knowledge base of feminism. I had my own sense of feminism already, but it wasn't organized by an educated sense of it. But I think eighties feminism has much to recommend it. I tire of broad statements about second-wave feminism being narrow, which then gets corrected with third-wave feminism and Judith Butler. I think, "Well, that's inaccurate."

Margaret: I agree! It was a really important moment. Most people think the eighties was this incredibly conservative, Reagan-Bush–era decade. They don't realize the incredibly dynamic social movements going on, solidarity with Central America, anti-nuclear movements, and feminism and the anti-racism work that was going on.

Krista: Yes, and white feminists trying to reckon with *This Bridge* or Gloria Anzaldúa.

Margaret: Right after college, I got a job with a group called Clergy and Laity Concerned. The group started during the Vietnam War, against it. I had moved up to Eugene, Oregon. I'd gotten a job with them as, of all things, a development director. Here I was, like, twenty-two, twenty-three, but I didn't know the first thing about how to raise money. I wanted a job and I wanted to work for a nonprofit progressive organization. By the time I joined their staff, their primary focus was anti-racism. It wasn't anti-war. They had done a remarkable job of creating a multiracial coalition. This was not one of those white groups that had a token Black person or token Indigenous person. They truly had done incredible work and had a multiracial staff, multiracial advisory board.

When I started working for CALC, as we called it, Clergy and Laity Concerned, we were taking stands, even though our main focus was on anti-racism. We were asked constantly to take a stand on this or that—whatever the issues were of the day. One day, we got a letter from a women's group in town that had asked us to come out in support of abortion rights. I felt very strongly that we should do that. I believed very strongly that we should have reproductive justice and I assumed our organization would do that, because we were taking progressive stances on everything. Well. [sigh]

I brought it up at a staff meeting, I said, "Has anybody answered this letter? Are we going to join them?" And this silence came over the group. One of my colleagues on the staff, a woman I adored—her name was Guadalupe but we called her Lupe. I was trying to remember her last name. She was Mexican American and a devout Catholic. She was very upset that we would consider taking this position in support of abortion. But I was adamant that we should do something, even though, you know, I was twenty-three or twenty-four. Lupe was probably in her late thirties, and Marian, who was the director, probably in her late forties by then.

Krista: But in the center of reproductive lifecycles.

Margaret: Yeah. A couple other staff people said, "Why don't we bring it to our board?" We did, and it became the most divisive thing you can imagine. Lupe quit. Some people on the board felt as strongly as I did that we should be supporting this. Other people thought, "No, we can't do this, because we're a coalition of people from many different religions and many different racial backgrounds." Not everybody agrees on this issue.

I was so torn up about it. It was formative because it pitted my strong commitments and passions against racism against my strong commitments and passion for reproductive justice and feminism. I don't know if I would react differently now than I did then. I may now be more compromising about it and realize that every part of my life doesn't have to be a place where I support abortion rights. But I don't know, maybe I would feel just as strongly. But it was a really tough time. I hated that Lupe felt she had to leave the organization because we had started discussing abortion and she didn't feel like it was a safe place anymore.

That was an important moment when it made me doubt or think about: Was I imposing my views as a white feminist on different women who had different views? Who were people I loved and adored and respected greatly and admired.

Krista: What ultimately happened?

Margaret: They didn't take a stand on the issue. Lupe quit. I went back to graduate school and they did not resolve it at all. A lot of other people were pulled out of the organization because of the issue. I think the organization rebuilt itself. Marian kept it going.

Krista: In many ways that was a stymying moment across organizations and for feminism generally. I wonder if a figure like Lupe would have taken the same position today? Knowing what we know all the more clearly about reproductive justice especially for women of color. And what the absence of it costs.

Margaret: Well, it was an interfaith organization.

Krista: Right, and it's so interesting to think of interfaith organizations able to do coalitions around anti-racism and yet not center what we might think of as a fundamental civil right for women. This moment is one that stays as a strong memory more than the earlier one of being at Stanford and doing a newspaper together across differences?

Margaret: Feminism has been or became for me very much about a commitment to the liberation and transformation and emancipation of all oppressed people. It was easy to be a feminist at Stanford with a small group of people who shared values. We were committed anti-racists, and also committed to reproductive justice and spoke out against violence against women.

But after Stanford, I realized that there were tricky things about being a feminist, and feminism had been and could be used as a weapon against people of color. That moment, which happened a year or less before I went back to grad school to study women's history, was influential because I realized that people who have a shared commitment to justice might have these wedges. They might have places where they couldn't agree on everything. That challenge was interesting to me. It was something that's harder to do.

I feel like I'm still doing that hard work of trying to find where people have long-standing disagreements or conflicts but want to create spaces where they can dialogue and come together.

Krista: Speaking of wedge issues, I wonder what your thoughts are about the tendency to identify "white feminism" or "white feminist history" with white-reformer-good-deed-policy-doing action, when there are lots of women of color who lead issues of reproductive justice.

Margaret: Absolutely, the leadership.

Krista: I don't know if you want to think aloud with me about the way in which "the wedge" attaches to a sense of white feminist cluelessness? Or about the fact that lack of abortion rights might be a problem for women of color?

Margaret: Things have changed immensely since then. We don't just use abortion rights or pro-choice language anymore. We talk about reproductive justice, because we realize that involuntary sterilization, which happened against Latinx women, Indigenous women, and Black women so much, is a form of restricting women's reproduction and their rights as much as restricting abortion is. I come across so many women of color now who are taking primary leadership roles on reproductive justice.

Krista: The Women's March organization is very self-consciously forwarding that leadership in all of its major public moments.

Margaret: Yeah, that's a tired cliché, that abortion is a white women's issue. But at that earlier moment in my life, it very much seemed to be. There wasn't yet that growing consciousness about how reproductive justice is a much broader issue and something that greatly affects women of color and Indigenous women.

Some of those early experiences in childhood, college, and right after college, had a lot of impact on my scholarship. When I went back to get my PhD in history, I knew I wanted to do women's history. But I didn't have a sense of what, though probably American history. My first seminar was with Vicki Ruiz, and she was teaching a class on the New Western history, as it was called then. This was 1990, at UC Davis. One of the books she assigned turned out to be influential for me, Peggy Pascoe's *Relations of Rescue*. In that class, I decided to study Western history.

Krista: New Western Historians made such a case for it, that's what it was for me too, the case they made.

Margaret: I never thought I'd study it, or think of it as a "field."

Krista: But the New Western history made it a desirable thing.

Margaret: Yeah. Sexy.

Krista: Sexy in a certain edgy and pissed-off way.

Margaret: Yes. And Patty Limerick's *Legacy of Conquest* was also important. Both books made me realize that I wanted to study this fraught question of women and race in history. Vicki was just such an amazing mentor. She helped me so much to attach my interest to something specific.

Another important person from that era who is still is an important person in my life is Annette Reed. She's a Tolowa woman from Northern California, and she was in my cohort. And I loved being in class with her. She would bring up stuff about American Indian history that I'd never learned. As a history major at Stanford, I never learned a thing about Native Americans. It was incredible for me to learn from Annette. I started to realize I was very interested in this history. I used the term "white people" and "Indigenous peoples" and their "encounters" at the time. I used that innocuous term. Only later was I able to find other frameworks like a settler colonial framework to understand the nature of these relationships.

Krista: When did settler studies come in for you? Was it with Patrick Wolfe?

Margaret: It predated Patrick Wolfe. It was through two feminist scholars from Canada and the UK, Daiva Stasiulis and Nira Yuval-Davis, who edited *Unsettling Settler Societies: Articulations of Gender, Race, Ethnicity and Class* in 1995. They were writing in the early 1990s about settler colonialism and feminism and women and gender. But Patrick Wolfe is who is known, from Australia. I love his work, it's super important, but he never had a real strong gender or feminist approach.

Krista: And I think settler studies still is not really particularly gender-conscious.

Margaret: Right? Ironic given that these Canadian scholars were doing this early work from a feminist perspective. I got interested in the phenomenon of white women's interactions with Indigenous people. Then I expanded that to looking comparatively at Australia and Canada, and that's when I discovered the settler colonial framework and how useful it would be to have it in an American context.

Krista: I have a thought, or a question, if you would entertain it with me. What do you think is good about white women's relations with one another? I've been thinking about the way that white women understand themselves as being allies to Others. But what about being allies to one another? In the *Living West* project, one piece of the "feminist rest area" concept is to have white women talk to one another about whiteness.

We were talking before we turned on the video about having a "rest area" for white women. You talk in *One Hundred Winters* about the need for white settlers to learn reciprocity and responsibility and that those reckonings bring gifts—they are not by definition forms of humiliation. They're forms of—well, relief is the term I would use. Accountability or responsibility are different forms of freedom to build the future without trying to run away from settler legacies, which is not possible. I think this would be a good conversation among white women, though we're still at a place where you have to convince white women that we're white, white feminists.

I wonder, rather than talk about the difficulties of that kind of conversation, where do you *not* have that experience? Because that would be the place to build.

Margaret: That's a really important point.

Krista: I have thought about our *Living West* project as having principles of reconciliation coming from anyone who wants to contribute them, and it would be helpful to have specifics for white feminists. There are lots of Indigenous protocols for reconciliation or participation in different national and sovereign tribal contexts. We need something directive or proactive for white women so we are not stuck apologizing for vague things that don't give anybody relief from historical wrongs.

Margaret: Yeah, the scholarship I've done, I feel like white women have a lot to be accountable for. Maybe not actions now. But actions in the past that white women took in the name of being feminists or maternalists.[8]

It's interesting that you ask this question because I find it really uncomfortable and I intentionally avoid all-white groups. I feel like if as a white person I am hanging out almost entirely with other white people, something's wrong. I bristle. Of course, it used to be it was comfortable to be around other white people, and not so comfortable to make an effort to go into a non-white space or a mixed space.

But I think you're right how important it is for white women to have these discussions with each other. But not "Oh, let's get together. We have a lot in common." No, but "What does this mean to be white? And what is the proper feminist response to whiteness?" I think that could be an incredibly rich conversation if it's done with people who are serious and intentional about wanting to dismantle racism and challenge white supremacy.

Krista: Coming back to the feminist rest area concept, and to conversations about "care" and "maternal thinking" we were having off-video. You used the term "taking care of" and "being careful" with one another.

Margaret: I remember "care ethics" was the term, early in the eighties. Nel Noddings's work on the feminist ethic of care.[9] Other people since then built on her work. There's been critiques of that strand of work, but I think part of the work of reconciliation is about deep respect for one another, deep care for one another, and a real commitment to make connections and form relationships. That's so much what we need in this world right now.

There was an album *Testimony* I used to listen to all the time in college by Ferron, a Canadian feminist singer-songwriter. I heard that album again recently and became reacquainted with a song, "Our Purpose Here." And one line goes: "It's a woman's dream, this autonomy where the lines connect, but the points stay free." I love that because I feel it's a great expression of a certain kind of feminism. That it's still about women's bodily autonomy, integrity, but it's also about this connection. And how important that is.

It is important white people don't get defensive and that we're open to critique. But it's frustrating to see grandstanding among white people about who can be more anti-racist. That's where a kind of carefulness comes in. Of taking care or being careful. Because white people sometimes want to get points or stars, "You're a good, good white person!" Instead of being willing to interrogate themselves, and to see that we're all complicit. Many of us are struggling too and trying and wanting to do something different.

It's funny. I would very much claim to be a feminist, but I'm also extremely critical of aspects of feminism. And I don't think I've ever used the term "feminist West." I can't wait to see how you think about it and work and use it. Because for me, West has come to mean something more like settler colonialism.

Krista: Oh, yeah.

Margaret: Feminist settler colonialism, when you call it that, it's so complicated.

Krista: I wouldn't want to call it that. It's like the term "white feminism" as stand in for mainstream feminism. I use the term "white feminist" as a descriptive term for myself but I do not stand for a politics of white feminism. But these teasings are the necessary work. And I have retained that term "West" from the beginning of my scholarly writing. It has put me at odds at times with friends—some of whom even wrote blurbs for my first book, like José David Saldívar. Fifteen, twenty years ago, he didn't work in U.S. West studies as much as he worked in borderland studies. But I have been of the opinion that we shouldn't sacrifice or concede the term "West" to people who want to make it a triumphalist achievement. I want to work with "West" as a provocation.

Margaret: I have to think more on that. The West is a space of conquest. The West is a settler colonial site. What does it mean to be a feminist in that site? I'm truly thinking about these issues with the *Playing Pioneer Woman* book, about being so into Laura Ingalls Wilder and trying to act that out in my play and the kind of feminism that was.

ROAD FINDS
Coming Full Circle

José and I have one last trip for this project, not an interview.

We head to Santa Fe for the 2022 Western Literature Association Conference. COVID has interrupted the annual conference for the last couple of years, imperiling membership numbers, organizational finances, the progress of scholarship, and training and mentoring of graduate students. Every email about the conference speaks a pent-up desire to get together. José and I feel the desire too, even if we have covered all these miles and connected with lots of people over the last couple of summers and in between.

This time driving to Santa Fe I do not leave my favorite black shirt behind in the Lubbock Best Western. From José's side of the van, he's saying something about Littlefield, where Waylon Jennings was born. I would say it's been a helluva semester, but that's how it always is.

Our cat, Mr. Kitty, is having a holiday at home with Tia Lala, or José's sister Laura. Our boys are settled in DC and San Francisco. Our older son will finish a program this year and has found a sweetheart. Our younger son has landed on his feet on the other side of work upheavals.

The boys have heard their mom has received two awards, and my own mother and sisters have heard. A lot of proud love and congratulations on the family chats. The first is the Wylder Award for Exceptional Service to the organization. The other is the Walker Prize for the year's best essay, for the "Staying with the White Trouble" piece—very unexpected. The Walker Prize is not complicated. I feel the satisfaction of having put an idea through its paces in writing, and of course I'm grateful for recognition for a feminist essay about whiteness. I'm glad especially to see affirmation of Amy Hamilton as *Western American Literature*'s new editor.

But the Wylder Award for long-term service comes with more of a lump in the throat. Thirty years of conferences, excluding two for babies. For a lot of us, WLA becomes a thread of life. I grew up as a young scholar with WLA, and repeatedly the organization took chances on me. It took a big chance when I was elected president only five years after I got the PhD. Encouraging my idea to have a conference focused on the twenty-first century at the Houston Galleria mall![1] For outdoorsy scholars, the mall was a stretch. We honored three Chicano studies siblings—the Saldívars—as Distinguished Achievement Award Critics. There was a Saturday surf venture to the Gulf Coast on Galveston Island, a place with sloppy wind waves if there are waves.

That's how things went—WLA left the door open for risk-taking and I asked it, and us, to take risks too. It's gone both ways.

These are memories and ideas I work out as we drive to Santa Fe. I'm pleased, yes. But nervously figuring out what to say at the awards ceremony. I ask José: "Can't you just please write remarks and deliver them for me?"

Lisa Tatonetti and Audrey Goodman, WLA co-presidents, have spent two years putting the program together, held at the splendid Santa Fe Convention Center.[2] The conference opens with the 1931 experimental film *A Day in Santa Fe* by the Cherokee author, playwright, and poet Lynn Riggs. Comments about the film, Riggs's queering of that place and time, come from James Cox, Kirby Brown, Andy Couch, and Joanna Hearne. How meaningful it is to keep company with these folks.

In an amazing stroke of good fortune, every one of the participants in the *Living West* project comes to Santa Fe for the conference. I have invited people to speak on two panels, but who imagines everyone can or will come? Ours is a sort of unruly thrilled reunion event for a group that has never before met as whole. One event is a roundtable with eight participants and a big audience, and last-minute "excitement," as Kalenda Eaton might call it, when her plane is delayed. But with a few minutes to spare, she arrives smiling, towing her suitcase. Our editor Clark Whitehorn, hosting Nebraska's book exhibit, enthusiastically waves from the back of the big room.

Spirits during the roundtable are high, people talk about the project as nerve-racking but worthwhile. The conversations about the work of the "I" expands our sense of the possible. It's good, people say, but a challenge. Even if we agree to making our work more relatable, to getting better at revealing ourselves, talking about our relations to places we love and who we are in them needs prodding. The word "push" comes up several times, how I have pushed people to examine certain questions, and what we get from pushing ourselves outside of comfort zones. It helps to do it as a collective. Ours is a space of learning and uncertainty but also security—a legitimate feminist rest area at WLA for whatever time it lasts.

Other memorable moments are part of coming full circle. Eight graduate students from Rice are in Santa Fe for four nights, going to panels, presenting research, supporting each other. They make José and me proud.

A plenary I am on, "Editing in a Moment of Crisis," details how people kept projects together through the crises of COVID including family deaths. Kirby Brown talks about "generosity" as a resource, a structure, and a sort of methodology of the new book *North American Indigenous Modernisms*. After that panel I am talking with James Cox, a friend and senior colleague in Native studies. We trade the statement that we won't do noncollaborative research at this point of our work lives when so much depends on building better relations. We talk about needing to be senior to embrace this commitment since humanities promotion standards value monographs, single-author models of authority.

Another panel, for the *Gender and the American West* collection edited by Susan Bernardin, allows me to talk about a theory piece I've done, knowledges derived from specific places via feminist "standpoint."[3] I look back at notes jotted on my program, see a starred phrase from Christine Bold: "reconceptualizing the archive . . . a fifth keyword for this volume."

The nervy evening event finally arrives. Bill Handley, WLA's esteemed and endearing secretary, does the honors of introducing people who staff the awards committees, like Emily Lutenski, who chairs the Walker Committee. I admire Emily, her work and leadership of WLA. In St. Louis, when she cohosted the 2018 conference with Michael L. Johnson, Emily introduced many of us to *Whose Streets?*, a documentary about the police murder of Michael Brown.[4]

Steve Tatum and Kathy Tatum sit at our table during the banquet dinner, when awards are presented. Susan Bernardin is also sitting with us tonight. Susan together with Steve will present me with the Wylder Award. Dina Gilio-Whitaker, Priscilla Ybarra, and Chas Jewett also share our table. All of them are reassuring—my stomach is a mess. Having Priscilla and Dina near seems right because when I was doing the "White

Troubles" essay that wins the award we were meeting and doing group writing for our "Climates of Violence" symposium proposal for coalitional feminism. At the last minute, before I go on stage, I realize that finally I have my feet on the ground.

So many times, I've written things as a way to figure them out, or take issue with something. Sometimes it's been a labor of love. But this piece about "white troubles" comes out of anger, despair, and at some point, I realized I needed not, and that white people needed not, be stuck there, defeated. As I joined in protests, #MeToo, protests against the murder of George Floyd, marches to stop gun violence, I realized something had changed for white people; I was far from alone. The essay came out of not being alone.

Accepting the awards I say some version of these things, and take in the moment. I find out later that Priscilla has had the presence of mind to video the awards presentations and I know how happy my mother will be, so gratified, to see the goings-on.

The next morning, Saturday, the *Living West* project hosts an early panel on the concept of feminist rest areas. The idea has been to apply it to people's own evolving work, see what the concept helps us notice. Dina Gilio-Whitaker does a piece on American Indian Women, Environmental Activism, and Outdoor Sports. Elena Valdez presents a creative nonfiction piece on *enjarradoras*, mud and abode-making with her daughter, as a feminist rest area in northern New Mexico. Randi Tanglen continues to think about rest areas through sitting with the discomfort of settler white histories. And Linda Karell, sharing "Stories for the Rest of Us" from an in-process memoir, tells a mother/daughter tale about addictions and the need for maternal relief.

The conference is inspirational, so much so that José puts forward his name for president in 2027. As we drive back to Houston, I take stock of WLA as a continuing community that supports my efforts to push boundaries on issues of feminist accountabilities to places and to one another. Without naming it as such along the way, WLA always encouraged me to put relationality and place accountabilities at the center of a research ethics and practice, and that philosophy allowed me to find the right footing for my convictions.

If I came to WLA years back as a kind of anti-West figure, I hope that as I exit, whenever that may be, we are more on the side of the future Wests that I was trying for all along. I do think we are decolonizing our knowledges and relations—too slowly always, but that is kind of the way things go. We pay it forward.

Conclusion

Relational Work Ahead

In a project that sees itself as living and not "done" when its book version is published, it's important to think about where or how we go forward.

Toward what do our relations move?

In certain circles, it's a truism to say settler colonialism is ongoing, a structure and not an event. What's not a truism, though it is true, is that movements opposing colonial structures also are ongoing. Five to seven million women marching worldwide the day after the inauguration of Donald Trump in 2017. Two to three hundred tribes with thousands of other allies coming together at Standing Rock to protest the Dakota Access pipeline construction. Millions in the streets globally to protest the murder of George Floyd. At least a million standing with U.S. high school students against gun violence. Millions, including so many school children, for Global Climate Marches. There are many keepers of the flame.

In 1981, speaking in the disillusioned time after the election of Ronald Reagan, Bernice Johnson Reagon declared, "It is our world, and we are here to stay. And we are not on the defensive."[1] She was talking to audiences at the West Coast Women's Music Festival about discouraged media people and writers of books who perpetuated the wrong idea that the civil rights movement "was a dream," that "nothing happened" in the 1970s.

"It's a lie," she insisted; if you have a better job than your mother had, who else did that? "Of course they don't tell you *you* did that [changed the country, stopped the war], and so you keep trying to figure out what went wrong!" The lie only becomes true if "you believe them and do not take the next step." The next step is building new relationships.

For Reagon, an "offensive movement" began in the United States in the 1960s and continued, and if it faltered under the cloud of the Reagan election, it's because in order to go forward, "we've got to do it [make politics] with some folk we don't care too much about." Coalitions for the twenty-first century, she told festival-goers, need clarity about what the work of coalition is—it's relational work, it's the work of care.

The social worlds of summer 2023, when I write these lines, are a great distance from the era of global civil rights movements of 1968 or even from living memory of them. Perhaps we are less far off, in the United States, from the 1980s. But for me, Bernice Johnson Reagon's thinking is medicine. I take from her a sense that the world belongs to the people, that justice movements play offense not defense, and that relations and care, coalitional work, are building-block political strategies, maps to new places. How have millions of people gotten to the streets in recent years? The massive scale only happens through coalition, collaboration.

In a time of political despair in the United States, it's heartening to notice coalitional lessons have been embraced—however imperfectly. Indeed, the design of this *Living West* project represents an attempt in real time to experiment with lessons learned. As scholars we have come together not by way of single issues or argumentation but by way of relationality. And because of that, I envision us still talking. We have more to talk about now, to get to know one another about.

I have learned from contributors how to think anew about the U.S. West and care practices of feminism. I hear more clearly what Priscilla Solis Ybarra has been saying for a long time about the geography and history of the West as the enabling (Anglo/imperial) imaginary of American environmentalism. I appreciate, in fresh ways, that the West, as a concept and an analytic, tells us how we got to where we are now politically. It continues to shape lives and relations to places.

The question of belonging that is present so often in discussions of place offers many surprises. In the east Texas land legacies of Kalenda Eaton's family, I see the depth of western histories that remain occluded, unforwarded, which shake understandings of reality. Another surprise is how much the political decision to not belong, for example to disassociate from sexist gender norms or colonialist communities, is a reminder of the critical distances that can be opened up or made available through a feminist standpoint. All the white feminists here wrestle with the problem of white supremacy and implications in its social webs. Whatever common language we forge comes about through interactivity, as Dina Gilio-Whitaker observes, and coalitional conversations. Talking with, toward, and in awareness of one another buffers the wedge issues, as Margaret Jacobs calls them, that arise when different political priorities strain a common purpose. While the iconic settler West of cinema, popular history, and current geopolitics, is always present, so too our relations with one another are real-time exercises in a collective vision of futures that take us elsewhere.

One takeaway for me is a sense of how much more fundamentally our relations need to change. I am speaking broadly. I mean they need to change in this country. But more locally, they need to change in the organizations in which any of us recognize accountability relations. For some of us that will be the Western Literature Association.

A 2023 essay by Hillary Rodham Clinton, "The Weaponization of Loneliness," is one marker of a decent bit of mainstream thinking that shows nonetheless how far there is yet to go on a path of better relations and accountability. The piece is a diagnosis of the political character of the divisive present. Clinton sees "loneliness" or frayed relationalities as toxic for national well-being, democracy, and the functioning of institutions. She links the rise of strong-man authoritarianism to the vulnerability of people who suffer existential crises of belonging and purpose, who are falling through cracks of imploded communities and disconnected kin systems. We might say Clinton updates, with less edge and style, Joan Didion's diagnosis of 1968 in *Slouching Towards Bethlehem*: that the "center was not holding." Progressive people should not dismiss Clinton's essay out of hand because it will be read widely and expresses popular political thought.

Clinton is a profoundly capable white feminist. But as one reads into her gloss on U.S. history, she lapses into a surprisingly dated, even *Pollyanna*, sense of the past. She talks about "us" as Americans "working together" in a grand experiment. Of laborers who stand up for a better workday. Of enslaved people shepherding others through the Underground Railroad toward "freedom." Of pioneers who "stick together in wagon trains." It's breathtaking to encounter wagon train families as patriots in what becomes a happy history of America, getting better and better by remembering "we're all in this together."

I pause on Clinton's essay because her identification of the disrepair of national relationality is right. Violence, greed, exploitation, grievance politics, mental health breakdowns—these are relations gone wrong. But what is not grappled with are the core problems: white supremacy and how it lives and reproduces itself inside of a patriarchal settler state. Who among us can imagine being in conversation with the Hillary Clintons of the world? Many white people today will prefer to work across race or Indigeneity rather than inside the social worlds of whiteness. This problem of white people with white people is one to take seriously because the coalitions needed now do not look like those of years past.

In U.S. West studies, the transformation to perceiving western geopolitical space as settler space has been a paradigm shift in understanding space, place, history, and knowledge itself. All the activist and scholarly organizations taking seriously the impacts of settler frameworks are faced with this reckoning. It's a call to recreate not only our knowledges but our relationships with one another, including among white people. The presence at times of "ugly feelings" in scholars' conversations about university life might well also describe the discomfort expressed by some of us about their own whiteness and white histories. We might call it (in affect language) "shame." Shame, as my colleague Rosemary Hennessy and I discuss, is distinct from guilt, is more of a social category, an effect of social censure and judgment. She reminds me, guilt says: I did something wrong. Shame says: I am wrong. Shame places us in social networks and relations. It can be excruciating to talk about shaming topics. One can't hold on long to feelings of shame and allow their presence.

To the degree one evades shame, and why not evade it unless there is a reason, it can interrupt memory or create disremembering and denials, elisions—which is to say perhaps those areas become stuck, unevolved. In the *Living West* project, living beyond the initial strong discomforts of talking publicly about whiteness has hoped to serve a purpose. The implication of white people in white supremacy is well beyond us as individuals to repudiate. In an important if seemingly different vein related to white power movements, the historian Kathleen Belew makes the case that so-called lone wolves who perpetrate white violence are mischaracterized as 'lone' since they leave behind manifestos, call-outs, to networks of extremism.[2] They never act alone. They perceive a social glue between white people that other white people strive to dismantle.

White feminists may disavow certain belongings out of political commitments, but disavowal cannot erase one's whiteness. We are "glued in" with the rest of white people. If we are to be active as feminists against white racism and settler unawareness in the everyday places we go about our lives, accountability to whiteness might be reevaluated as a political asset. Not in the sense of self-congratulation, but in the sense that better allies are less timid, defensive, and anxious about whiteness, less vulnerable to silence and hiding.

I am convinced that many white feminists do not claim their feminism because they are stymied by how to engage whiteness in ways that do not eclipse the violence they know is occasioned by white supremacy. They know that they don't know the lived experience or threat of that violence. It is not in their or in my bones. *Living West*, I hope, offers ways to remember whiteness together, in concert with other feminists, as a strategy of intervention on not remembering or standing alone in one's white shame (so to speak).

This kind of philosophy or group charge of "calling in" white people, not only "calling out" white people, is being expressed increasingly, with admirable nuance, in large organizations like Stand Up for Racial Justice (SURJ), led by coalitions of young activists. The commitment to persist in these conversations as white feminists, to "stay with the white trouble," is key to being in feminist relation and not being passive about either feminism or whiteness. White feminists are not "just white girls" any longer—many of us have grown up. As insufficient as that phrase is in 2023, it perhaps surfaces a moment, earlier, along the way to more overt anti-racist or decolonial feminist standpoints. A form of feminist care work.

Returning to the blind spots of Hillary Clinton about "pioneers," and the blind spots of white people about settler life generally, they are not remarkable. They are everywhere, every day. Pioneers as iconic figures of a national history, and "Pioneer Parks," celebrate colonial claims on land. Their ubiquity relegitimizes those claims. Controversy rarely accompanies parks and monuments commemorating pioneers. They do not call up comparisons to Confederate monuments. Which means that the takeover of Indigenous land, and the fact that treaty agreements (unenforced) still govern land disputes, lives in plain sight; it is not hidden in plain sight. The blind spot normalizes settler presence and makes settlers invisible to themselves, unremarkable.

José and I have talked a lot about the Pioneer Parks of our travels. I write about a few specific instances, in Bend, Oregon, and in Lincoln,

Nebraska. There is a Pioneer Obelisk in Houston's Hermann Park where, as a part of my regular "US West and Its Others" classes, I take students so we can notice together what most of us are trained to walk past. My abilities as a tour guide, with the help of Indigenous studies, have gotten better. In the last assignment of the class in spring of 2023, I asked students to use our tour in Hermann Park as a model for doing a walking tour of memorials in their hometowns. What did the memorials tell them, or not tell them, about American history in the places they call home? What land acknowledgment could they come up with? Watching students grapple with questions about settler history and Indigenous presence in their homeplaces was revealing to all of us—we barely scratched the surfaces of what knowledge is needed to make different worlds.

Perhaps the most interesting and difficult questions going forward, again in terms of relationality, are how to make feminist rest areas in the complicated spaces of settler imaginaries. Relationships in this project are not by definition political—in the sense that no one signed up for a particular campaign when we decided to do interviews. The fact that I have done particular political actions with some of the contributors may be a bonus, but we came together for conversations and consciousness raising. How our relations participate in other processes of reconciliation or justice remains to be seen.

Without designing it as such, the overall affect of the *Living West* project has been hopeful. We might say people have felt cared about. Is it something I have done, José has done, groups of people have done for one another? Is it a tone, or a practice of listening? Certainly everyone has given something, as Reagon counsels activists to do in coalitions: give. In any case, optimism in a moment of political despair is a valuable resource for individuals and for groups. Hopefulness, as an offensive ideal (in Bernice Johnson Reagon's sense of playing "offense"), keeps people going, us going; it shows the value of our work, ourselves, and our relations with one another.

Most of us act in places where we have agency and cause, with people we know, and with the talents we have. Transforming relationality is itself a very ambitious charge. When I reflect on what it means for me personally, how much I need to grow from the raised Protestant efficient woman I have been all my life, I am genuinely humbled. Others hopefully can help me, care for me, as I learn more about how to care and be a good neighbor. One priority for me, at this point in my life, is to slow down enough, still myself enough, to listen to what people around me are saying. Grievance politics and reasons for despair are everywhere. Maintaining a sense of possibility and willingness for risk seem ways to keep in fighting shape. Another is practicing gratitudes. There are always places and people to celebrate, reasons to keep fighting, and reasons to fight for one another.

ACKNOWLEDGMENTS

The generosities of the contributors to this project appear across the pages of this book. I feel most fortunate to have memories for a lifetime and to anticipate future conversations. Unlike many research projects that unfold over long periods and involve talks given and archives consulted, this one was relatively quick, and involved only one talk outside of Rice University, at the University of Colorado Boulder's Center of the American West. I did that talk, and so much of the project, with Zainab Abdali, a smart and good-humored PhD student and contributor who served as the Clancy Taylor Public Humanities summer intern in 2021 and 2022. In all else, I've had the faithful support of José Aranda, my partner in life, whose presence and substantive conversations ground me in all I do.

I appreciate research support from Rice's Dean of Humanities, Kathleen Canning, as well as from Rice University's Humanities Research Center. I appreciate Sabine Barcatta for manuscript expertise and kindness. The writer Liz Rosner has become a regular part of my writing life, sharing her talents as a writer and a teacher of writers, and I am grateful to have new projects on the horizon and imagine Liz as part of them. The scholar Rosemary Hennessy, my writing partner and close friend, always can be counted on to clarify stakes. Clark Whitehorn at the University of Nebraska Press has been a supporter from the start, working to fulfill our joint vision. Susan Kollin, always a generous colleague, offered a bounty of insightful suggestions as a press reader.

My sister-in-law, Laura Aranda, held down the home front for long stretches when José and I traveled. She kept our beautiful Mr. Amiga happy and fed. In these last weeks he lived out the last days of his life; they were content. My older son has a group of close friends who, with him, raised Amiga. A friend to all—that's how he lives on in their memories. José and I miss him.

Sometimes one hears about land acknowledgments as too performative. I personally find it meaningful to feel out the localities and griefs of these statements. I pay respects to the lands and people of the Karankawa and Atakapa-Ishak, original inhabitants of today's Gulf Coast South region; I pay respects to their elders and strive to be a good neighbor in the now.

INTERVIEW PROTOCOL

Thank you so much for sharing yourself and your thinking.

Our interviews, I'm hoping, are organic conversations. The video of the interview is a sixty-to-seventy-five-minute record, an archive. It's up to you and us where the conversation goes.

The questions are prompts for thinking beforehand, reflecting. The goal is not for anyone to "answer the questions," per se. Each one could be an all-day conversation. Rather we begin here, knowing these are prompts for you, us, and for people's work later. Also, one of the biggest gifts for me is to learn about questions you would prioritize instead, so interview *me*, please, or reorient us as the process unfolds.

The decision to name this project *Living West as Feminists* is a way to generate discussion of the very problems invoked by the terms "U.S. West" and "feminism." I will write in the blog about why the terms seems strategically valuable to me and also limited. I expect we will address the limits at length as well as take up alternatives you all envision.

One aspiration of the project is to speak ourselves across the ranges of the personal, intellectual and scholarly, and the political. In the one-page summary I sent that is a kernel of the book proposal, I focused on how scholars live their feminisms and live their relation to places and land. I wanted us to think aloud together about how we inhabit our feminisms and how they inhabit us. To me these seem *not* like simple or straight-forward considerations. But a blending of the intellectual, personal, and political likely helps open us to the overlapping layers of our lives—not dislocate one part from another, or remove our histories and families and misgivings from our writing, teaching, and politics. Feminist research practices encourage positioning ourselves in our work, locating ourselves somehow. Situating the self and our communities in place can enrich our work, complicate its stakes, and force the issue of accountabilities. Hope-fully it moves the "us" of the project toward one another.

Questions

Let's talk about the place or land we are on for the conversation. Start with the where of the here. How do you feel linked to it (e.g., early memories of place or land in your family, as a child, other strong memories of place)?

More generally, what places do you feel comfortable in or welcome—or not? What places are your places or your peoples' places? Alternatively, on what land or lands do you feel you belong, or not belong?

What is your association of these places with the U.S. West? Associations might be feelings, memory, body knowledges, historical and cultural legacies, language or sound legacies, senses of kin and ancestry, any of which inevitably might include violence.

What do you think of when you think about "feminism" (an image, idea, anything that comes to mind)? How do you characterize your own feminism (e.g., politics, theory work, institutional change in university, ways of being or writing, environment practices, relation to economics, maternity, sexuality, care work, women and girls)?

Share an example or a story about the ways you personally live your feminism and your relation to places and/or land. Maybe it was imperfect—that's part of the story. What is the where of how you inhabited feminism and how feminism inhabited you? The story could be now.

What kinds of readings help you think about place, land, or feminism?

In response to worries about the current status of the humanities in universities, administrators and university research centers often encourage scholars to engage in public-facing work more so than in years past. Are you interested in this public work, or already doing it? What are its challenges for you and your practices as a scholar?

Let's assume you have a chance to talk about feminism and the U.S. West to a gathered group of interested nonuniversity people. What are your priorities in these discussions? What do you want people to know?

What surprises you about this project? What follow-up ideas do you have, or what queries do you have, for Krista or José?

NOTES

Feminist Road-Tripping

1. The thought about the many trails of tears comes from Harjo, *An American Sunrise*, xiv.
2. For examples of the framework, see Comer, "Thinking Otherwise," and Van Houten, "bell hooks."
3. This essay eventually was published as Comer, "Staying with the White Trouble of Recent Feminist Westerns," and was awarded the Western Literature Association's Don D. Walker Prize for best essay published in western American literary and cultural studies in 2021.
4. I respect "intersectionality" as a term used by antiracist and decolonial feminists. At the same time, I am persuaded by Wendy Brown that feminists benefit from distinguishing between the descriptive capacity of "intersectionality" and the need to theorize the relatively autonomous forms of institutional power that produce injustice (family, medicine, law, education, religion, economics). See Brown, "The Impossibility of Women's Studies."
5. For a discussion of the compatibility of feminism and hard-line conservatism, see the introduction to Schuller, *The Trouble with White Women*, 1–12.
6. Ruíz and Dotson, "On the Politics of Coalition."
7. King, *The Black Shoals*.
8. Quoted in King, "Interview with Dr. Tiffany Lethabo King," 66.
9. Again see Comer, "Thinking Otherwise," and Comer, "The Problem of the Critical in Global Wests." In understanding the new political economy of regions under globalization, both essays draw from Tatum, "Spectrality and the Postregional Interface."
10. Comer, "Toward a Feminist Turn."
11. See "Code of Conduct," https://www.westernlit.org/code-of-conduct/.
12. See Women's March, "Women's Agenda."
13. Kendall, *Hood Feminism*.
14. Kirk Siegler, *Roots of U.S. Capitol Insurrectionists Run through American West*, National Public Radio, January 12, 2021, https://www.npr.org/2021/01/12/955665162/roots-of-u-s-capitol-insurrectionists-run-through-american-west.

15. Harding, "Philosophy and Standpoint Theory."
16. See Smith, *Decolonizing Methodologies*. Also see Kirkness and Barnhardt, "First Nations and Higher Education."
17. For more on the methodology of "listening to white stories as such," see Comer, "Staying with the White Trouble," 103.
18. For a discussion of "grinding" as the culture of white supremacy and capitalism today, see Hersey, *Rest Is Resistance*.
19. Duggan, "Academe's Ugly Feelings."
20. Federici, *Re-enchanting the World*, 2.
21. Institute for Women Surfers, http://www.instituteforwomensurfers.org/.
22. For more on Brown Girl Surf today, see https://browngirlsurf.com/.
23. Ahmed, "Once We Find Each Other."
24. Ahmed, "Once We Find Each Other."

The Blog Launches Us

1. Krista Comer, *Living West as Feminists* (blog), https://feministwests.blogs.rice.edu/.

The Relations Holding Us

1. Ybarra, "A Farm for My Mother, a Farm for Meme."
2. The term conceptualizes cultural geographies for people of Mexican descent that spill beyond the national boundaries of the United States or Mexico, and is coined by the great border thinker Américo Paredes, in *A Texas-Mexican Cancionero: Folksongs of the Lower Border*.
3. For a relevant discussion of land banks and Chicana feminism, see Ybarra, *Writing the Good Life*, 96–117.

Querencia across Generations

1. The website for Tewa Women United can be found at https://tewawomenunited.org/ and the "Indigenous Wisdom Curriculum Project" is run by the Indian Pueblo Cultural Center, available at https://indianpueblo.org/indigenous-wisdom-curriculum-project/.
2. Please see Knapp, "O'Keeffe Museum, Pueblo-Indigenous Groups Oppose NM Tourism Dept."

Remaking the Heart of Aztlán

1. Vizcaíno-Alemán, "Growing Up Chicana," 172.
2. Vizcaíno-Alemán, 172.

3. Vizcaíno-Alemán, "Resisting the Darkness of Boxes."
4. Learn more about EspinoZa's mural here: Denver Public Library, Western History Resources, "Important and Historic Mural by Chicana Artist."
5. Cisneros, *The House on Mango Street*.

Feminist Homing and Unhoming

1. Estés, *Women Who Run with the Wolves*.
2. Ahmed, "Once We Find Each Other, So Much Else Becomes Possible."
3. Kolodny, *The Lay of the Land*.
4. Comer, "Standpoint, Situated Knowledge, Feminist Wests."
5. Hamilton, "Colonialism and Gendered Violence," 390–92.
6. Hamilton, "Gender, Affect, Environmental Justice, and Indigeneity in the Classroom."

Road Finds: On Keeping Company

1. Minnie Bruce Pratt Obituary, https://obits.syracuse.com/us/obituaries/syracuse/name/minnie-pratt-obituary?id=52388716.
2. Pratt, "Identity," 18.

Outside the Picture Window

1. *Institute for Women Surfers*, accessed June 3, 2022, http://www.instituteforwomensurfers.org/.

Deciding to Remember

1. Karell, "Spokane Kitten."
2. Ivan Doig, "The Collection—Ivan Doig Archive," *Montana State University Library*, accessed June 3, 2022, http://ivandoig.montana.edu/collection/.
3. See program at Western Literature Association, "WLA 2016 Conference Program: The Profane West," October 2016, http://www.westernlit.org/wp-content/uploads/2010/01/2016-Conference-Program.pdf.

Lunch

1. Cates-Carney, "Montana Students React to Texas School Shooting."

For Me, the West Is Rural

1. Tanglen, "Guest Column."
2. For more on Humanities Montana, see "Humanities Montana," June 17, 2019, https://www.humanitiesmontana.org/.

3. Please see, Tanglen, "Teaching Confederate Monuments as American Literature."
4. Please see Tanglen, "Reconfiguring Religion."
5. Tanglen, "Reconfiguring Religion."
6. Bergman, *The Motherless Child in the Novels of Pauline Hopkins*.
7. Jennifer Bendery, "Montana GOP Gov. Taps Far-Right Conspiracy Theorist for State Humanities Board." *HuffPost*, May 9, 2023, https://www.huffpost.com/entry/greg-gianforte-jeremy-carl-white-nationalism_n_64592fede4b094269baed3fa.
8. Walter Criswell, "Randi Tanglen 'Hopes and Keeps Busy,'" UND *Today* (blog), March 7, 2023, https://blogs.und.edu/und-today/2023/03/randi-tanglen-hopes-and-keeps-busy/.

Road Finds: What Lingers in the Air

1. For a review of Stegner's thinking and writing in his later years see Comer, *Landscapes of the New West*, 38–49.
2. A full discussion of this controversy can be found in Comer, "Exceptionalism, Other Wests, Critical Regionalism," especially 166–69.

Finding Community through Transcription

1. Fadda-Conrey, *Contemporary Arab-American Literature*.
2. Anzaldúa and Keating, *This Bridge We Call Home*.
3. Moraga and Anzaldúa, *This Bridge Called My Back*.

A Rendezvous

1. Melody Graulich's short story "Wishful Thinking" was published in *Front Range Review* in spring 2020.
2. Graulich, "Prepositional Spaces."

A Fighting Zapotec Feminism

1. Alberto, "Mestizaje desde Abajo."
2. Nicolas, "'Soy de Zoochina.'"
3. Stephen, *Transborder Lives*.
4. To learn more about Citlali Fabián and her work, see Fabián.

Colville Women

1. Gilio, "Panhe at the Crossroads."
2. Gilio-Whitaker, "American Settler Colonialism 101."

3. See the website for San Onofre Parks Foundation, "San Onofre Parks Foundation," accessed January 14, 2023, https://sanoparks.org/.
4. Mackenzie, *The Exiles*.
5. Gilio-Whitaker, *Illegitimate Nation*.
6. Dina has written about the Colville case for ICT *News*, "Native History."
7. Gilio-Whitaker and Comer, "Being Good Relatives."
8. Gilio-Whitaker, "What's in a Name?"

Road Finds: Slowing Down for Home

1. Mountz et al., "For Slow Scholarship."

Retracing the Western Black Family

1. Find more about the "Oklahoma Black Homesteader Project" online.
2. See Eaton, "Djeli."
3. Eaton, *Womanism*, 8.

The Archives of Gardens

1. Goodman, "What Is a Feminist Landscape?"
2. For more, see Campbell's introduction to *The Rhizomatic West*, 1–40.
3. See "Charis Wilson Journal, Letters, and Notes."
4. Goodman, "What Is a Feminist Landscape?"
5. LeMenager, *Living Oil*, 2.

The Both/And

1. Dr. Cristina Eisenberg, for instance, was hired in the inaugural role of associate dean in the College of Forestry for Inclusive Excellence and Tribal Initiatives. See "Eisenberg, Cristina | College of Forestry Directory," Oregon State University, accessed July 12, 2023, https://directory.forestry .oregonstate.edu/people/eisenberg-cristina.
2. The guest-edited volume by Krista Comer and Susan Bernardin is *Western American Literature* 53, no. 1 (2018).
3. Bernardin, *The Routledge Companion to Gender and the American West*.
4. Nudelman, "Marys Peak Creek."
5. Forest Service, *The Kalapuya and Marys Peak*.
6. Hank Sims, "Klamath Dam Removal Clears Final Federal Hurdle; Historic Decommissioning of Four Hydropower Dams to Begin Next Year," *Lost Coast Outpost*, November 17, 2022, https://lostcoastoutpost.com/2022/nov/17 /klamath-dams-coming-down/.

7. Bernardin, "Introduction."

8. LeCocq, "Indigenous Studies Minor to Start at OSU."

Roads Finds: Falling Rocks

1. National Park Service, "The 24 Associated Tribes."

2. Hofstaedter, "Abortion Was Already Inaccessible on Reservation Land."

3. For one of the most recognized discussions of this history see Federici, *Caliban*.

4. Pacia, "Reproductive Rights vs. Reproductive Justice."

5. See *"The Opposite Side of the River,"* accessed September 12, 2023, https://www.youtube.com/watch?v=K8R3Ny4wvzE.

Returning to Pueblo as Myself

1. For more information about the Sangre de Cristo Arts Museum, see https://www.sdc-arts.org/about-arts-center.

2. Ripley, "Assault on Wife of a Legislator."

3. Thomsen and Baker, "The Importance of Talking about Women."

4. Ross and Solinger, *Reproductive Justice*.

5. Thomsen, Baker, and Levitt, "Pregnant?"

6. Tolentino, "We're Not Going Back to the Time Before Roe."

Road Finds: El Pueblo Museum

1. "Borderlands of Southern Colorado // El Pueblo History Museum," accessed September 13, 2023, https://www.historycolorado.org/exhibit/borderlands.

2. Museum of Fine Arts, Houston, "The Hogg Brothers Collection," accessed July 12, 2023, https://emuseum.mfah.org/groups/Hogg-Brothers-Collection/results.

3. "Women of the Borderlands | History Colorado," History Colorado, February 25, 2021, https://www.historycolorado.org/story/borderlands-southern-colorado/2021/02/25/women-borderlands.

4. See Conan, "Chicano Movement's Denver Roots Run Deep."

True Confessions

1. Lamont, *The Bower Atmosphere*.

2. Lamont, "'More Than She Deserves.'"

3. Lamont, *Westerns*.

Reconciling Feminism

1. Center for Great Plains Studies, "Contemporary Indigeneity."
2. See more at Genoa Indian School Digital Reconciliation Project.
3. Find out more on their website; see Reconciliation Rising.
4. Reconciliation Rising, "'Return of the Pawnees' Film."
5. Deloria, *Playing Indian*.
6. "See Up with People III," *Colorado*, https://www.youtube.com/watch?v=9kuCnrSkeao.
7. Thomas and various artists, *Free to Be You and Me*.
8. Jacobs, *White Mother to a Dark Race*.
9. Noddings, *Caring*.

Roads Finds: Coming Full Circle

1. For an archived program, see https://www.westernlit.org/wp-content/uploads/2022/09/wla-Conference-Program-2003-The-West-of-the-21st-century.pdf.
2. https://www.westernlit.org/wp-content/uploads/2022/10/Program-2022-for-distribution-side-by-side.pdf.
3. Comer, "Standpoint, Situated Knowledge, Feminist Wests."
4. See Gabbatt, "Whose Streets?"

Conclusion

1. Reagon, "Coalition Politics," 368. Quotes drawn from pages 367–68.
2. Belew, *Bring the War Home*.

BIBLIOGRAPHY

Ahmed, Sara. "Once We Find Each Other, So Much Else Becomes Possible." Interview by Adam Fitzgerald. *Literary Hub*, April 10, 2017. https://lithub.com/sara-ahmed-once-we-find-each-other-so-much-else-becomes-possible/.

Alberto, Lourdes. "Coming Out as Indian: On Being an Indigenous Latina in the US." *Latino Studies* 15 (2017): 247–53.

———. "Mestizaje desde Abajo: Zapotec Visual Cultures and Decolonial Mestizaje in the Photography of Citlali Fabián." *Aztlán: A Journal of Chicano Studies* 46, no. 2 (Fall 2021): 235–50.

Amadahy, Zainab, and Bonita Lawrence. "Indigenous Peoples and Black People in Canada: Settlers or Allies?" In *Breaching the Colonial Contract*, edited by Arlo Kempf, 105–36. Dordrecht: Springer Netherlands, 2009.

Anaya, Rudolfo. *Heart of Aztlán*. 1976. Reprint, Albuquerque: University of New Mexico Press, 1988.

Anzaldúa, Gloria, and AnaLouise Keating. *This Bridge We Call Home: Radical Visions for Transformation*. New York: Routledge, 2002.

Aranda, José F., Jr. *The Places of Modernity in Early Mexican American Literature, 1984–1948*. Lincoln: University of Nebraska Press, 2022.

Barker, Joanne. "Water as an Analytic of Indigenous Feminisms." *American Indian Culture and Research Journal* 43, no. 3 (2020): 1–40.

Belew, Kathleen. *Bring the War Home: The White Power Movement and Paramilitary America*. Cambridge MA: Harvard University Press, 2019.

Bergman, Jill. *The Motherless Child in the Novels of Pauline Hopkins*. Baton Rouge: Louisiana State University Press, 2012.

Bernardin, Susan. "Introduction." In *In the Land of the Grasshopper Song: Two Women in the Klamath River Indian Country in 1908–09*, 2nd ed., by Mary Ellicott Arnold and Mabel Reed, ix–xviii. Lincoln: University of Nebraska Press, 2011.

Bernardin, Susan, ed. *The Routledge Companion to Gender and the American West*. New York: Routledge, 2022.

Bernardin, Susan, and Krista Comer. "Introduction: Pasts, Presents, Futures." *Western American Literature* 53, no. 1 (2018): xi–xix.

Brooks, Joanna. *The Book of Mormon Girl: A Memoir of an American Faith*. New York: Free Press, 2012.

Brown, Wendy. "The Impossibility of Women's Studies." *differences: A Journal of Feminist Cultural Studies* 9, no. 3 (1997): 79–101.

Campbell, Neil. *The Rhizomatic West: Representing the American West in a Transnational, Global, Media Age*. Lincoln NE: Bison Books, 2008.

Cates-Carney, Corin. "Montana Students React to Texas School Shooting." *Montana Public Radio*, May 21, 2018. https://www.mtpr.org/montana-news/2018-05-21/montana-students-react-to-texas-school-shooting.

Center for Great Plains Studies. "Contemporary Indigeneity." Accessed July 12, 2023. https://www.unl.edu/plains/contemporary-indigeneity.

"Charis Wilson Journal, Letters, and Notes Documenting the Whitman Trip with Edward Weston." Accessed January 14, 2023. https://oac.cdlib.org/findaid/ark:/13030/c8g44vx6/entire_text/.

Cisneros, Sandra. *The House on Mango Street*. New York: Knopf Doubleday, 1991.

Clinton, Hillary Rodham. "The Weaponization of Loneliness." *The Atlantic*, August 7, 2023. https://www.theatlantic.com/ideas/archive/2023/08/hillary-clinton-essay-loneliness-epidemic/674921/.

Conan, Neal. "Chicano Movement's Denver Roots Run Deep." With guests Lisa Martinez and Antonio Esquibel. *Talk of the Nation*. NPR, June 30, 2011. https://www.npr.org/2011/06/30/137529484/the-chicano-movements-denver-roots-run-deep.

The Combahee River Collective. "The Combahee River Collective Statement." In *Home Girls: A Black Feminist Anthology*, edited by Barbara Smith, 264–74. New Brunswick NJ: Rutgers University Press, 2000.

Comer, Krista. "Exceptionalism, Other Wests, Critical Regionalism." In *American Literary History* 23, no. 1 (2011): 159–73. https://doi.org/10.1093/alh/ajq043.

———. *Landscapes of the New West: Gender and Geography in Contemporary Women's Writing*. Chapel Hill: University of North Carolina Press, 1999.

———. *Living West as Feminists: Conversations about the Where of Us* (blog), n.d. https://feministwests.blogs.rice.edu.

———. "The Problem of the Critical in Global Wests." In *A History of Western American Literature*, edited by Susam Kollin, 205–22. New York: Cambridge University Press, 2015.

———. "Standpoint, Situated Knowledge, Feminist Wests." In *The Routledge Companion to Gender and the American West*, edited by Susan Bernardin, 114–24. New York: Routledge, 2022.

———. "Staying with the White Trouble of Recent Feminist Westerns." *Western American Literature* 56, no. 2 (2021): 101–23.

———. *Surfer Girls in the New World Order*. Chapel Hill NC: Duke University Press, 2010.

———. "Thinking Otherwise across Global Wests: Issues of Mobility and Feminist Critical Regionalism." *Occasion: Interdisciplinary Studies in the Humanities* 10 (December 7, 2016): 1–18. https://arcade.stanford.edu/occasion/thinking-otherwise-across-global-wests-issues-mobility-and-feminist-critical-regionalism.

———. "Toward a Feminist Turn." *Western American Literature* 53, no. 1 (2018): 11–20.

———. "West." In *Keywords for American Cultural Studies*, 3rd ed. New York: New York University Press, 2020. https://keywords.nyupress.org/american-cultural-studies/essay/west/.

Cotera, Maria, director, with co-director Linda Garcia Merchant. *Chicana por Mi Raza Digital Memory Project*. https://chicanapormiraza.org/.

Davis, Angela Y. *Abolition Democracy: Beyond Empire, Prisons, and Torture*. New York: Seven Stories Press, 2011.

———. *Freedom Is a Constant Struggle: Ferguson, Palestine, and the Foundations of a Movement*. Chicago: Haymarket Books, 2016.

Deloria, Philip Joseph. *Playing Indian*. New Haven CT: Yale University Press, 1998.

Denver Public Library, Western History Resources. "Important and Historic Mural by Chicana Artist, Carlota Espinoza Back on Display," September 22, 2020. https://history.denverlibrary.org/news/carlota-espinoza-mural.

Didion, Joan. *Slouching Towards Bethlehem*. New York: Farrar, Straus, and Giroux, 1968.

Duggan, Lisa. "Academe's Ugly Feelings: Navigating Passive Aggression and Competitive Envy." *The Chronicle of Higher Education*, February 7, 2022. https://www.chronicle.com/article/academes-ugly-feelings.

Eaton, Kalenda. "Djeli: Memories Tell Us Everything and Nothing at All." *Oklahoma Humanities* 14, no. 1 (2021): 14–17.

———. *Womanism, Literature, and the Transformation of the Black Community, 1965–1980*. New York: Routledge, 2008.

Ehrlich, Gretel. *The Solace of Open Spaces: Essays*. New York: Viking, 1985.

Estés, Clarissa Pinkola. *Women Who Run with the Wolves: Myths and Stories of the Wild Woman Archetype*. New York: Ballantine Books, 1995.

Fabián, Citlali. "Citlali Fabián." Accessed January 14, 2023. http://www.citlalifabian.com.

Fadda-Conrey, Carol. *Contemporary Arab-American Literature: Transnational Reconfigurations of Citizenship and Belonging*. New York: New York University Press, 2014.

Federici, Silvia. *Caliban and the Witch: Women, the Body, and Primitive Accumulation*. New York: Autonomedia, 2004.

———. *Re-enchanting the World: Feminism and the Politics of the Commons*. Oakland CA: PM Press, 2018.

Finney, Carolyn. *Black Faces, White Spaces: Reimagining the Relationship of African Americans to the Great Outdoors*. Chapel Hill: University of North Carolina Press Books, 2014.

Friedan, Betty. *The Feminine Mystique (50th Anniversary Edition)*. New York: W. W. Norton, 2013.

Forest Service. *The Kalapuya and Marys Peak*. YouTube. 2021. https://www.youtube.com/watch?v=k0ea80bvzyE.

Gabbatt, Adam. "Whose Streets? Powerful Ferguson Film Focuses on 'Flashpoint Moment.'" *The Guardian*, August 11, 2017, sec. Film. https://www.theguardian.com/film/2017/aug/11/ferguson-documentary-whose-streets-michael-brown-race-protests.

Genoa Indian School Digital Reconciliation Project. "Home Page: Genoa Indian School Digital Reconciliation Project." Accessed July 12, 2023. https://genoaindianschool.org/.

Gilio, Dina. "Panhe at the Crossroads: Toward an Indigenized Environmental Jus-

tice Theory." *American Studies E T Ds*, February 1, 2012. https://digitalrepository
.unm.edu/amst_etds/15.

Gilio-Whitaker, Dina. "American Settler Colonialism 101." *ThoughtCo*. Accessed
January 14, 2023. https://www.thoughtco.com/american-settler-colonialism
-4082454.

———. *As Long as Grass Grows: The Indigenous Fight for Environmental Justice, from
Colonization to Standing Rock*. Boston: Beacon Press, 2019.

———. *Illegitimate Nation: Privilege, Race, and Belonging in the U.S. Settler State*.
Boston: Beacon Press, forthcoming.

———. *Indians for Sale: Pretenders, Disenrollment, and Native American Identity
in Late Capitalism*. Boston: Beacon Press, forthcoming.

———. "Native History: The Epic Termination Battle on the Colville Indian Reservation." *I C T News*, September 2, 2015. https://ictnews.org/archive/native-history
-the-epic-termination-battle-on-the-colville-indian-reservation.

———. "What's in a Name? What It Means to Decolonize a Natural Feature." *Sierra:
The Magazine of the Sierra Club*, March 17, 2022. https://www.sierraclub.org
/sierra/2022-1-spring/feature/whats-name-what-it-means-decolonize-natural
-feature.

Gilio-Whitaker, Dina, and Krista Comer. "Being Good Relatives: A Story of Indigenous and Settler Surfeminist Collaboration and Legislated Land Acknowledgments." In *Waves of Hope, Waves of Belonging: Indigeneity, Gender, and Race in
the Surfing Line Up*, edited by Lydia Heberling, David Kemper, and Jess Ponting.
Seattle: University of Washington Press, forthcoming.

Goodman, Audrey. *A Planetary Lens: The Photo-Poetics of Western Women's Writing*. Lincoln: University of Nebraska Press, 2021.

———. "What Is a Feminist Landscape? A Vocabulary for Re-Visioning Place in the
US West." In *The Routledge Companion to Gender and the American West*, edited
by Susan Bernardin, 422–35. New York: Routledge, 2022.

Graulich, Melody. "Prepositional Spaces." In *Western Subjects*, edited by Gioia Woods
and Kathleen A. Boardman, 386–419. Salt Lake City: University of Utah Press,
2005.

———. "Wishful Thinking." *Front Range Review*, Spring 2020. Accessed June 3, 2022.
https://cpb-us-e1.wpmucdn.com/blogs.rice.edu/dist/b/12404/files/2021/08
/Graulich-Writing-Sample-Wishful-Thinking.pdf.

Habell-Pallán, Michelle. *Womxn Who Rock: Making Scenes, Building Communities*.
Accessed September 12, 2023. https://womenwhorockcommunity.org/.

Hamilton, Amy T. "Colonialism and Gendered Violence in the Grassy, Bloody West."
In *The Routledge Companion to Gender and the American West*, edited by Susan
Bernardin, 384–98. New York: Routledge, 2022.

———. "Gender, Affect, Environmental Justice, and Indigeneity in the Classroom."
In *Teaching Western American Literature*, edited by Brady Harrison and Randi
Lynn Tanglen, 89–104. Lincoln: University of Nebraska Press, 2020.

———. *Peregrinations: Walking in American Literature*. Reno: University of Nevada Press, 2018.

Harding, Sandra. "Philosophy and Standpoint Theory: Negotiating with the Positivist Legacy; New Social Justice Movements and a Standpoint Politics of Method." In *The Politics of Method in the Human Sciences*, edited by George Steinmetz, 346–65. Durham NC: Duke University Press, 2005. https://read.dukeupress.edu/books/book/2082/chapter/242829/Philosophy-and-Standpoint-TheoryNegotiating-with.

Harjo, Joy. *An American Sunrise: Poems*. New York: W. W. Norton, 2019.

Hennessy, Rosemary. *In the Company of Radical Women Writers*. Minneapolis: University of Minnesota Press, 2023.

Hersey, Tricia. *Rest Is Resistance: A Manifesto*. Boston: Little, Brown, 2022.

Hofstaedter, Emily. "Abortion Was Already Inaccessible on Reservation Land. Dobbs Made Things Worse." *Mother Jones*, August 12, 2022. https://www.motherjones.com/politics/2022/08/abortion-dobbs-tribal-land/.

Indian Pueblo Cultural Center. "Indigenous Wisdom Curriculum Project." Accessed June 3, 2022. https://indianpueblo.org/indigenous-wisdom-curriculum-project/.

"Institute for Women Surfers." Accessed June 3, 2022. http://www.instituteforwomensurfers.org/.

Jacobs, Margaret D. *After One Hundred Winters: In Search of Reconciliation on America's Stolen Lands*. Princeton NJ: Princeton University Press, 2021.

———. "Western History: What's Gender Got to Do with It?" *Faculty Publications, Department of History*, October 1, 2011. https://digitalcommons.unl.edu/historyfacpub/114.

———. *White Mother to a Dark Race: Settler Colonialism, Maternalism, and the Removal of Indigenous Children in the American West and Australia, 1880–1940*. Lincoln: University of Nebraska Press, 2009.

Justice, Daniel Heath. *Why Indigenous Literatures Matter*. Waterloo, Canada: Wilfrid Laurier University Press, 2018.

Karell, Linda K. "Spokane Kitten." In *Bright Bones: Contemporary Montana Writing*, edited by Natalie Peeterse, 143–51. Helena MT: Open Country Press, 2018.

———. *Writing Together/Writing Apart: Collaboration in Western American Literature*. Lincoln: University of Nebraska Press, 2002.

Kendall, Mikki. *Hood Feminism: Notes from the Women That a Movement Forgot*. London: Penguin, 2021.

Kimmerer, Robin. *Braiding Sweetgrass: Indigenous Wisdom, Scientific Knowledge and the Teachings of Plants*. Minneapolis: Milkweed Editions, 2013.

King, Tiffany Lethabo. *The Black Shoals: Offshore Formations of Black and Native Studies*. Durham NC: Duke University Press, 2019.

———. "Interview with Dr. Tiffany Lethabo King." *feral feminisms: Complicities, Connections, and Struggles: Critical Transnational Feminist Analysis of Settler Colonialism* 4 (Summer 2015): 64–68. https://feralfeminisms.com/lethabo-king/.

Kirkness, Verna J., and Ray Barnhardt. "First Nations and Higher Education: The

Four R's—Respect, Relevance, Reciprocity, Responsibility." *Journal of American Indian Education* 30, no. 3 (1991): 1–15.

Knapp, Rachel. "O'Keeffe Museum, Pueblo-Indigenous Groups Oppose NM Tourism Dept." Video. *KRQE News*, April 20, 2021, sec. New Mexico News. https://www.krqe.com/news/new-mexico/okeeffe-museum-pueblo-indigenous-groups-oppose-nm-tourism-dept-video/.

Kollin, Susan. *Thelma and Louise*. Reel West Series. Albuquerque: University of New Mexico Press, 2023.

Kolodny, Annette. *The Lay of the Land: Metaphor as Experience and History in American Life and Letters*. Chapel Hill: University of North Carolina Press, 1975.

Lamont, Victoria. *The Bower Atmosphere: A Biography of B. M. Bower*. Lincoln NE: Bison Books, forthcoming.

———. "'More Than She Deserves': Woman Suffrage Memorials in the 'Equality State.'" *Canadian Review of American Studies* 36, no. 1 (2006): 17–43.

———. *Westerns: A Women's History*. Lincoln: University of Nebraska Press, 2016.

LeCocq, Riley. "Indigenous Studies Minor to Start at OSU as Three Indigenous Faculty Members Are Given Tenure Track." *The Daily Barometer* (blog), May 12, 2022. https://dailybaro.orangemedianetwork.com/16753/daily-barometer-news/indigenous-studies-minor-to-start-at-osu-as-three-indigenous-faculty-members-are-given-tenure-track/.

LeMenager, Stephanie. *Living Oil: Petroleum Culture in the American Century*. Oxford University Press, 2013.

Liboiron, Max. *Pollution Is Colonialism*. Chapel Hill NC: Duke University Press, 2021.

Limerick, Patricia Nelson. *The Legacy of Conquest: The Unbroken Past of the American West*. New York: W. W. Norton, 2011.

Long Soldier, Layli. *Whereas: Poems*. Minneapolis MN: Graywolf Press, 2017.

Lugones, María. "The Coloniality of Gender." *Worlds and Knowledges Otherwise* (Spring 2008). Duke University Web dossier. Accessed September 10, 2023. https://globalstudies.trinity.duke.edu/projects/wko-gender.

Mackenzie, Kent, director. *The Exiles*. Milestone Films, 1961.

Macoun, Alissa, and Elizabeth Strakosch. "The Ethical Demands of Settler Colonial Theory." *Settler Colonial Studies* 3, no. 3–4 (2013): 426–43. https://doi.org/10.1080/2201473x.2013.810695.

Martin, Biddy, and Chandra Talpade Mohanty. "Feminist Politics: What's Home Got to Do with It?" In *Feminist Studies/Critical Studies*, edited by Teresa de Lauretis, 191–212. London: Palgrave Macmillan, 1986.

Maynard, Robyn, and Leanne Betasamosake Simpson. *Rehearsals for Living*. Chicago: Haymarket Books, 2022.

"Montana Students React to Texas School Shooting." *Montana Public Radio*, May 22, 2018. https://www.mtpr.org/montana-news/2018-05-21/montana-students-react-to-texas-school-shooting.

Moraga, Cherríe, and Gloria Anzaldúa. *This Bridge Called My Back: Writings by Radical Women of Color*. Albany: State University of New York Press, 1981.

Mountz, Alison, et al. "For Slow Scholarship: A Feminist Politics of Resistance through Collective Action in the Neoliberal University." *ACME: An International Journal for Critical Geographies* 14, no. 4 (2015): 1235–59.

National Park Service. "The 24 Associated Tribes of Mesa Verde." Visit Mesa Verde. Accessed July 12, 2023. https://www.visitmesaverde.com/media/399909/mesa -verde-associated-tribes.pdf.

Nicolas, Brenda. "'Soy de Zoochina': Transborder Comunalidad Practices among Adult Children of Indigenous Migrants." *Latino Studies* 19, no. 1 (March 1, 2021): 47–69.

Noddings, Nel. *Caring: A Relational Approach to Ethics and Moral Education*. Berkeley: University of California Press, 2013.

Nudelman, Geoff. "Marys Peak Creek Naming Honors the Indigenous Heritage of the Willamette Valley." *Willamette Valley*, June 20, 2021. https://willamettevalley .org/articles/marys-peak-creek-naming-honors-the-indigenous-heritage-of -the-willamette-valley/.

Okin, Susan Moller. "Is Multiculturalism Bad for Women?" *Boston Review*, October 1, 1997. https://www.bostonreview.net/forum/susan-moller-okin-multiculuralism -bad-women/.

"Oklahoma Black Homesteader Project | Center for Great Plains Studies | Nebraska." Accessed January 14, 2023. https://www.unl.edu/plains/oklahoma-black -homesteader-project.

Pacia, Danielle M. "Reproductive Rights vs. Reproductive Justice: Why the Difference Matters in Bioethics—Bill of Health." *Bill of Health* (blog), November 3, 2020. https://blog.petrieflom.law.harvard.edu/2020/11/03/reproductive -rights-justice-bioethics/.

Paredes, Américo. *A Texas-Mexican Cancionero: Folksongs of the Lower Border*. Champaign–Urbana: University of Illinois Press, 1976.

Pascoe, Peggy. *Relations of Rescue: The Search for Female Moral Authority in the American West, 1874–1939*. New York: Oxford University Press, 1990.

Porsild, Charlene L. *Gamblers and Dreamers: Women, Men, and Community in the Klondike*. Vancouver: University of British Columbia Press, 1998.

Pratt, Minnie Bruce. "Identity: Skin Blood Heart." In *Yours in Struggle: Three Feminist Perspectives on Anti-Semitism and Racism*, by Elly Bulkin, Minnie Bruce Pratt, and Barbara Smith, 1–57. Chicago: Long Haul Press, 1984.

Prescott, Cynthia Culver. *Pioneer Mother Monuments: Constructing Cultural Memory*. Norman: University of Oklahoma Press, 2019.

Reagon, Bernice Johnson. "Coalition Politics: Turning the Century." In *Home Girls: A Black Feminist Anthology*, edited by Barbara Smith, 354–68. New York: Kitchen Table, Women of Color Press, 1983.

Reconciliation Rising. "Home Page: Reconciliation Rising." Accessed July 12, 2023. https://www.reconciliationrising.org.

———. "'Return of the Pawnees' Film." Accessed July 12, 2023. https://www.reconciliationrising.org/return-of-the-pawnees-film.

Rich, Adrienne. *Diving into the Wreck: Poems 1971–1972*. New York: W. W. Norton, 1973.

Ripley, Anthony. "Assault on Wife of a Legislator. Linked to Colorado Racial Row." *New York Times*, January 30, 1970, sec. Archives. https://www.nytimes.com/1970/01/30/archives/assault-on-wife-of-a-legislator-linked-to-colorado-racial-row.html.

Ross, Loretta, and Rickie Solinger. *Reproductive Justice: An Introduction*. Berkeley: University of California Press, 2017.

Ruíz, Elena, and Kristie Dotson. "On the Politics of Coalition." *Feminist Philosophy Quarterly* 3, no. 2 (July 6, 2017). Article 4. https://doi.org/10.5206/fpq/2017.2.4.

Sandoz, Mari. *Old Jules*. Boston: Little, Brown, and Company Publishers, 1935.

Sangre de Cristo Arts and Conference Center. "About the Arts Center." Accessed July 12, 2023. https://www.sdc-arts.org/about-arts-center.

Schuller, Kyla. *The Trouble with White Women: A Counterhistory of Feminism*. New York: Bold Type Books, 2021.

Sedgwick, *Shame and Its Sisters: A Silvan Tomkins Reader*. Chapel Hill NC: Duke University Press, 1995.

Silko, Leslie Marmon. *Almanac of the Dead*. New York: Simon & Schuster, 1991.

Smith, Linda Tuhiwai. *Decolonizing Methodologies: Research and Indigenous Peoples*. London: Zed Books, 2021.

Stasiulis, Daiva, and Nira Yuval-Davis, ed. *Unsettling Settler Societies: Articulations of Gender, Race, Ethnicity and Class*. Thousand Oaks CA: Sage Publications, 1995.

Stegner, Wallace. *The American West as Living Space*. Ann Arbor: University of Michigan Press, 1987.

Stephen, Lynn. *Transborder Lives: Indigenous Oaxacans in Mexico, California, and Oregon*. Durham NC: Duke University Press, 2007.

Tanglen, Randi Lynn. "Guest Column: Sustaining the Humanities across Rural Montana." *Bozeman Daily Chronicle*, June 16, 2021, sec. Guest Columns. https://www.bozemandailychronicle.com/opinions/guest_columnists/guest-column-sustaining-the-humanities-across-rural-montana/article_3df4ec75-08c0-58b0-87b5-1293abe586ed.html.

——. "Reconfiguring Religion: Race, and the Female Body Politic in American Fiction by Women, 1859–1911." Dissertation, University of Arizona, 2008.

——. "*Sowing Possibility* Episode 8: Randi Lynn Tanglen, PhD." Apple podcast. Accessed September 12, 2023. https://podcasts.apple.com/us/podcast/sowing-possibility-episode-8-randi-lynn-tanglen-phd/id1501245840?i=1000558988800.

——. "Teaching Confederate Monuments as American Literature." In *Reading Confederate Monuments*, edited by Maria Seger, 230–49. Jackson: University Press of Mississippi, 2022.

Tatum, Stephen. "Spectrality and the Postregional Interface." In *Postwestern Cultures: Literature, Theory, Space*, edited by Susan Kollin, 3–29. Lincoln: University of Nebraska Press.

Tewa Women United. "Home Page—Tewa Women United." Accessed June 3, 2022. https://tewawomenunited.org/.

Thomas, Marlo, and various artists. *Free to Be You and Me*. Bell Records, 1972. YouTube. https://www.youtube.com/watch?v=7ps3nOcLbhi.

Thomsen, Carly. *Queering Reproductive Justice*. Berkeley: University of California Press, forthcoming.

Thomsen, Carly, and Carrie N. Baker. "The Importance of Talking about Women in the Fight against Abortion Bans." *Ms.* magazine, June 23, 2022. https://msmagazine.com/2022/06/23/women-abortion-bans-inclusive-language-pregnant-people/.

Thomsen, Carly, Carrie N. Baker, and Zach Levitt. "Pregnant? Need Help? They Have an Agenda." *New York Times*, May 12, 2022, sec. Opinion. https://www.nytimes.com/interactive/2022/05/12/opinion/crisis-pregnancy-centers-roe.html.

Tolentino, Jia. "We're Not Going Back to the Time Before Roe. We're Going Somewhere Worse." *New Yorker*, June 24, 2022. https://www.newyorker.com/magazine/2022/07/04/we-are-not-going-back-to-the-time-before-roe-we-are-going-somewhere-worse.

Truettner, William H. *The West as America: Reinterpreting Images of the Frontier, 1820–1920*. Washington DC: Smithsonian, 1991.

Valdez, Elena V. "Reclaiming Our Past, Sustaining Our Future: Envisioning a New Mexico Land Grant and Acequia Curriculum." The Acequia and Land Grant Education Project. Center for the Education and Study of Diverse Populations at New Mexico Highlands University, 2021. https://its.nmhu.edu/IntranetUploads/007370-algewhite-422202233432.07.02%20print%20version.pdf.

Van Houten, Christina. "bell hooks, Critical Regionalism, and the Politics of Ecological Returns." In *Materialist Feminisms Against Neoliberalism*, edited by Mary Ellen Campbell and A. L. McCready, Politics and Culture (2014) online. Accessed January 3, 2015.

Vizcaíno-Alemán, Melina. *Gender and Place in Chicana/o Literature: Critical Regionalism and the Mexican American Southwest*. Cham: Palgrave McMillan, 2017.

———. "Growing Up Chicana in the Heart of Anaya's Aztlán." *Aztlán: A Journal of Chicano Studies* 46, no. 1 (Spring 2021): 173–84.

———. "Resisting the Darkness of Boxes: A Conversation with María Teresa Márquez." *Blue Mesa Review* 43 (Spring 2021). https://issuu.com/bluemesareview/docs/blue_mesa_review_issue_43/s/12291587.

Woman Stands Shining (Pat McCabe) and Dr. Carolyn Finney. "Conversation at the Crossroads: The Intimacy of Right Relations." Franklin Environmental Center at Hillcrest, Middlebury College, November 17, 2020. https://www.youtube.com/watch?v=tDlJXxcN5UU.

Western Literature Association. "Code of Conduct." Accessed July 11, 2023. https://www.westernlit.org/code-of-conduct/.

Women's March. *Women's Agenda*. Accessed August 30, 2023. https://www.scribd.com/document/397727839/The-Women-s-March-2019-Women-s-Agenda.

———. "Women's March Calls for a Summer of Rage After Scotus Decision to Over-

turn Roe V. Wade." Accessed July 12, 2023. https://www.womensmarch.com
/newsroom/womens-march-calls-for-a-summer-of-rage-after-scotus-decision
-to-overturn.

Yazzie, Melanie, and Cutcha Risling Baldy. "Introduction: Indigenous Peoples and
the Politics of Water." *Decolonization: Indigeneity, Education & Society* 7, no.
1 (2018): 1–18.

Ybarra, Priscilla. "A Farm for My Mother, a Farm for Meme." HowlRound Theatre
Commons, December 21, 2020. https://howlround.com/farm-my-mother
-farm-meme.

———. *Writing the Good Life: Mexican American Literature and the Environment.*
Tucson: University of Arizona Press, 2016.

CONTRIBUTORS

ZAINAB ABDALI is a PhD student in English at Rice University. She researches South Asian Anglophone literature, with a focus on literary and cultural representations of resistance to the war on terror. Her work has been published in *Religion and the Arts* and in *Western American Literature*.

LOURDES ALBERTO is Zapotec from Yalalag, Oaxaca, Mexico. She was born and raised in Los Angeles. She is the inaugural director of American Indian studies at Cal State Los Angeles. Prior to returning to California, she held a joint appointment as an associate professor of English and Ethnic Studies at the University of Utah. Her research interests focus on the various crossings of Indigenous and Latino/a Studies, diasporic and migratory Indigeneities.

JOSÉ F. ARANDA JR. is a professor of Chicanx literatures at Rice University. He holds the Terrence Doody Chair in English and has a dual appointment in the Department of English and the Department of Modern and Classical Literature and Language. He is the author of *When We Arrive: A New Literary History of Mexican America* and *The Places of Modernity in Early Mexican American Literature, 1848–1948*. He is a board member of the Recovering the U.S. Hispanic Literary Project as well as a cofounding editor of the new journal *Pasados: Recovering History, Imagining Latinidad*.

SUSAN BERNARDIN is director of the School of Language, Culture, and Society at Oregon State. She has published widely in Native literary studies, visual arts, and comics. A former president of the Western Literature Association, she is editor of *Gender and the American West* in Routledge's Gender Companion Series.

KRISTA COMER is a professor of English at Rice University. In 2014 she cofounded the Institute for Women Surfers, a grassroots educational initiative in the feminist public humanities. She writes for scholarly as well as nonspecialist audiences. She has published over thirty essays, and her previous books include *Landscapes of the New West* and *Surfer Girls in the New World Order*. She is at work on *Feminist Surf Life in the Age of Climate Change* as well as a memoir.

KALENDA EATON is a professor at the University of Oklahoma in the Department of African and African American studies. She is a scholar of Black literary studies, studies of the American West, and Black social and cultural history. Eaton is noted for her teaching and public scholarship on African Americans in the Great Plains region and on Black women writers.

DINA GILIO-WHITAKER is a first-line descendant of the Colville Confederated Tribes. She is an independent educator and consultant on tribal environmental policy issues, and lecturer in American Indian studies at California State University San Marcos. She publishes widely as a journalist and is also author of *As Long as Grass Grows: The Fight for Environmental Justice from Colonization to Standing Rock.*

AUDREY GOODMAN'S research explores the lived, literary, and visual histories of the U.S. Southwest and U.S.-Mexico borderlands. Her most recent book is *A Planetary Lens: The Photo-poetics of Western Women's Writing.* She has served as co-president of the Western Literature Association and is a professor of English at Georgia State University in Atlanta.

MELODY GRAULICH is an author of many essays and books on such figures as Mary Austin, Wallace Stegner, Leslie Silko, and Louis Owens. Her favorite genre is autobiographical literary and cultural criticism, in which she has often used her own stories as points of departure or inspiration. Since retirement she has turned to fiction, largely place-based. Her New England story "Granite Ledges" is available on Amazon.

AMY T. HAMILTON is professor of English and director of gender and sexuality studies at Northern Michigan University. She is the editor of *Western American Literature.* Amy is the author of *Peregrinations: Walking in American Literature* and coeditor with Tom J. Hillard of *Before the West Was West: Critical Essays on Pre-1800 Literature of the American Frontiers.*

MARGARET JACOBS is the Charles Mach Professor of History and the director of the Center for Great Plains Studies at the University of Nebraska–Lincoln. She has published more than thirty-five articles and four books, most recently *After One Hundred Winters: In Search of Reconciliation on America's Stolen Lands.*

LINDA KARELL is an associate professor of English at Montana State University. She is the author of *Writing Together/Writing Apart: Collaboration in Western American Literature.* She teaches American literature, western American literature, literary theory, memoir, graphic novels, and is committed to her wife, her pets, her students. She is working on a memoir, *To Give Me Good Gifts.*

VICTORIA LAMONT is a settler scholar at the University of Waterloo in Ontario, Canada, in the traditional territory of the Neutral, Anishnaabeg, Haudenosaunee, and Mississauga peoples. She is the author of *Westerns: A Women's History* and *The Bower Atmosphere: A Biography of B. M. Bower.* In her spare time she helps look after a flock of one hundred sheep, and trains border collies to herd them.

RANDI TANGLEN is vice provost for faculty affairs at the University of North Dakota; she previously served as the executive director of Humanities Montana as well as a professor at Austin College. She coedited *Teaching Western American Literature*. Her essays on western American literature and pedagogy are published in *Western American Literature*, *Southwestern American Literature*, and several edited volumes.

ELENA V. VALDEZ earned her BA in English from the University of New Mexico and continued her study of literature at Rice University. After earning her PhD, she chose to return to her hometown of Santa Fe, where she serves as the Bilingual Seal Specialist in the Language and Culture Division at the New Mexico Public Education Department. She writes for scholarly and educational policy audiences. She and her husband are now raising a fierce Chicana feminist.

MELINA VIZCAÍNO-ALEMÁN is an associate professor in the Department of English at the University of New Mexico. She teaches courses in American literary studies and specializes in the Southwest and Chicanx studies. Her next project focuses on Chicana *revistas* published between 1968 and 1978 and rethinks Xicana poetics of the Chicano movement.

PRISCILLA SOLIS YBARRA is an associate professor in the Department of English at University of North Texas. She writes and teaches about Mexican American culture and how to dwell well with the Earth. Her publications include *Writing the Goodlife: Mexican American Literature* and the *Environment and Latinx Environmentalisms: Place, Justice, and the Decolonial*. Her current project documents her ecological foremothers.

INDEX

Page numbers with italics indicate illustrations.

Trump, Ivanka, xix

ugly feelings, as concept, xxvi
United Coalition to Protect Panhe, 111, 112
Unsettling Settler Societies (Stasiulis and
  Yuval-Davis), 216–17
U.S. West, as concept, 15–16, 32, 50, 60, 76,
  80, 97; Bernardin on, 160; Eaton on, 128,
  134–36; Gilio-Whitaker on, 115–16; Lam-
  ont on, 196. *See also* feminist Wests
Ute, 205
Ute Mountain Ute, 171

Valdez, Elena, 11–19, 224
Vasquez, Enriqueta, 8
Verenika (food), 75
violence against women, 180–81
Vizcaíno-Alemán, Melina, 21–28
vulnerability, xxvi, xxvii, 155

wages, xxvi, 162
Wagner, Sally, xl
Wakanim Artist Collaborative, 159
Walker Prize, 221
War on Terror, xl
"The Weaponization of Loneliness" (Clin-
  ton), 229
well-being, xxiv–xxvi, 2, 12, 22, 155, 166,
  171, 229. *See also* hopefulness
West. *See* U.S. West
West as America exhibition, 185
West Coast Women's Music Festival,
  xxxiii–xxxvii, 52, 116, 227
Western American Literature (publication),
  29, 42, 48, 87, 88, 159, 221
Western Literature Association, xvii, xx,
  xviii, 36, 80, 87, 147, 221–25
Western pioneer identity, 208–9
"Whereas" (Soldier), 37
the where of here. *See* place orientations
White, Helen Thatcher "Sitty," 178–79
white feminism: Comer on, xviii, xix, xxiv,
  29, 42–44, 173, 181; Hamilton on, 33–34,
  36, 37–39; Jacobs on, 215–16, 217–18; of
  Tanglen, 74

white fragility, 42, 44
Whitehorn, Clark, 63–65
Whitehouse TX, 127–40
Whitehouse Church of God and Christ,
  127
white nationalism, 65, 70
whiteness, xxix; in academia, 199, 200–
  201; accountability to, 230–31; in
  Canada, 200; Comer on, 48–49, 183–84;
  Hamilton on, 29, 31, 42; in Montana, 64–
  65, 70, 78; reproductive rights and, 172
White Shell Water Place, 148
white stories as such, as concept, xxiv
white supremacy, xix, 42, 44, 68, 128, 163,
  172, 181, 200, 230
Whose Streets? (film), 223
Why Indigenous Literatures Matter (Jus-
  tice), 98
Wichita peoples, 4
Wills, Drew, 45, 80
Winnebago peoples, 206
Wolfe, Patrick, 216–17
womanism, 133, 136–37
Woman Stands Shining (McCabe), xix–xx
women, politics of term, 182
Women's Marches, xxi, 215
women's movement, xix
women's studies courses, xl, 7, 34, 212
Women Who Rock project (Habell-Pallán),
  xi
Women Who Run with the Wolves (Estes), 33
working-class identity, 61. *See also* blue
  collar identity
Wright, Rigina, 26–27
Writing the Good Life (Ybarra), 6
Writing Together/Writing Apart (Karell), 62
Wylder Award for Exceptional Service, 221

Yalalag, Oaxaca, Mexico, 98–99, 102–5
Ybarra, Priscilla Solis, 1–10, xix, 228
Yellowstone (TV series), 76
Yellowstone National Park, 99–100

Zapotec feminism, 97–108